Praise for *Heritage and Hate*

Heritage and Hate investigates the origins and contemporary uses of "a panoply of Old South words and symbols," studying the cheers, university slogans, and online messages of students as well as the words and silences of university leaders. The volume's unique contribution is to analyze those words and symbols as rhetoric that, whether or not it was obvious, was and is always making arguments about power, race, and belonging.

—Ted M. Ownby, William Winter Professor of History, University of Mississippi, and author of *American Dreams in Mississippi: Consumers, Poverty, and Culture, 1830–1998*

Stephen Monroe has elegantly articulated the racial friction that surrounds much of the iconography of the South. As Confederate monuments and memorials are taken down daily in the midst of the antiracism movement that has swept across America, the timing of this book is perfect.

—Charles K. Ross, professor of African American studies and history, University of Mississippi, and author of *Mavericks, Money, and Men: The AFL, Black Players, and the Evolution of Modern Football*

Stephen Monroe has written a superb study of the history, cultural power, and traumatic effects of what he terms "confederate rhetoric," the racist language and chauvinistic verbal codes that have saturated the South from the Civil War to the present day. Focusing on how such rhetoric thrives on the campuses of southern colleges and universities, Monroe reveals the learned nature of the phenomenon and its tendency to hide in plain sight.

—Craig A. Warren, author of *The Rebel Yell: A Cultural History*

Heritage and Hate shows vividly that nostalgic histories of the Old South have long functioned as historical propaganda, preserved and nurtured in association with southern colleges and universities, and that confederate rhetoric is deeply embedded in popular language choices and symbols. Stephen Monroe's thoroughly researched and clearly argued book is an important contribution to scholarship and public affairs alike. It demonstrates that confederate rhetoric is stubbornly persistent in present-day political discourse and that the struggle to overcome it and tell a more accurate, representative version of southern history matters profoundly to the nation as a whole.

—Bradford Vivian, author of *Commonplace Witnessing: Rhetorical Invention, Historical Remembrance, and Public Culture*

This smart and bold book confronts "formative and active" usages of paternalistic and plantation-born terms like "Ole Miss" and explores the ritualistic meanings embedded in seemingly innocuous cheers like the Hotty Toddy, linking those phenomena across time and region to make a persuasive and, at times, alarming case that Lost Cause retentions still affect the futures of southern peoples.

—John T. Edge, author of *The Potlikker Papers*

This is a very important book that offers insights into the historical development of confederate rhetoric on southern college campuses, as well as the ways in which it is sustained and resonant in the contemporary era. Monroe skillfully explicates its hidden nature and offers abundant evidence pointing to the ways in which its subtlety functions to "protect" it from the forces of modernization, even in the setting of academic institutions (ostensibly) committed to the progressive ideals of inclusion, critical thinking, and fairness.

—Patricia G. Davis, author of *Laying Claim: African American Cultural Memory and Southern Identity*

HERITAGE AND HATE

HERITAGE AND HATE

Old South Rhetoric at Southern Universities

STEPHEN M. MONROE

THE UNIVERSITY OF ALABAMA PRESS
Tuscaloosa

The University of Alabama Press
Tuscaloosa, Alabama 35487-0380
uapress.ua.edu

Typeface: Adobe Caslon Pro

Cover design: Lori Lynch

Cataloging-in-Publication data is available from the Library of Congress.
ISBN: 978-0-8173-2093-5
E-ISBN: 978-0-8173-9357-1

To Mom and Dad

To George and Ann

To every person who loves the University of Mississippi

front confederate tag tells all I need to know
about the soul of this South / get it young country
bumpkin / make grandpa proud / push that pedal
like propaganda / like a hate you can't understand

Derrick Harriell, "Links Rd to HWY 6 to Jackson Ave"

The old signs are still over the minds of men. Custom and conscience still divide our children and southern tradition is a ghost that many still believe in.

Lillian Smith, *Killers of the Dream*

Contents

Figures

Preface

Words and symbols rooted in the Lost Cause continue to influence individual and communal identities across the US South. These words and symbols make up a vital and dynamic regional semiotic collective that I label "confederate rhetoric." Far from inactive or languorous, confederate rhetoric has exerted a formative power throughout much of the region's history and remains lively and energetic. It is a southern example of what rhetorician Laurie Gries has called "an ongoing activation," a rhetoric that is "a distributed event, an energetic and generative process in which single things become multiple and vital." Elaborating on this concept, Gries noted in *Still Life with Rhetoric*, "If we actually take time to trace things as they circulate and enter into various relations, we can come to discover that many things are unpredictably active and still on the rhetorical move."[1] Such is the case with Old South words and symbols, and so in this book I trace examples of confederate rhetoric as they have circulated across time and catalyzed human action and reaction. By charting some of these circulations, relations, and cultural impacts, this book demonstrates how confederate rhetoric has been—and continues to be—an influential and ongoing landmark "event" in the history of the US South.

One doesn't have to look far for a notable example of the ongoing influence of confederate rhetoric. Recall the 2016 presidential election and the years that followed when Russia's social media campaign became apparent. This extended attack against the United States relied, in part, on confederate rhetoric. Russian operatives, based in St. Petersburg, generated and spread propaganda and misinformation using digital personas imitative of American citizens or American interest groups. Russia's goal was to create dissent and turmoil within the US, and it pursued that goal by leveraging existing cultural and racial conflicts. Scholars from the University of Oxford and Graphika found that "the Russian effort targeted many kinds of communities within the

US, but particularly the most extreme conservatives and those with particular sensitivities to race and immigration. [Russia] used a variety of fake accounts to infiltrate political discussion in liberal and conservative communities, including Black activist communities, in order to exacerbate social divisions and influence the agenda. Accounts posing as liberal and as conservative US users were frequently created and operated from the same computers." These efforts had a remarkably broad impact. From 2015 to 2017, on Facebook alone, thousands of Russian posts, disguised as American posts, were shared by actual Facebook users nearly 31 million times. Users responded with nearly 39 million likes, 5.4 million emojis, and 3.5 million textual comments.[2]

The social media campaign was rhetorically thoughtful and strategic. The Russians deployed mixtures of culturally provocative words, symbols, and images in specific geographic and demographic patterns. For example, operatives targeted Black communities with visual and textual messages promoting Black Lives Matter while simultaneously targeting white communities with visual and textual messages promoting Confederate history and southern pride (fig. 1). These efforts relied heavily on memes, which distill big ideas into evocative and digestible snippets. As analysts from the American think tank New Knowledge have concluded, "While many people think of memes as 'cat pictures with words,' the Defense Department and DARPA have studied them for years as a powerful tool of cultural influence, capable of reinforcing or even changing values and behavior." It seems that Russia has been studying memes, too, as it is now deploying them against the United States.[3]

Although the popular media has focused mostly on whether the Russian social media campaign affected the outcome of the 2016 presidential election, scholars who have analyzed the available data have not established such a specific connection. What is clear is that the Russian effort was (and is) massive, coordinated, and ongoing. Darren Linvell and Patrick Warren, professors at Clemson University, are among a group of scholars studying the Russian social media operation. Their early analysis concludes that Russia is interested in goals bigger than influencing any single election. It is, instead, attempting to "distract, divide, and demoralize" American citizens. "There were more tweets in the year after the election than there were in the year before the election," said Warren in a 2018 interview. "I want to shout this from the rooftops. This is not just an election thing. It's a continuing intervention in the political conversation." Russia has spent millions of dollars per year on this operation, all in an effort to sow discord in America.[4]

In pursuing its goal of dividing Americans, Russia seems to have focused on energizing "identity groups on opposing sides of the American electorate . . . to reinforce or expand existing divisions."[5] Many of the memes featured

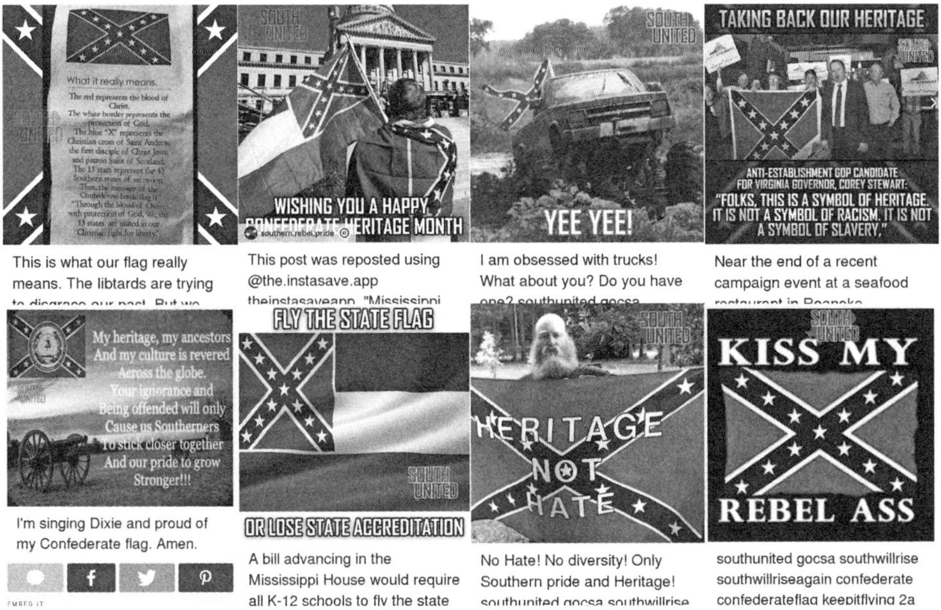

Figure 1. Various memes created by Russian agents at the Internet Research Agency in St. Petersburg. These—and hundreds of others—were distributed across social media platforms under the guise of an account called South United. Although many Russian ads may be lost forever, having been removed by Twitter, Facebook, and Instagram, a significant sampling has been preserved by those companies and by researchers and journalists. The examples depicted in this montage by Joanne Mitchell were collected and archived by researchers in an online repository of South United content begun in October 2017 and hosted at Medium.com by user UsHadrons.

confederate rhetoric: Old South words and symbols that carry forward, preserve, and promote racist ideologies. This rhetoric has been an extremely powerful force in the US South, one that has helped shape (for the worse) the history of the region. Indeed, confederate rhetoric is an old but active American weakness, one recently recognized and exploited by a contemporary American adversary: Russia.

Russia's adoption and deployment of confederate rhetoric is instructive insofar as it highlights the ongoing relevance of Old South words and symbols. Russia was tapping into an existing tradition when it created memes and messages like those discussed above. How and why did confederate rhetoric gain such cultural traction? As an operative force, how has it influenced individuals and communities? How has it shaped the history of the region? For those lessons, we must look not to St. Petersburg but to the US South.

To find salient and enlightening examples of confederate rhetoric, I first turned to Mississippi, a place with a rich rhetorical landscape. Why begin in Mississippi? In many ways, the state represents the US South in its purest and most potent form. One of the original states of the Confederacy, Mississippi has long been marked by conflict and tension; it has been and continues to be fertile land for racial injustice and codified inequities. The writer Walker Percy once observed that Mississippi is "renowned for murder, church burning, dynamiting, assassinations, night-riding, not to mention the lesser forms of terrorism."[6] With its long history of turmoil, the state is an easy place to find dynamic and complex rhetorical artifacts. They litter the ground.

But again, this study is not about unearthing inactive and forgotten shards of linguistic history. It is, instead, about understanding a blaring and ongoing rhetorical event. In Mississippi, confederate rhetoric remains active, loud, and influential. While writing this preface, I witnessed a jolting example of confederate rhetoric, one pointed out on social media by the Mississippi writer Angie Thomas. On Twitter, Thomas quoted and condemned an official tweet issued by the Mississippi Department of Revenue (@MSDepartmentRevenue) on January 17, 2019: "In honor of General Robert E. Lee's birthday and Martin Luther King Jr. Day, we will be closed on Monday, January 21."[7] With this statement, we see that Old South words and symbols remain, to again quote Gries, "unpredictably active and still on the rhetorical move" in Mississippi. The unnamed tweeter, writing on behalf of the state government, in a single sentence managed to invoke and privilege Robert E. Lee, the Confederacy's primary hero, and thereby undercut and sully a national holiday designed to celebrate Dr. King and our country's ongoing progress toward civil rights. In 2019, this tweeter used a communication platform invented in 2006 to deliver a discriminatory and marginalizing message with roots dating back to 1861. I often turn my attention to Mississippi because of moments like these, prosecuted not by Russians or other outsiders but by Mississippians themselves. As a rhetorician, there is no more interesting, disturbing, or enticing place on earth.

But I am not interested in repeating or strengthening false assumptions about Mississippi's uniqueness or singularity. Yes, Mississippi has earned a particularly foul reputation. When the writer V. S. Naipaul made his journey through the US South, he reported that "even in Alabama I found that Mississippi had a reputation for poverty and racial hardness." Or, as writer Richard Grant noted after coming to Mississippi, "no state is more synonymous in the rest of the country with racism, ignorance, and cultural backwardness."[8] Mississippi is infamous for its mistakes, as it should be. But casting the state as something different from the rest of the South (or from the rest of the country) is a convenient falsity, a misleading tradition that often serves to merely obscure or excuse racism and institutionalized discrimination in other places. The truth is that Mississippi *is* America and that Americans can learn more about their broader culture whenever they learn more about Mississippi. Faulkner believed this, as did Richard Wright, Eudora Welty, Robert Kennedy, and Dr. King.

In its tradition of racism, Mississippi may be exemplary, but it is also merely *an* example. Certainly Mississippi should not be relegated to the role of national scapegoat. Yet, it should be dwelled on and studied as a stark illustration. For my own purposes, I find that confederate rhetoric is particularly lively and accessible in Mississippi. It can be observed and traced (in its vitality and influence) quite easily. But I also find that confederate rhetoric can be found without much difficulty in other southern states. In this book, I start in Mississippi, but I also trace Old South terms and images now circulating in Alabama, Georgia, Missouri, and elsewhere.

Rather than approaching Mississippi as a unique rhetorical landscape, I look into and from Mississippi for its rhetorical representativeness, for what its rhetoric can teach us about the broader South, a region that scholars continue to untangle. I believe that rhetoricians and language scholars have many contributions to make to the ongoing conversation about the US South, a conversation now dominated by insightful historians, literary scholars, sociologists, creative writers, and other academicians. I also believe that rhetorical approaches will be welcomed and embraced by current scholars of southern studies, an incredibly productive, open, and interdisciplinary field.

Of course, as many scholars have pointed out, there is no single "South." Instead, the South has always been a network of communities: states, towns, churches, clubs, schools, and so on. Each southerner identifies with a number of these nested communities before identifying more broadly with the South at large. Kwame Anthony Appiah's observation about Rome, a place where "every civilized person belonged to a community among communities," could thus be applied to the US South.[9] In this way, the South is like the classical world where Roman citizens identified first with a particular polis and subsequently with the larger empire. This is certainly true in Mississippi, where the notion of nested communities still governs life.

Individual Mississippians, upon meeting for the first time, usually ask each other, "What's your hometown?" The question immediately creates conditions of credibility and commonality. What typically follows are other questions: "Do you know so and so?" "Are you related to so and so?" By way of this name game, two strangers in Mississippi can make multiple connections within only a minute or two of meeting, thereby reassuring each other of some shared membership and reifying feelings of hospitality and order. This is a tangible benefit of the rural South. If urban modernity is often unfriendly, creating in its pace and scale the discomforting conditions of anonymity, rural modernity in Mississippi often feels slow, small, and friendly.

Personal transactions and their resulting connectedness are possible in contemporary Mississippi, in part, because the state's population is small. Mississippi does not have even one major metropolitan city. Here is a colloquial and self-effacing joke: What are the two largest cities in Mississippi? The punch line: Memphis and New Orleans. Instead of having cosmopolitan anchors, Mississippi has a collection of small towns, and these small towns are usually only twenty or thirty miles apart, divided by expansive fields and forests but connected by uncongested roads and by shared lifestyles and customs. Almost all Mississippi towns have a central square or main street. County seats have a courthouse—or at least an empty plot where the courthouse once stood. There is likely a monument to the Confederate dead erected in the early 1900s by a local chapter of the United Daughters of the Confederacy or some other nostalgic organization. There is probably a Walmart on the edge of town or on the edge of the town nearby. New businesses are rare but almost always located near the highway or interstate, if the town is economically lucky enough to be near a highway or interstate. Neighborhoods usually remain segregated by race. Schools, churches, police departments, and public libraries tend to be the best-functioning institutions. There is probably a bank or two and a still-local drugstore, a hardware store, and several gas stations. Even in the Mississippi Delta, where the soil is among the most fertile in the world, small towns are commonly classified as food deserts. Farmers' markets are popping up in some towns, but they are still fairly rare. Overall, the economy of small-town Mississippi is struggling. The weather is oppressive in the summer and dreary in the winter. Life is languid and lugubrious. There is not a lot of change or excitement, and so the young people are leaving in droves, whenever they are able. Newcomers rarely arrive.

These are broad generalizations, of course, but most Mississippians would recognize them as familiar. Such commonalities partially explain the deep sense of affiliation and community felt by Mississippians. Pride is an elusive concept, particularly on the communal level, but Mississippians are undoubtedly a proud people who are often bound together primarily by a shared understanding of adversity. Mississippians know about their bad reputation. People of all colors and creeds bristle at this status, which often feels like an inherited and unshakable stigma. It is a stigma that compounds more immediate and material problems in the state, for Mississippians have long suffered together under difficult socioeconomic conditions.

Of course, conditions in Mississippi are far more difficult—and hostile—for Black Mississippians than for white Mississippians. To this day, life is often structured and governed according to inherited and enforced conceptions of race. Students of American history will not be surprised by this reality, as Jim Crow was stronger in Mississippi than anyplace else in the South, "an invisible hand" determining "that white people were in charge and colored people were under them and had to obey."[10] As a system of division and oppression, Jim Crow was comprehensive and ingrained in Mississippi. So much so that even today, decades removed from the victories of the civil rights movement, Jim Crow's legacy sometimes seems more immediate than Dr. King's.

Progress has been made, and many Mississippians both Black and white continue to push for improvements, but Mississippi remains an antagonistic place, on the whole, for its African American inhabitants. The political, social, educational, and economic structures of the present were constructed by Lost Cause traditionalists of the past. Mississippi today has laws protecting the rights of African Americans, but it rarely has policies or institutions that encourage those same African Americans to maximize their rights, to fully pursue life, liberty, and happiness. Inequality of opportunity remains very real throughout Mississippi, and those realities have been well documented by historians, sociologists, poets, political scientists, journalists, and others. This book adds to our knowledge of such inequities by describing the ways in which Old South words and symbols have generated, strengthened, and preserved portions of Mississippi's antagonistic racial environment. Part of my thesis is that confederate rhetoric has consistently promoted whiteness and oppressed otherness.

Again and again, I will return in this story to one particular community within Mississippi: the University of Mississippi, also known as "Ole Miss." Founded in 1848, UM is Mississippi's flagship university, serving more than twenty-three thousand students in 2018. It is also one of the most prestigious social networks in the state, one that joins together educated people from every town in Mississippi and that has governed—and continues to govern—the intellectual and cultural standards of Mississippi more than any other single institution or collective group. If the South can, indeed, be understood as a series of nested communities, UM is a key part of the sequence, a community within the community that is very prominent in the collective imagination and memory. When the African American writer Anthony Walton traveled to Mississippi to research his family's southern roots, he noticed the ubiquity of the state's largest university: "Ole Miss seemed to be a theme throughout my journey, touching in one way or another most of the people I talked to, surfacing again and again in historical accounts and looming in my imagination as a symbol of Mississippi's social culture. Ole Miss, with its redbrick buildings (some built by my mother's relatives), its groves of trees, its winding roads and pretty coeds, seemed to represent 'the South' and all its preoccupations with history, romance, and order."[11]

Indeed, for many people, the university is emblematic not only of Mississippi, but of the genteel and educated South at large. Today, UM represents both progress and continuity. It is a research university with an accomplished faculty and an impressive list of academic accolades. It is also a place where the Old South lives on in the landscape, in the customs, and in a localized set of deeply embedded confederate rhetoric.

While the University of Mississippi is my primary case study, I also highlight confederate rhetoric at other major universities in the US South. Every southern state has a predominantly white university or two standing prominently in the imagination and culture. These institutions dot the map of the South and are usually located in small, rural towns away from urban centers. As educational historian Clarence Mohr has noted, "By design most southern colleges were located in small, interior towns where students could supposedly be shielded from the moral temptations and intellectual heresies of city life."[12] Today, many of these universities remain, persevering as the region's oldest intellectual and social hubs. The University of Georgia, the University of Alabama, the University of Missouri, the University of Tennessee: such schools have been strong influences on the history of the region and to this day are lively communities with weighty lists of alumni and supporters. Useful for my purposes, such universities are also communities with rich recorded histories, places where I found plenty of artifacts and easily tracked some of confederate rhetoric's dynamism and impact. They are discourse communities that have always spent some time and energy navel-gazing, recording and reflecting the intricacies of their discourse. After researching and writing this book, I view the South's major universities as nexuses between rhetoric and culture, sites where southern identities—personal and communal—are formed and proliferated.

This book presents evidence for the deeply intertwined nature of language and identity. By analyzing certain artifacts of public memory at southern universities, I show how words and symbols have churned actively above and beneath the surface of the South's conflicted history. These words and symbols have consistently performed cultural and ideological work during critical moments of crisis and during mundane periods of peace. In my analysis of the University of Mississippi, for example, I find a community where semiotic traditions are cherished and where identity has been formed, reified, changed, and transmitted by words and symbols across many generations. I find a community that clings stubbornly to Old South words and symbols while simultaneously struggling against the darker legacies of those words and symbols in a recursive attempt to become a viably modern and new university. I find insights relevant to confederate rhetoric's influence at other southern universities, and I find lessons about how rhetoric can limit racial progress and its pace. This book concludes with reasons for hope and examples of rhetorical progress now ongoing within the region. First, though, it begins with a full explanation of the concept of confederate rhetoric, which is used throughout the book to better understand the rich and troubling linguistic and semiotic space known as the US South.

Acknowledgments

I AM THANKFUL TO HAVE RECEIVED encouragement from many people while writing this book.

I am most grateful to my family for their love and support. My mom and dad have influenced me more than any other people in the world. They have never let me down, and they have always encouraged me to work hard and to put others before myself. I thank them for everything.

Over the last few years, George has often accompanied me to the office on weekends, reading a book or doing his homework in the comfy chair across from my desk while I typed away on my manuscript. George is a kind person and a good friend, and he never hesitated to say, "Dad, your book will be great." Ann pushes and inspires me in everything. I am lucky to have her as a colleague, reader, friend, and wife. Without her, I would be stuck someplace else in life. I'm bolstered knowing that Ann will like me even if this book receives terrible reviews. Other family members have helped me so many times over the years, providing varied examples of goodness. I love and thank them all.

In some ways, this book is a strong critique of the University of Mississippi. In other ways, it is an endorsement of the university's great strength and potential. UM means so much to me. It is the place where I became my full self, where I learned to be a scholar and teacher, where I count my largest number of friends. I am grateful to the people of UM for teaching and inspiring me every day. Special thanks to John Mayo, Edward and Amanda Wilson, Meredith Creekmore, Allen and Susan Spore, Reba and Lance Greer, David and Claire Crews, Renvy Pittman, and Dave and Reba White Williams.

My academic mentors have taught me skills and kept me focused. Joe Urgo was my primary guide through graduate school, and he continues to model the best of academia. Joe brings a zeal to his work that I have tried to emulate in my own professional life. His advice about academic writing still resonates with me: "Make it interesting. What's to lose?" Don Kartiganer, Jaime Harker, Katie McKee, Verbie Prevost, Barry Hannah, Ann Fisher-Wirth, Ben Fisher, Colby Cullman, Greg O'Dea, Tayo Alabi, Karen Raber, Irv Resnick: all world-class professors who taught me generously. I owe them very much.

Many UM administrators have encouraged and supported me over the years. Maurice Eftink taught by example and never turned me away from his office. I asked too many questions, but he always gave me instructive answers. He taught me about the combined value of patience and persistence within a bureaucracy. I learned the most about leading with integrity from Glenn Hopkins, a dean who never pursued the spotlight but who always tried to improve the institution, even when no one was looking. Many others have mentored me along the way, including Don Cole, Morris Stocks, Ann Abadie, Rich Forgette, Carolyn Staton, Robert Khayat, Thomas Wallace, and Noel Wilkin.

The University of Mississippi has outstanding students. I thank the graduate students in my recent seminars for helping me sharpen some of the ideas in this book. I thank many undergraduate students for inspiring me with their hard work and determination. Special thanks to Lakeith Faulkner and Curtis Hill.

While writing this book, I have been buttressed by my colleagues in the Department of Writing and Rhetoric at the University of Mississippi. Glenn Schove, Joanne Mitchell, and Karen Forgette have often protected my time and sacrificed their own priorities for mine. Without Glenn, Joanne, and Karen, this book would still be many years from completion. Our department is a supportive and collaborative place, truly, and my faculty colleagues have never hesitated to cheer me on. Thanks to Guy Krueger, Wendy Goldberg, Angela Green, Kate Hooper, Ashley Jones-Bodie, Chip Dunkin, Don Unger, Karla Lyles, Chad Russell, Andrew Davis, Tori Brown, LaToya Faulk, Alice Myatt, Amber Nichols-Buckley, Deidra Jackson, Ellen Shelton, and every other superb faculty member in our department. Thank you most especially to Robert Cummings. Bob has been a great friend, mentor, and fellow troublemaker over the years. I appreciate his feedback on an early draft of this book, and I am honored to be his colleague.

The College of Liberal Arts at the University of Mississippi provided me with research funding for this project. I thank Dean Lee Cohen and everyone in the dean's office, including my esteemed colleagues Holly Reynolds, Don Dyer, Kirsten Dellinger, Chuck Hussey, and Jan Murray. I also thank my FAS-Track colleagues: Susan Nicholas, Gray Flora, Camp Best, Suzanne Wilkin, Sharon Levine, Maura Scully Murry, and Jackie Certion.

Librarians have been critical to this project, of course. From the UM Libraries, I thank Jennifer Ford for her wisdom and ongoing encouragement.

Leigh McWhite is not only a librarian but also a fine historian, and she often pointed me to valuable resources and nudged me toward good ideas. I also thank Alan Munshower for his help. At the University of Tennessee at Chattanooga, Carolyn Runyon in Special Collections patiently answered my questions and tracked down valuable resources. Thanks to Kevin Ray at the University of Alabama Libraries, Mary Linnemann at the Hargrett Rare Book and Manuscript Library at the University of Georgia, and Kari Hallford at the Alabama Department of Archives and History.

At a critical moment in the development of this book, Frankie Barrett became my collaborator. Her research assistance and perceptive feedback improved my ideas and gave me new momentum on the project. I am grateful to Frankie, and I look forward to reading her first book, which I predict will be amazing. Elizabeth Sweeney has also made many contributions, and I appreciate her editorial insights.

Finally, I thank Daniel Waterman, editor in chief at the University of Alabama Press, who believed in this book before anyone else. Dan has been an incredible guide throughout the process, and I see him as the sagacious grandfather to this book. He is one of the country's great editors; he is also patient and attentive. Everyone at the University of Alabama Press has been wonderful. Special thanks to Kelly Finefrock, Blanche Sarratt, and Clint Kimberling.

I began working on this book in 2016 and have stolen time whenever possible to push it along. I know there are gaps and weaknesses, and those belong solely to me. I thank you, the reader, for giving of your time. I hope something in this book will spark your own ideas, and I hope those ideas improve upon my own.

HERITAGE AND HATE

Introduction

ACROSS THE US SOUTH, COMMUNITIES are struggling with words and symbols rooted in a deeply problematic past. The reckoning is difficult, recursive, and inherently rhetorical. This book focuses on southern university communities to explore how they have struggled with their linguistic and symbolic inheritance: a panoply of Old South words and symbols. My analysis begins with Reconstruction and ends just after the presidency of Barack Obama. A complicated and instructive tale unfolds: one that foregrounds issues of language, identity, ideology, and race. At universities throughout the South, multiracial communities are attempting to reconcile and contextualize symbols generated and entrenched by previous generations who institutionalized nostalgia for the Old South and enforced racial exclusion.

Some of the resulting rhetorical conflicts began decades ago during the civil rights movement when African American students first pushed their way perilously into all-white southern universities and colleges. Other conflicts are more recent, brewing as African Americans (and progressive white Americans) begin to attain and cement genuine agency and voice in those communities. Tensions have been and remain high. Remnants of the old majority continue to recruit and indoctrinate modern adherents. White traditionalists may be in decline by some measures, but their legacy proves powerful and resilient, especially within the closed systems of southern universities, places where identities have often been constructed on nostalgia and tradition. As these institutions become more diverse and modern, white alumni and their allies often feel disoriented and besieged. In their view, everything that has publicly and privately defined their beloved university communities—from anthems to buildings to flags to monuments to mascots—seems to be under attack. In the vocabulary of my primary case study, when "New Miss" collides with "Ole Miss," the resulting discourse is sometimes civil, sometimes violent.

In 2017, Americans watched in horror as the tragedy in Charlottesville played out on television. There, in modern America, people were still dying in battles over Old South symbols and language. And these battles are common. On August 9, 2017, just a few days before Charlottesville, the *New York Times* ran a story about the University of Mississippi under the headline "Ole Miss Edges Out of Its Confederate Shadow, Gingerly." Reporter Stephanie Saul rightly pointed out that problems at the university are both emblematic and unique: "Ole Miss's identity is intertwined with slavery and the Jim Crow era, partly because of the state's history, but also because the school vigorously embraced Confederate symbols." To some extent, the same can be said of every public university in the US South. These institutions spent decades making ideational and emotional investments in terms and symbols that many modern stakeholders regard as hateful and offensive. For present-day university leaders, the path toward harmony is treacherous, and the struggle with inherited symbols and language (what I term "confederate rhetoric") is both unsettled and unsettling.

What Is Confederate Rhetoric and What Does It Do?

The concept of confederate rhetoric is developed and used throughout this book to better understand the ways in which certain words and symbols operate within the US South. What do I mean by the term "confederate rhetoric"? Readers will notice that confederate rhetoric encompasses many modes of communication, including words, sounds, colors, statues, flags, photos, architecture, and more. As a concept, it is historical, gathering any and all symbolic behavior that is rooted in or that recalls the Old South. The concept is also interdisciplinary and inclusive, something similar to Jan Blommaert's concept of discourse, which "comprises all forms of meaningful semiotic human activity seen in connection with social, cultural, and historical patterns and developments of use."[1] But my concept of confederate rhetoric is also focused and exclusive, in that my purposes are specifically regional. I seek to draw on and contribute to, from a semiotic stance, the field of southern studies, which is notably interdisciplinary and flexible and which focuses first and foremost on analyzing and understanding the complexities of the US South.[2]

The South is a rich linguistic and semiotic space, one where people of all backgrounds know and feel the importance of words and symbols. Michael Montgomery and Ellen Johnson have described the tremendous value that southerners place on language: "For many Southerners, the way they speak English marks their loyalties, their upbringing, their roots, and their identity."[3] In other ways, too, southerners have long been hyperlinguistic, sensitive to and considerate of language. One manifestation is the South's unmatched literary tradition, a lens through which the outside world has looked at the South and a mirror in which many southerners have pondered their own identity. C. Vann Woodward put it this way: "After Faulkner, Wolfe, Warren, and Welty no literate Southerner could remain unaware of his heritage or doubt its enduring value."[4] Indeed, artful language of all kinds is produced and valued in the US South. Past and present writers, songwriters, storytellers, preachers, and speechmakers are revered and rewarded in the South. Outsiders still sometimes follow H. L. Mencken's lead from 1917, attacking the South as a literary and intellectual desert, but such myopia is no longer the norm. The South does struggle with educational funding and attainment, but even its least-educated citizens value the power of words and symbols. Southerners of all backgrounds, religions, and political persuasions tend to be sophisticated rhetors and hearers, people who understand the power and flexibility of language. In the South, a Chomskyan or Saussurean stability of meaning does not seem to match the popular consciousness. Instead, language in the South continues to be alive and dynamic: a polite "yes" can actually mean "go to hell."

The South is a place where words and symbols have always held the power to index, or refer to, multiple meanings. In my view, southerners understand and use the indexicality of language for various purposes. In fact, to whatever extent the US South can be defined as a regional culture, words and symbols play a critical role in the formation and propagation of that culture, both on the personal and communal levels. Lillian Smith wrote that the South "cannot get along without symbols, it would be unthinkable. But they are full of strange power. . . . They need to be handled as carefully as nuclear energy."[5]

Studying this energy—a rhetorical energy—is one of the purposes of this book. I have chosen the term "confederate rhetoric" because my interest lies in contestations, those situations in which words and symbols stir conflict. Here again, the region proves rich and fertile. It is a place where marble statues can be argumentative, flags discriminatory, and etiquette hateful. Untangling the complicated rhetorical conflicts of the South has necessitated a multidisciplinary approach, but my methodology is built first and foremost on a key assumption from the fields of rhetoric and critical discourse analysis: namely, that language and society are comprehensively intertwined. Norman Fairclough, Jan Blommaert, Stephanie Kerschbaum, and Laurie Gries are a few of the many scholars who have mapped, in other contexts, the nuanced relationships between identity, language, and power. Words, images, and symbols are not simply reflective and passive; they are formative and active. To understand and trace some of their many consequences in the US South, I apply theories and methods developed by such scholars of rhetoric and critical discourse analysis.

This book also relies on and extends scholarship in southern studies and history, including work by Grace Elizabeth Hale, James C. Cobb, Charles Reagan Wilson, Karen Cox, and Ted Ownby. My goal is not simply to understand rhetoric, but to understand rhetoric in the particular context of the US South. In so doing, I build from scholarship by those who know the most about the region. Indeed, some historians and popular writers have already written perceptive books about my primary case study, the University of Mississippi community (fig. 2). These include *The Price of Defiance* by Charles Eagles, *An American Insurrection* by William Doyle, and *The Band Played Dixie* by Nadine Cohodas. My research relies on such sources, which recount many episodes ripe for additional analysis. It also takes the examination of the UM community in a new direction by foregrounding language and symbols, which I argue are primary catalysts in the history of the institution and region. In my view, language and symbols do not simply reflect historical stasis or change; they generate historical stasis or change.

Promoting words and symbols to such a prominent position, my analytical approach complements traditional historical accounts of the US South. If historians see Confederate monuments as symptoms or artifacts, I see them as active rhetorical agents. Charles Reagan Wilson asked of the South, "Is there something in the culture here that has fostered a tolerance for symbols

FIGURE 2. Fall football pep rally at the University of Mississippi in 1966. This photograph was printed in the 1967 yearbook alongside a caption that read, "Unbridled enthusiasm is rampant at first pep rally." (University of Mississippi, *Ole Miss, 1967*, 24. Special Collections, University of Mississippi Libraries.)

of racial antagonism?"[6] I ask a similar question but in a different way: Is there something *in* the symbols that has fostered and protected a tolerance for a culture of racial antagonism? In my reading of southern history, southern language and symbols are Wilson's elusive "something," the very force that has fostered and protected the South's disturbing (and stubborn) culture of racism.

Eight Common Characteristics of Confederate Rhetoric

Just how do words and symbols generate and animate human behavior? How do they control communities and institutions? How has confederate rhetoric shaped the history and culture of the US South? In the following chapters, I share my search for answers to these questions. Through close and careful readings of historical episodes from particular southern communities, I have found that confederate rhetoric has played a formative role in creating and re-creating southern identities across time, slowed progress toward racial harmony, and reinforced racial barriers built by previous generations. Furthermore, it has performed this work while often obfuscating its purpose and protecting its own existence. Before exploring these complex consequences, and before narrowing my focus to southern university communities, let me offer eight broad introductory observations about confederate rhetoric in the hopes of establishing a working definition.

Confederate rhetoric has tremendous emotional power. This may be an obvious point, but it is also foundational. Old South terms and symbols evoke, for southerners, strong and motivating feelings. These affective responses are oftentimes more compelling than any accompanying intellectual responses. And, of course, these affective responses vary depending on one's perspective and position. Take, for example, the song "Dixie," which begins "I wish I was in the land of cotton, / Old times there are not forgotten." Nostalgic white southerners can be brought to tears by what they hear as a beautiful and profound anthem. Black southerners, on the other hand, are more likely to feel disgust and revulsion by what they hear as a reminder of slavery and oppression. One set of lyrics leads to two very strong but divergent emotional responses. Take, as another example, the phrase "cotton-picking." For many white southerners, even in recent history, this is a lighthearted adjectival phrase used nonchalantly in situations of teasing or joking (fig. 3). For many Black southerners, however, the term "cotton-picking" is grim and heavy, evoking the painful history of agrarian enslavement. Again, one term leads to two strong but divergent emotional responses. Confederate rhetoric stirs powerful emotions, but those emotions are never singular, never simple.

Figure 3. Party at the University of Tennessee during the 1949/50 school year. The photograph shows students drinking outside a building labeled "Cotton Pickers Cabin" and featuring a caricature of an enslaved Black man. Such racist humor, including many blackface parties and performances, was a prevalent part of southern university life during the twentieth century. (University of Tennessee, *The Volunteer, 1950*, 240. University of Tennessee, Knoxville, Libraries.)

The catalog of confederate rhetoric includes overtly racist language like the n-word alongside subtler words and symbols. The n-word resonates powerfully when deployed by white people against Black people, but other, less-glaring words and symbols also deliver significant emotional content and serve to reify—on a very personal level—the region's long tradition of racism. Take, for example, the Confederate battle flag and its derivatives. The flag remains a pervasive symbol in the modern South, seen along country roads and above state capitols. Many white people who would never defend or use the n-word do feel comfortable defending the flag, especially when it is embedded within a state flag, as was the case still in Mississippi in 2019. Further down the scale of overtness, there are other examples of confederate rhetoric that have thus far escaped scrutiny. Chapter 3, for example, uncovers the complicated history and oppressive power of an extant college football cheer, the Hotty Toddy at the University of Mississippi, an example of confederate rhetoric that continues to hide in plain sight, even while performing powerful cultural work. The Hotty Toddy is not controversial per se, but it can be racially oppressive. Revealing the full spectrum of confederate rhetoric—from the overt slur to the subtle fight song—is important to understanding power and language in the US South. Indeed, to paraphrase Jane Hill, covert confederate rhetoric may be the most interesting and pernicious, for it has yet to be compromised or questioned in its power.[7]

Confederate rhetoric has perpetuated the simplification of racial categories in the US South. Indeed, in this region, race has usually been artificially defined as a binarism: a person is either white or Black. Of course, this is a reductive identity practice, one that fixes individual identities and ignores or downplays racial complexities. The simplification of race in the history of the US South has served important purposes, becoming what Grace Elizabeth Hale has called "the founding metaphor" that made possible a "new collective white identity across lines of gender and class and a new regional distinctiveness." The false binary of race is one of the cornerstones of the South's comprehensive system to privilege white people and oppress Black people. Like all binaries, the white/Black worldview is straightforward and comprehensible, and as such, it is an effective rhetorical strategy for marketing and perpetuating the orthodox order.[8] Confederate rhetoric has played an important role in creating, strengthening, and preserving this false binary by establishing and guarding stark linguistic and semiotic barriers between the races. Think of the powerful images of "White" and "Colored" signage on public water fountains during much of the twentieth century. Water fountains, in and of themselves, are not very important to societal order. When racialized and labeled, however, water fountains in the US South became prominent signposts of identity enforcement, declarative reminders of a system that considered white people to be better than Black people and that viewed everyone in society as one or the other, white or Black. Subtler, but just as demarcating, are many contemporary practices in the US South. On southern university campuses, for example, there are magisterial fraternity houses for white men and, nearby, either very humble or entirely absent fraternity houses for Black men. As symbols, as confederate rhetoric, these architectural counterpoints serve as a visual argument for the perpetuation of the South's simplified binary of race.

Confederate rhetoric is a rhetoric of whiteness, a rhetoric of power. For generations, white southerners have crafted and used confederate rhetoric to establish, exert, and maintain power over Black southerners. Thus, confederate rhetoric is a regional example of Norman Fairclough's "discourse," in that confederate rhetoric has been (and continues to be) a means for "exercising power over others in ways which are illegitimate, unjust or otherwise harmful."[9] The rhetoric of southern whiteness has its roots in Reconstruction and has experienced growth spurts during eras like the civil rights movement. In times of trouble, white traditionalists have become more creative, more rhetorical, conceiving new and innovative words and symbols or reviving previous words and symbols, all as defensive stratagems to fight off unimaginable and unwanted social and racial changes. Of course, white people have traditionally had more linguistic range and power in the US South than Black people, who were (and are) systematically discouraged from educational attainment. White utterances of confederate rhetoric highlight these privileges. Just as there have been places in the South where Black people were not welcome and they knew to avoid, confederate rhetoric is off-limits to Black southerners. As a set of words and symbols, confederate rhetoric is a white tradition. It is extraordinarily rare, for example, to see a Black southerner doing the rebel yell or uttering the regional cliché "Southern by the Grace of God" or calling anyone "boy" or shouting "The South will rise again!" or wearing a shirt imprinted with the rebel flag or driving a car with a "Cotton" novelty plate on the front. Confederate rhetoric is a semiotic club that admits only white members. Here again, confederate rhetoric creates and emphasizes racial divisions. Indeed, this power to sort by race, to enforce and reinforce the racial order of the Old South, is perhaps this rhetoric's most important and enduring function. Working as guardians against acts of racial reconciliation and progress is, in the (J. L.) Austinian sense, what these words and symbols do best and most often.

Confederate rhetoric encourages and unifies white people, thereby protecting their majority status and preserving traditional orthodoxies. Confederate rhetoric creates and strengthens a sociolinguistic confederacy, one in which white people remain more powerful than Black people. Symbols, genres, music, and statuary, at one time or another, have all been rallying points—or simply reassuring touchstones—for white people in the US South. White southerners who defend the Confederate battle flag (and its state-specific derivatives) often describe it as "our" flag. White southerners who tell "black jokes" rarely do so with Black people in the room, and white people who attend country music concerts can look across stadiums without seeing a single Black face. Traveling across the region, white southerners can find Confederate statues in nearly every small town. Such mechanisms promote white unity and offer potential retreat to every white southerner, even to those who do not fly the flag or tell the jokes or listen to the music or revere the statues. All white people in the South have access to this rhetorical umbrella of protection. All are, to some extent, sheltered beneath confederate rhetoric, and this benefit cannot be abdicated. Symbols and language that evoke the Old South offer ongoing encouragement and unifying shelter to white people, even to those who reject explicitly racist practices.

While confederate rhetoric offers benefits to white people, it offers discouragement and punishment to Black people. In this respect, confederate rhetoric complements racial violence. Of course, any conversation about the imposition of racism in the US South must acknowledge the incredible power of white-on-Black violence. Bryan Stevenson has noted, "Racial terror and the constant threat created by violently enforced racial hierarchy were profoundly traumatizing for African Americans."[10] My intention is not to minimize the horrible role of actual violence in the US South. Instead, I argue that confederate rhetoric has worked alongside this violence to enforce and reinforce similar traumas. Acts of terror are effective strategies for punishing individuals and groups and for preserving order. But order must also be enforced daily, hourly, and weekly. While acts of public violence such as lynchings required planning and coordination within the white community, confederate rhetoric has been deployed far more frequently and with far less effort. Confederate rhetoric was (and is) less disruptive than terroristic approaches because it has been incorporated seamlessly into daily life. Lynchings and murders have played a critical role in punishing and discouraging Black people in the US South, and confederate rhetoric has served as a constant and effective partner in that oppression (fig. 4). White southerners have punished and discouraged Black people with violence—and with words and symbols.

As other forms of oppression have waned in legality and acceptability, confederate rhetoric has remained popular and active. There are many reasons for this (un)healthy trajectory. White people seeking to preserve old hierarchies of power have lost the legal standing to physically exclude Black people from institutions that white people once controlled. Southern universities, for example, were forced to integrate in the 1960s. Even so, those impositions do not mark the end of white resistance within the US South. This is an obvious but important point. Words and symbols have always been reliable tools for enforcing control, but during times of incursion, words and symbols become even more valuable and effective to the controlling majority. In fact, in the US South, confederate rhetoric is one of the last retreats for projects and agendas of discrimination. This reality has played out in southern universities: Black students now attend, but through language and symbols the definition and terms of full belonging remain in the control of the white majority. Confederate rhetoric sets the parameters of complete inclusion and opportunity, and that regulatory power has proven quite resilient, even into the twenty-first century.

Confederate rhetoric has survived and thrived, in large part, because of its ability to conceal itself. Often confederate rhetoric is hiding in plain sight. Two chapters of this book deal with related but distinct examples: the term "Ole

FIGURE 4. "Encores" page from the 1932 University of Georgia yearbook. The text reads in part, "Students at the University just after the Civil war enjoyed a day of real sport when the newly freed Negroes set out to unfold for themselves the mysteries of the college buildings. . . . The fun started when the students charged from their classes armed with pistols, rifles, and clubs to chase the greatly enlightened Negroes away once and for all." (University of Georgia, *Pandora, 1932*. Courtesy of Hargett Rare Book and Manuscript Library/University of Georgia Libraries.)

Miss" and the Hotty Toddy cheer. Even today, within the University of Mississippi community, it is taboo to question these foundational traditions. I break this taboo by looking beyond orthodox etymologies. In the case of the Hotty Toddy, I interrogate the cheer, uncovering a previously unacknowledged history, one that might surprise today's student body, who revere the Hotty Toddy as a wholesome and unifying tradition. The truth, however, is darker and far more complicated, as there have been moments when the cheer has been used by white people on campus to register hate and foment racialized violence. Consider, for example, how in 1963 the Hotty Toddy was used by white students in spontaneous jubilation to celebrate the assassination of President Kennedy and how in 2012 the cheer was hurled by white students against their Black peers in a late-night rally to protest the reelection of President Barack Obama. The Hotty Toddy is one example of confederate rhetoric that has hidden for decades in plain sight, cloaking itself as a harmless university tradition, avoiding scrutiny, but always remaining available as a tool for racial power.

Why Is Confederate Rhetoric a Concept Worth Development and Study?

A few years before she died, poet Lucille Clifton visited the University of Mississippi to speak to the English department. I was in the audience, an impressionable young graduate student in those days. Clifton opened her talk by playing with the university's popular and traditional nickname. "Ole Miss," she began. "Here I am at Ole Miss. [Pause] I guess I'd rather be at New Miss, but I'm happy to be at Ole Miss, too, I suppose." Poets like Clifton are powerful because they use language to cut through life's illusions. Clifton did so for me that day, using straightforward and disarming language to expose deep problems within a central tenet of my community's orthodoxy: our very name for ourselves. It was a gentle rumination for Clifton; for me, it was the profound genesis of the present book. If our very name—our brand, our public identity—pushed people away, what about our other words and symbols? What pernicious work were they performing?

As the years wore on, I stayed at UM, playing various administrative and faculty roles, and I am still here, writing these words from my office overlooking the Grove. I have not forgotten Lucille Clifton's playful but critical interrogation of "Ole Miss," and I have often wondered if others (insiders or outsiders) would question the term. Few ever do. Indeed, "Ole Miss" remains a fixed orthodoxy, a label so deeply interwoven with the identity of the school and community as to be commonsensical, natural, preternatural, even. Except for a few lonely voices, like that of history professor Charles Eagles, few people ever publicly question "Ole Miss," which is most often described as an "affectionate" nickname.[11] That adjective, "affectionate," has been a controlling description of the term for decades, but as Clifton understood and communicated years ago, it tells only part of the story.

This book grew from my discomforting reaction to Clifton's playfully poetic insight. I knew then, and I know now, that southern university communities are full of white people with progressive racial agendas. Many white students, faculty, administrators, and alumni want to move their institutions toward racial harmony and are working alongside their African American peers every day to increase opportunities and build on the progress of the civil rights movement. And, of course, real gains have been made: over the last half century, African American students, faculty, administrators, and alumni have become (nearly) equal members of these once exclusionary institutions. When viewed optimistically, southern university campuses seem poised to defeat, once and for all, the racism of their problematic pasts. This is true at schools across the region, including the University of Mississippi, the University of Alabama, the University of Georgia, and the University of Missouri.

Yet the promise of defeating racism—of moving on—has proven illusory. For every gain, there is a loss. Southern universities continue to struggle with profound problems of racial inequity. Decade after decade, progress is interrupted by jarring episodes of campus hate speech, by racially motivated crimes, by micro- and macroaggressions. White and Black people who desperately want to be free from their institutions' problematic histories grow frustrated and fatigued. It can feel to them like a vicious and unending cycle. In 2014, after a noose and rebel flag were placed around the neck of a campus statue honoring James Meredith, the first African American student to attend the University of Mississippi, the student editors of the campus newspaper expressed their exhaustion and disheartenment:

> This is disgraceful. But what makes it all the worse is that it is another disgraceful moment in a series of disgraceful moments. We are racking them up and bolstering the stereotypes that are ingrained within the national consciousness. And we, *The Daily Mississippian*, continue to write editorials about them. The campus continues to hold candlelight vigils. The administration continues to create committees, send apologetic emails and preach to us. . . . But still nothing has changed. These events continue to happen semester after semester, and year after year. All of our actions seem fruitless and impotent, leaving us broken, scared, humiliated and with burning, difficult questions: What do we do about it? How do we stop these events from transpiring? How do we fight an idea?[12]

The sense of confusion and bewilderment in this statement recalls Charles Reagan Wilson's speculation that there is "something" vague—some anchoring force—that allows for the preservation of the South's culture of racism. That force is, I argue, confederate rhetoric. By tracing specific examples as they circulate and influence, we can see how confederate rhetoric drags institutions backward or slows progress. Dynamic and powerful, Old South words and symbols often create stasis or even reversion.

This book does not forward facile arguments. I do not suggest that most white people in the modern South are racists or that anyone who uses a term connected to the Old South is a racist. Such claims are false, counterproductive, and harmful. This is not a book about blame. Instead, the concept of confederate rhetoric has the potential to empower progressive white people, to encourage a new kind of reflection on traditions of language and symbols that often seem commonsensical and harmless from the safety of the majority perspective. This book intends to push readers firmly away from passive acceptance of semiotic traditions and toward purposeful consideration and confrontation of those semiotic traditions.

How can leaders and administrators in the US South stop the frustrating cycle of racism within their institutions? How can they battle an idea? How can they contribute more wholeheartedly to continued racial progress? What can they do to further empower Black southerners and overcome frustrating setbacks in race relations? For one, they can recognize and reflect on their own traditions. They can critically examine their own linguistic and semiotic inheritance. They can stop defending harmful words and symbols and begin revising them. For in the US South, it is the white majority who still controls the language of power and privilege.

The first step is recognition, and the concept of confederate rhetoric can be a tool for this. Confederate rhetoric—words and symbols rooted in and evocative of the Old South—remain pervasive within southern universities, and part of my mission with this book is straightforward exposure. Although often hidden or overlooked or minimized, this rhetoric is, indeed, present. Even when unrecognized (or especially then), confederate rhetoric creates, preserves, and promotes the chronic enforcement of outdated racial norms. This rhetoric sustains a status quo that is more than a century old. It warns and punishes Black people, even as it serves to reassure and shelter white people. In obvious ways, and in many more subtle ways, confederate rhetoric offers punitive reminders to Black southerners that they are still considered inferior within southern systems and institutions. Confederate rhetoric is not harmless. Instead, it is a dangerous and effective weapon for excluding and oppressing Black people. Its presence and power should not be ignored or underestimated.

White supremacists continue to understand the value and importance of Old South words and symbols. When Eli Mosley co-organized the 2017 white supremacist rally in Charlottesville, he was thinking in rhetorical terms. "I decided that the left was winning with identity politics, so I wanted to play identity politics too," Mosley shared with ProPublica reporters. Physical violence grabs the headlines and is one important tactic of groups like Vanguard America and Identity Evropa, but it would be a dangerous mistake to view the white supremacist movement as pure barbarity. Instead, the people involved are often savvy, self-aware, and skillfully rhetorical. Sometimes they use violence, but more often they engage in symbolic and linguistic fights. They read and write books, rally on message boards, network on college campuses, protest the removal of Confederate statues, advocate for the preservation of tradition, wave the Confederate battle flag, and yell racial slurs. As ProPublica has shown, participants originate from both the political left and the political right.[13] They become united by and through their words and symbols.

In the US South, many white people have grown tired of talking about race. From the perch of the majority position, conversations and debates about racism may seem no longer necessary, or, as some argue, such discussions merely propagate racial problems. In 2017, when Mississippi's largest newspaper, the *Clarion-Ledger*, covered racial reconciliation and contextualization efforts at the University of Mississippi, many (presumably white) commenters expressed disdain for both the efforts and the coverage. A poster calling himself Randy Craig wrote, "People it's time to move on, can't you find anything else to write about to help contribute to fixing real problems in our society (crime, killing, raping, the murder of babies every day, the destruction of the American family, etc.)." Other online commenters were even more pointed in their criticism. Another poster calling himself John Irwin Reston wrote, "I swear, if Mississippi blacks didn't have slavery in their unknown ancient ancestors' ancient history to read, study, complain about, lament, embrace, reject, rehash, live through vicariously and write about on a daily basis (did I miss anything) and continually pound their grief, anger, resentment, rage, unhappiness, sense of great loss and whatever else they're thinking, over the heads of the rest of society as if the practice still existed, I truly believe they would have nothing at all to complain about."[14] Such dismissive attitudes are, of course, only available to white people who can navigate the world without facing racism themselves. One major privilege of inhabiting the majority group within an unequal system is the privilege of dismissing inequality.

But such dismissiveness from within the white majority is not merely a symptom of privilege; it is a perpetuator of privilege. When white people defend or tolerate Old South words and symbols, for example, they are in effect asserting cultural dominance over the parameters of public memory. Scholars Carole Blair, Greg Dickinson, and Brian Ott have shown that such assertions over public memory—over the past—are always "activated by concerns, issues, or anxieties of the present. That is, groups tell their pasts to themselves and others as ways of understanding, valorizing, justifying, excusing, or subverting conditions or beliefs of their current moment."[15] In other words, some white southerners seek to control the public memory of the past for many fresh and current reasons, both affective and intellectual. They make choices and seek to prioritize public memories based on their anxieties for the present. In the dismissiveness of Reston and Craig, we can hear those manifested anxieties. Take, for example, Craig's assertion that people should move beyond considerations of the past in order to fix "real problems in our society (crime, killing, raping, the murder of babies every day, the destruction of the American family, etc.)."

First of all, the premise that reconciling the reality of the past will distract us from solving problems of the present is false. Second, we can hear in Craig's comment, and in Reston's, the common fantasy that we now live in a postracial world. That myth underpins the dismissiveness and seems something akin to what Tammie M. Kennedy, Joyce Irene Middleton, and Krista Ratcliffe have labeled a "haunting whiteness." In *Rhetorics of Whiteness*, these scholars show how whiteness functions "as a trope with associated discourses and cultural scripts that socialize people into ways of seeing, thinking, and performing whiteness and nonwhiteness."[16] When commenters like Reston and Craig dismiss racial reconciliation as unjustified complaining, they are performing whiteness, asserting control, and giving readers of the story (in this case Mississippi readers) a clear pathway toward dismissal and away from engagement with the difficult process of racial reconciliation. Reflecting on the weaknesses of your own inherited culture is difficult work; it is a cultural script adversarial to the status quo, and one that can be avoided through the facile process of looking away. All of this is at play within the discourse of the *Clarion-Ledger* story and comment section. Perhaps the most important point for the present discussion is that such rhetorical ploys are nothing more than silencing methods. In such emotional dismissals of discussions of Old South symbols, the white majority is attempting to shame, shun, and marginalize those in the Black minority—and their allies—who dare to forward public memories divergent from accepted, traditional, and white orthodoxies.

What's more, when white people dismiss or ignore institutional efforts to reconsider or contextualize traditional terms and symbols, they are wittingly or unwittingly aligning themselves with more extreme white voices. Furthermore, they are denying minority voices opportunities to enact the kind of "commonplace witnessing" to historical tragedy or injustice that can be therapeutic and reconciling. They are limiting what Bradford Vivian has called "a means of pursuing a more just, humane, or inclusive future."[17] Certainly, some white people in the US South are purposefully against justice, humanity, or inclusivity, but just as certainly, many more white people are simply reluctant to confront the status quo for less sinister reasons. These could include subject fatigue, laziness, or a regional predilection for not making waves, for not talking about impolite or unpleasant realities like religion, money, or, in this case, race. The causes are far less important than the consequences. Whenever white people tolerate confederate rhetoric, no matter their reasons, they are helping perpetuate racist attitudes and practices.

Such tensions, conflicts, alliances, and consequences are most apparent when diverse southerners gather together within a single organization or institution. That is one reason that this book focuses on southern universities, which are finite gathering places with long, rich, and complicated histories. For much of the nineteenth and twentieth centuries, state universities in the South were white retreats, key sites for the reproduction of southern power and white identity. And, in fact, white elites have often imagined, founded, and developed state universities as official state instruments, as training grounds for future white leaders.

This focus manifested early in southern history, even within the 1785 charter of the University of Georgia. Writing in 1949, campus historian Thomas Walter Reed noted that the Georgia legislature chartered UGA to embrace "all the citizens of the State (slaves never being citizens)" and "to educate its youth for the benefit of the State itself." Reed saw this foundational mission as "novel and so outstanding as to challenge profound consideration." He viewed the purposefulness of the university's charter as "the first instance in history where a State undertook by the establishment of a state university to furnish the sinews of war by which ignorance should be eradicated." He further praised the legislature's foresight in realizing "that really educated citizens are among the greatest assets in the commonwealth of any country," and lauded the legislature for fulfilling its "duty to provide the means of a liberal education within the State so as to guarantee homogeneity in the ideals of our youth and patriotic devotion to the State."[18]

Indeed, many state universities in the US South sought to "guarantee homogeneity" of thought and ideals among their all-white student bodies. In *The Price of Defiance*, Charles Eagles details how the "Ole Miss" of the 1950s and 1960s "stressed social life, encouraged conformity, and emphasized institutional traditions." Eagles quotes alumnus and journalist Curtis Wilkie's observation that "Ole Miss functioned as a . . . finishing school for the young women [and men] who would marry the elite and preside over their mansions." This concern was foundational and purposeful at the University of Mississippi, a school founded by and dominated by "Mississippi's wealthy planters and elite lawyers. . . . The central purpose of their university was not to introduce students to new and exciting ideas but to perpetuate conformity to established ones."[19]

No surprise, then, that students themselves have often embraced the idea that they are attending the South's public universities to prepare for leadership and to perpetuate conformity. The editors of the 1961 *Corolla*, the yearbook at the University of Alabama, celebrated this concept in their introduction: "[This yearbook] commemorates one hundred years of progress and change at the University of Alabama. The 'capstone of southern learning' played a vital role in the War for Southern Independence, and this issue of the *Corolla* seeks to remind us of our heritage, our traditions, and our destiny as an institution dedicated to educating men and women for future leadership."[20] Their commemoration statement was printed directly below a visual pairing of the American flag and the Confederate battle flag (fig. 5). There, in full color, the Confederate battle flag emphasized the regional and racial dimensions of their investment in continuity. The student editors at the University of Alabama were using confederate rhetoric to regionalize and racialize their communal identity. This was a typical rhetorical move at southern universities, which were founded to develop a specific kind of leader, one who respected regional heritage and traditions, and was, of course, white.

During the late twentieth century, as newcomers to these southern institutions, African American students had to fight against many words and symbols that were deeply embedded, exclusionary, marginalizing, and antagonistic. This book is the story of how such words and symbols have remained active and influential into the present, long after exclusionary laws and other racist customs have been abolished. It is the story of how southern universities have opened their doors but have often failed to reconcile their rhetoric.

Indeed, university leaders—and entire university communities—across the US South are struggling publicly with issues of identity and change. The stories are similar at the University of Mississippi, the University of Virginia, the University of Missouri, the University of Georgia, the University of Alabama, and elsewhere. No matter how modern or progressive their aspirations, southern university leaders and their constituents are often imprisoned by a sociolinguistic inheritance that is wily, sturdy, and stubbornly unreconstructed. The institutions have spent more than a century building and fortifying connections between their identities and confederate rhetoric. Often, they now seek to overcome those rhetorical legacies without confronting or understanding them.

In this book, I trace and clarify some of the complicated dynamics of confederate rhetoric within southern universities. More generally, I see the rhetoric of the US South as a fertile and still developing field of study. When I look across the region, I see undiscovered rhetorical realities and neglected primary source documents. I see many communities and organizations with dynamic words and symbols that have yet to be examined. I see possibilities for extracting fresh insights from existing scholarship in history and other disciplines. And I see countless ways in which linguistic and semiotic traditions have reified power and helped defend ideologies over time. With this book, I present one contribution to this potentially vast field of study.

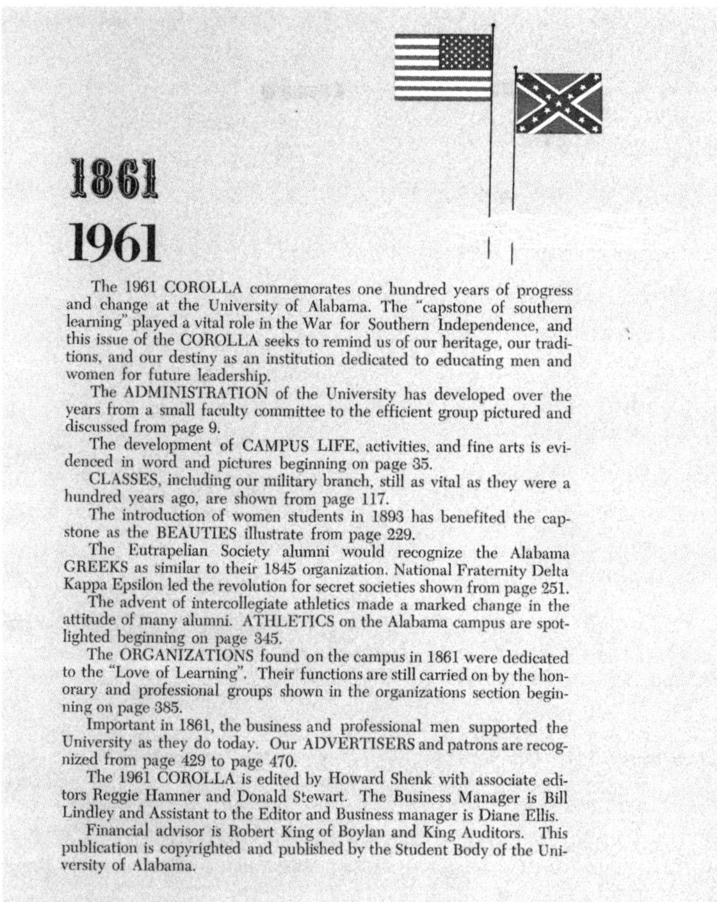

1861

1961

The 1961 COROLLA commemorates one hundred years of progress and change at the University of Alabama. The "capstone of southern learning" played a vital role in the War for Southern Independence, and this issue of the COROLLA seeks to remind us of our heritage, our traditions, and our destiny as an institution dedicated to educating men and women for future leadership.

The ADMINISTRATION of the University has developed over the years from a small faculty committee to the efficient group pictured and discussed from page 9.

The development of CAMPUS LIFE, activities, and fine arts is evidenced in word and pictures beginning on page 35.

CLASSES, including our military branch, still as vital as they were a hundred years ago, are shown from page 117.

The introduction of women students in 1893 has benefited the capstone as the BEAUTIES illustrate from page 229.

The Eutrapelian Society alumni would recognize the Alabama GREEKS as similar to their 1845 organization. National Fraternity Delta Kappa Epsilon led the revolution for secret societies shown from page 251.

The advent of intercollegiate athletics made a marked change in the attitude of many alumni. ATHLETICS on the Alabama campus are spotlighted beginning on page 345.

The ORGANIZATIONS found on the campus in 1861 were dedicated to the "Love of Learning". Their functions are still carried on by the honorary and professional groups shown in the organizations section beginning on page 385.

Important in 1861, the business and professional men supported the University as they do today. Our ADVERTISERS and patrons are recognized from page 429 to page 470.

The 1961 COROLLA is edited by Howard Shenk with associate editors Reggie Hamner and Donald Stewart. The Business Manager is Bill Lindley and Assistant to the Editor and Business manager is Diane Ellis.

Financial advisor is Robert King of Boylan and King Auditors. This publication is copyrighted and published by the Student Body of the University of Alabama.

FIGURE 5. Opening page of the 1961 University of Alabama yearbook. The university is described as the "capstone of southern learning," and the yearbook's first stated goal is to "remind us of our heritage, our traditions, and our destiny as an institution dedicated to educating men and women for future leadership." (University of Alabama, *Corolla, 1961*. The University of Alabama Libraries Special Collections.)

CHAPTER 1

"A Name So Beautiful and Appropriate"

"Ole Miss" and the Ideology of Self-Identification from 1897 to 1971

> I love Ole Miss. I love the words Ole Miss. . . . The affectionate term Ole Miss is an important part of our identity and will continue to be. . . . There's never been any confusion internally about who we are. Those of us who have loved this university for a long time use these terms Ole Miss and University of Mississippi interchangeably. . . . Those of us who've been around this university a long time don't have to stop and think consciously am I going to use Ole Miss or am I going to use University of Mississippi.
>
> Chancellor Dan Jones, 2014

> If you bill yourself as Ole Miss and you call yourself the Rebels and the first thing a visitor to campus sees is a Confederate monument, whether intentionally or not, it conveys an image. . . . If I could do one thing, the place would never be called Ole Miss again.
>
> Professor Charles Eagles, 2014

In the early 2000s, when Lucille Clifton questioned the term "Ole Miss," I was surprised, even jolted. At the time, I had been at the University of Mississippi for a few years as a full-time graduate student. I was teaching and taking classes, attending events, and spending my spare time in the library. Since I was frequently on campus, my life revolved around the university, yet I had never heard any doubts about the ubiquitous "Ole Miss." Like seemingly everyone around me, I had accepted the commonplace description of the term as an "affectionate nickname." Perhaps if I had thought any more about the subject, I would have assumed, like many others, that "Ole Miss" was merely an abbreviation for "Old Mississippi." But Clifton was suggesting a serious oversight. She was suggesting that "Ole Miss" had a deeper meaning, something darker and more disturbing than simple affection or straightforward abbreviation.

In the ensuing years—and especially during the research and writing of this book—I have developed a more nuanced understanding of the term. Once I began listening, I heard that not everyone within the UM community regarded "Ole Miss" as an affectionate nickname. The name may have been pervasive, but it was not uniformly understood or deployed. As the dual and dueling epigraphs to this chapter illustrate, by 2014, this disagreement had become public. The majority of people at UM still loved, accepted, and embraced "Ole Miss," but a previously silent minority was beginning to speak up.

In this chapter, I trace part of the 115-year history of the term "Ole Miss," focusing on salient moments when its rhetorical nature has jutted into view. While the term is a concise abbreviation for the University of Mississippi, it is also something far more potent. "Ole Miss" is confederate rhetoric, a powerful actant that has prosecuted an ongoing argument into the very nature of the people and place it represents. For most of the school's history, that argument has been decidedly one-sided, with a white majority in firm control of the communal discourse. Over the years, "Ole Miss" has been invoked to glorify and defend the Old South and its outmoded ways of life, used to punish and exclude Black people (and white people on the side of progress), and served as code, container, and protector of nostalgic feelings for the Lost Cause. For Mississippians and other southerners on the losing end of history—those looking back fondly on old times not forgotten—"Ole Miss" has become an increasingly important semiotic bastion, a linguistic preserve for a doomed but stubborn ideology.

Widespread Acceptance, Quiet Concern

Unaware perhaps of the term's rhetorical and ideological history, those in power at today's University of Mississippi promote "Ole Miss" as a marker of equanimity and harmony, not of conflict. Theirs is a vocal majority that treasures the name for its emotional potency and clubby cachet. For this group, "Ole Miss" encapsulates all that is good, traditional, and unique about their alma mater, a university proudly regarded by insiders as "the most Southern school in our most Southern State." "Ole Miss," the term, reminds this majority of vaguely defined better times when the South was peaceful, prosperous, and genteel. As one school official said in 2014, the name has "got a good, Southern, friendly feel. It connotes hospitality and a lot of good things about being in the South." Such benevolent interpretations, which present "Ole Miss" as nonracial language, characterize the current orthodoxy, which regards the name as a distinctive and entirely positive university tradition. Chancellor Dan Jones promulgated this majority view in 2014 when he said, "I love Ole Miss. I love the words Ole Miss. . . . The affectionate term Ole Miss is an important part of our identity and will continue to be. . . . There's never been any confusion internally about who we are. Those of us who have loved this university for a long time use these terms Ole Miss and University of Mississippi interchangeably." This "affectionate" usage of "Ole Miss" is, indeed, an old and established tradition within the community. As a writer pointed out in the school newspaper in 1929, "Whatever else may be said in comparison of Ole Miss with other schools, it cannot be denied that in respect to name it stands prominent. Nowhere else is there a name so beautiful and appropriate."[1]

For most people associated with the University of Mississippi, "Ole Miss" remains an unsullied heirloom, a positive and unifying label for their university collective, "a name so beautiful and appropriate." That majority has often chosen to dismiss or ignore the unsavory fact that before the 1848 founding of the university, at plantations throughout the Deep South, enslaved people used "Ole Miss" and its derivatives to refer to the wife of the plantation owner. Among the majority of the UM community, this fact is a whispered rumor most often treated like a shameful family secret. Even so, a small minority within the community has broken protocol to express reservations or objections to the use of "Ole Miss." In recent years, some of these stakeholders have been bold enough to share their dissenting views in public, as Professor Charles Eagles did when he told a *New York Times* reporter, "If I could do one thing, the place would never be called Ole Miss again."[2]

Most other opponents of the term have expressed their opposition using quieter methods. An undocumented but growing number of UM faculty, students, and staff avoid using it entirely, choosing instead to always say or write "The University of Mississippi," thereby marking their opposition through elision. One longtime staff member, Mrs. Jacqueline Certion, cited her moving reasons for adopting this approach:

> In 2014, I read the Mississippi Slave Narratives from the WPA Records for the first time. I have been employed at the University of Mississippi since 2001. Up until 2014, I boldly and with much pride told anyone who asked that I worked at Ole Miss. I am the great-great-granddaughter of Polly Turner Cancer. She was born into slavery and as a freed slave was interviewed for the Slave Narratives when she was 100 years old. *"My name is Polly Cancer an' I was born a slave; I b'long'd to de Turners; my Ole Marster was named Bill an' my Ole Mistus was named, Florena; she was a Rankin an' dey lived on Woodson's Ridge; I waited on my Ole Miss 'til she died."* As I read her words, tears ran down my face and it felt as though my breath was leaving my body. I had always heard where the name "Ole Miss" originated. Never had I heard it and understood so clear until that day. It was on that

> day that I began to work for The University of Mississippi. I vowed to my Great-Great-Grandmother Polly that I would NEVER work for the same employer ever again.[3]

This interpretative conflict (between those who love and embrace "Ole Miss" and those who revile and reject the term) is one with roots dating back to 1897, when the words were first applied to the University of Mississippi. Unlike other battles related to Old South imagery and UM identity, rarely has this conflict been made public. Those embracing the term far outnumber those opposing it, and those in the minority are usually reticent about their views—and for good reason. The most zealous defenders of this linguistic tradition can be aggressive or even hostile, especially online and through social media. Overall, there remains tremendous support and inertia for the orthodox view that "Ole Miss" represents all that is good and wholesome about the UM community. What explains the great divide between the prominent majority view and the quieter minority view?

Using methods of critical discourse analysis, I intentionally reconsider the term "Ole Miss," giving prolonged and methodical consideration to dissenting interpretations and latent meanings. Even though "Ole Miss" has become the popular, mainstream name for the University of Mississippi, it has avoided sustained criticism. While other university symbols associated with the Old South have been attacked, defended, and either extirpated or preserved, "Ole Miss" has, for the most part, avoided semiotic scrutiny. If most modern-day speakers and hearers in the community embrace the name, they do so without much information about its history. In this chapter, I address the void by tracing the term's ideological roots and utility from 1897 to 1971. My research reveals that "Ole Miss" is far from inert, straightforward language. It is not, as newcomers and outsiders often assume, a simple abbreviation for "Old Mississippi." Nor is it merely a benign linguistic relic from history or a sweet and endearing nickname. Instead, the term is complicated and volatile rhetoric—confederate rhetoric—containing profound (perhaps existential) threats for the community it names and divides.

Norman Fairclough has shown that "ideology invests language in various ways at various levels." Groups in power often use words to inscribe and reinforce their dominance. This practice works best when the ideological utility of language is partially or fully disguised. Building on Louis Althusser and Antonio Gramsci, Fairclough has demonstrated that "ideology is most effective when its workings are least visible." Words most often strengthen power structures when their ideological functions can be obfuscated, confused, denied, or forgotten. Language that achieves such a position works continually in the background—as assumption—to quietly influence and frame every act of interpretation. Words are most powerful in service to ideology when those words become "naturalized, automatized," when they come to be viewed as commonsensical and irreproachable.[4]

"Ole Miss" is an instructive, regional example of this sociolinguistic truth. After living a long life (one that continues today), the term's ideological roots and utility have become blurred over time, hidden beneath multiple interpretations and misunderstandings. As a community of speakers and hearers, the vast majority of students, alumni, and friends of the University of Mississippi have come to accept "Ole Miss" as something natural and traditional. For most, the name is not controversial at all. As *the* self-identifier of choice for this community, "Ole Miss" has become commonsensical through its ubiquity. It is used pervasively as the conventional label for everything related to the university; it is a term that stands prominent everywhere but that is rarely contextualized or explained. Thus "Ole Miss" resists casual analysis. It has become what Fairclough calls "naturalized," and its deep ideological complexities are now hiding in plain sight. To a large extent, this chapter is a description of the term's long process of naturalization.

Jan Blommaert points out that critical discourse analysis (CDA) can "result in a heightened awareness of hidden power dimensions and its effects: a critical language awareness." CDA can also provide entrances into ideological language that has become mundane and normalized, giving us actionable insights into previously unregistered relationships between language and power.[5] I use CDA to better understand "Ole Miss" in relation to the white southern majorities who have generated, renewed, and reinvigorated the term across more than a century. For the majority groups in this long lineage, the term has offered affordances of power both comforting and reifying. I begin with an examination of the name's moment of origin, near the end of the nineteenth century, when its rebellious and ideological nature was most clearly on display. Next, I survey its ideological utility until 1971, a time when "Ole Miss" was reinvigorated by an influential act of public rhetoric. If the term "Ole Miss" has begun to evolve, to outgrow and hide its racist and ideological roots, most of its long life has been devoted to preserving and glorifying Mississippi's particularly repressive corner of the white hegemony known as the US South.

The Birth of a Viral Term

"Ole Miss" comes from African American Vernacular English and was first appropriated by the students of the University of Mississippi in 1897. Firsthand accounts and previous scholarship have established that Elma Meek was the student who first imported the term into the university setting. She was responding to a contest (formal or informal, historians are uncertain) to nickname not the entire university but merely the university's new student yearbook.[6] Her suggestion won immediate praise and approval from the editors, who were among her student peers. For a variety of reasons, the editors believed "Ole Miss" to be the perfect name for their new publication.

The editors were not the only fans of Meek's creative import. Within a few short years, the broader student body had enthusiastically adopted the term, expanding its usage to personify the entire university. The term would continue to be used as the title of the yearbook, but it had by 1899 dramatically expanded its domain. "Ole Miss" has grown in popularity and breadth of usage ever since, becoming the self-identifier of choice for this university community and a strong national brand name. In other words, during the last 120 years, Meek's suggestion has gone viral.

Laurie Gries defines "virality" as "the tendency of things to spread quickly and widely." In her view, words and symbols "are especially contagious when they propagate affective desires that induce unconscious collective identifications and unconscious imitative feelings, thoughts, and behaviors."[7] Elma Meek suggested "Ole Miss" for the name of the university's yearbook, and then the term quickly spread within this community. To understand why this happened, one must understand why and how the term propagated the community's "affective desires" and induced the community's "collective identifications." What were the affective and ideational forces that fueled the rise and virality of "Ole Miss"?

The term's fascinating linguistic lifespan began during a time of psychological and social uncertainty for white southerners. The exclusively white students matriculating and studying at the University of Mississippi in 1897 had been born in the closing, tumultuous years of Reconstruction. A holistic upheaval for southern elites, Reconstruction was a civil, judicial, political, economic, and social addendum to the Civil War. White people who had previously wielded considerable political, social, and economic power continually faced threats to every aspect of their former order: free and empowered Black people were asserting themselves, carpetbaggers were stealing jobs, outsiders were imposing new laws and political practices, and agrarianism, which had been central to the South's economic and psychological foundation, was proving unreliable and erosive.[8]

White backlash to Reconstruction first became organized and effective during the 1870s. Historian Edward Ayers has called this South "an anxious place, filled with longing and resentment, for people had been dislodged from older bases of identity. . . . Many whites longed for a place where, holding unquestioned dominion, they could lead the South into stability and progress."[9] For white southerners, this was a time of jarring and externally imposed revolution and change. Before arriving at the University of Mississippi, Elma Meek and her peers had lived through and been shaped by this anxious and unsettling period.

Historians have exhaustively documented the various ways white southerners reacted to Reconstruction. White southerners organized politically, renewed commitments to familial and racial purity, created Confederate monuments and commemorations, and became violent through organizations like the Ku Klux Klan. White southerners also reacted, and reassured themselves, through language by telling stories and creating myths. These were linguistic reactions to Reconstruction, efforts in which writing and rhetoric became essential tools for repressing Black people, rejecting northerners and their ideas, and (imaginatively at least) returning to an old, reassuring order. As Grace Elizabeth Hale has shown, "Academic historians joined with amateur historians, antiquarians, Confederate memorialists, novelists, and short story writers to create a broad historical narrative that despite idiosyncrasies and differences of detail praised a romanticized past."[10] The editors and authors of the first yearbook at the University of Mississippi were engaging in just this kind of literary project, contributing locally to the growth of a false but appealing southern historical narrative: the Lost Cause. Along the way, students at the University of Mississippi adopted and nurtured the term "Ole Miss," a packet of language that was perfect for the mission of their day and one that has proven durable—and ideologically useful—into the present.

Why was the term "Ole Miss" so appealing in 1897? Why did the editors of that first yearbook unanimously rally behind Meek's suggestion, choosing it over other entries like the "Boll Weevil" and the "Cotton Boll"? Why was "Ole Miss" appealing enough to go viral—to jump contexts—and to continue trending across more than a century? For Elma Meek, the answers lay in the southern and racial origins and associations of the term. In a 1936 interview, Meek remembered her logic for the suggestion: "I had often heard old 'darkies' on the southern plantations address the lady in the 'Big House' as 'Ole Miss.' The name appealed to me, so I suggested it to the committee seeking a title for the annual." Her nostalgia for the antebellum past aligned perfectly with the mood and goals of the student editors. She won the contest because she intentionally or unintentionally anticipated her audience. In Gries's terminology, Meek was propagating affective desires and inducing communal identifications. Or, more exactly, the term Meek forwarded enacted these dynamics. As one yearbook editor, Maud Morrow Brown, recalled, "I was a member of the committee appointed to suggest names. . . . The name 'Ole Miss' appealed to us at once and it was adopted." Another student on the committee, Maurice Fulton, also recalled "Ole Miss" as being the clear student favorite: "At the time several names were under consideration, but none of them was distinctive enough. Someone . . . suggested Ole Miss, and those of the board who were present . . . heartily voted" for it.[11] From the first moment of its adoption, the term enjoyed a groundswell of community support.

Why? Other aspects of the first annual reveal an editorial preoccupation with glorifying and romanticizing the antebellum past. In addition to their nostalgic selection for the publication's title, the editors "affectionately" dedicated the yearbook to the "University Greys," students who had mustered in 1860 and then left the university soon after the outbreak of the Civil War to defend the Confederacy. The dedication at the front of the 1897 yearbook reads:

> To the "University Greys,"
> Who, under the leadership of that gallant
> Student=Soldier
> William Benjamin Lowry,
> resigned their college labors to battle for
> the cause of their fathers,
> this volume is affectionately dedicated.[12]

Dressed in a font that is lavish and romantic, this opening dedication clearly demonstrates the ideological and historical perspective of the student editors. They were looking backward—thirty-seven years into the past—to honor and memorialize a previous, rebellious generation. They were using confederate rhetoric to make an argument related to the present.

Throughout this first annual, the editors prosecuted the argument that old times were glorious. In doing so, they were willing (and perhaps eager) to promote the racism that was integral to the southern system. In one particularly jarring reference, in the section for fraternities and clubs, there is a sparse page devoted to the KKK (fig. 6). Less adorned than other club pages, the KKK page contains a small cartoon of five men carrying a black coffin. Beneath the uncaptioned image is a membership roll of sixteen students, one of whom was editor in chief G. G. Lyell, an early endorser of Elma Meek's title suggestion.

Given that Lyell, the editor in chief, was presumably the person with final authority over the annual's content and that he himself is listed on the KKK membership roll, it seems unlikely that the KKK entry was intended as a condemnation of the Klan. After all, why would Lyell include his own name in a condemnation? Without Lyell's reflections on this page or any other historical

K. K. K.

Members.

Wm. Britton,	J. V. Leitch,	L. McG. Porter,
J. G. Duke,	G. G. Lyell,	H. D. Priestley, Jr.,
W. W. Garth,	J. R. McDowell, Jr.,	B. S. Ricks,
J. E. Houston,	J. D. Miller,	R. W. Shipp,
W. P. Kretschmar,		J. F. Pope,
J. H. Thompson, Jr.,		R. P. Thompson,

116

Figure 6. Ku Klux Klan page from the 1897 University of Mississippi yearbook. (University of Mississippi, *Ole Miss*, 1897, 116. Special Collections, University of Mississippi Libraries.)

commentary from the time, it is not entirely clear whether the KKK page was a bad joke, a blatant endorsement of racial violence, an entry representing an actual campus affiliate of the notorious Ku Klux Klan, or something else. In all likelihood, the page did not represent an actual campus affiliate of the KKK, as the Klan was by 1897 a diminished organization, one that would not be broadly revived until 1920.[13] What is clear is that the KKK reference appeared first in the 1897 annual and reappeared in several subsequent volumes during the coming years (fig. 7).

Even if the KKK page was some kind of ill-advised joke, the direct reference to the Ku Klux Klan would have been obvious to the students of the time. Contemporary readers of the first *Ole Miss* would not have viewed the KKK reference as oblique allusion or deeply coded language. Instead, this page was a direct reference to a well-known terrorist organization, one devoted to preserving a key aspect of the Old South: white domination. As writers and editors,

FIGURE 7. Ku Klux Klan page from the 1912 University of Mississippi yearbook. KKK references appeared in annuals throughout the early twentieth century. See, among others, the 1905, 1908, 1909, and 1914 volumes for additional references. Fully analyzing these pages is an opportunity for future study. (University of Mississippi, *Ole Miss, 1912*, 228. Special Collections, University of Mississippi Libraries.)

the students who decided to publish the abbreviation KKK without explanation or context made a telling literary choice, inserting an obvious echo into their yearbook, an echo consistent with the goal of glorifying the Lost Cause.

Later in the inaugural *Ole Miss* is a page containing two caricatures of African American men, along with a derisive narrative written in a pejorative representation of African American dialect, under the title "Negro Philosophy" (fig. 8). One of the African American figures stands at a podium, presumably teaching philosophy to a university class: "Brer'rn, Some pussons say dat dere nar no niggers in de Bible, But I ken pruve dat dey is wrong, Per doant dey larn about dat nigger Demus (Nicodemus)." The detail of the punch line is supplied parenthetically, likely as editorial insurance for the joke's reception and success. Such demeaning and racialized wordplay was a popular mode of comedy during this era. Obviously deeply offensive by today's standards, the page is yet another example of an editorial preoccupation in the first *Ole Miss*: to glorify the old southern order and to reject the emerging one. Reconstruction might have temporarily empowered African Americans in Mississippi and elsewhere in the South, but not long afterward, the white students at UM were arguing against power and equality for Black people. Within their yearbook, white students at UM were recording their opinions that Black people were not worthy of education or opportunity.

Although the racism and nostalgia on display in the 1897 yearbook is not surprising, it is helpful in understanding and contextualizing "Ole Miss," a phrase that was invented, or more precisely appropriated, for the first time for this very publication. The inaugural *Ole Miss* marks and commemorates the term, just as it marks and commemorates the ideology of the day. In their selection of content, as in their selection of title, the students at the University of Mississippi were prosecuting a particular argument, foregrounding a world that was in some ways already imaginary. While a few students may have harbored false hopes for Confederate recovery, even the most zealous were no longer willing to take up arms in open rebellion against the United States, as

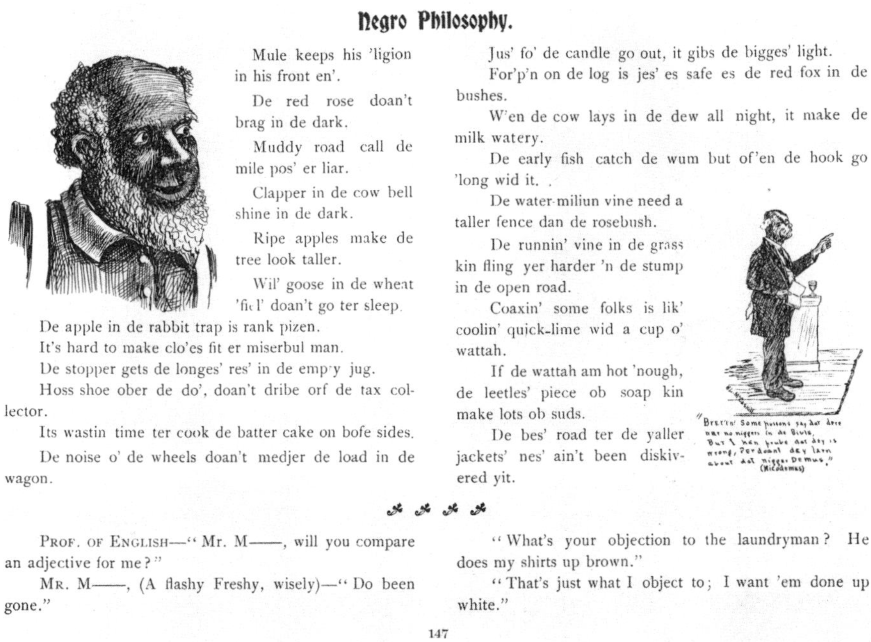

Negro Philosophy.

Mule keeps his 'ligion in his front en'.

De red rose doan't brag in de dark.

Muddy road call de mile pos' er liar.

Clapper in de cow bell shine in de dark.

Ripe apples make de tree look taller.

Wil' goose in de wheat 'fi l' doan't go ter sleep.

De apple in de rabbit trap is rank pizen.

It's hard to make clo'es fit er miserbul man.

De stopper gets de longes' res' in de emp'y jug.

Hoss shoe ober de do', doan't dribe orf de tax collector.

Its wastin time ter cook de batter cake on bofe sides.

De noise o' de wheels doan't medjer de load in de wagon.

Jus' fo' de candle go out, it gibs de bigges' light.

For'p'n on de log is jes' es safe es de red fox in de bushes.

W'en de cow lays in de dew all night, it make de milk watery.

De early fish catch de wum but of'en de hook go 'long wid it.

De water-miliun vine need a taller fence dan de rosebush.

De runnin' vine in de grass kin fling yer harder 'n de stump in de open road.

Coaxin' some folks is lik' coolin' quick-lime wid a cup o' wattah.

If de wattah am hot 'nough, de leetles' piece ob soap kin make lots ob suds.

De bes' road ter de yaller jackets' nes' ain't been diskivered yit.

PROF. OF ENGLISH—"Mr. M——, will you compare an adjective for me?"

MR. M——, (A flashy Freshy, wisely)—"Do been gone."

"What's your objection to the laundryman? He does my shirts up brown."

"That's just what I object to; I want 'em done up white."

147

FIGURE 8. Racist humor in the 1897 University of Mississippi yearbook. Humor at the expense of Black people was a common trope in yearbooks across the South during the nineteenth and twentieth centuries. Oftentimes, these cartoons, poems, and stories portrayed Black people as ignorant and uneducated. (University of Mississippi, *Ole Miss, 1897*, 147. Special Collections, University of Mississippi Libraries.)

had their revered academic ancestors, the University Greys, in 1861. By 1897, the student body at the University of Mississippi was content to inscribe their resistance onto the pages of their yearbook—and into its name. These students seized on "Ole Miss" as an apt expression of their clear and unified longing for what was in their minds better times.

Again, though, such confederate rhetoric was not merely intended to generate inactive nostalgia for the past. The student body was young and ambitious, and like most college students, they were looking ahead to the future. In part, their rhetorical choices were aspirational and forward-looking. They were not merely wallowing in a lost cause; they seemed to believe that parts of the southern cause could still be salvaged. In this view, they were aligning themselves with leaders like John Sharp Williams, who in 1897 was representing Mississippi in the US House of Representatives and who would soon be elected to the US Senate. In a 1904 speech to the United Confederate Veterans in Memphis, Williams emphasized that not every part of the southern cause was lost. "Slavery is lost," lamented Williams. "But the real cause for which our ancestors fought . . . the supremacy of the white man's civilization, the supremacy of the ethical culture . . . has not been lost."[14] Like their congressman, the students at the University of Mississippi had hopes and dreams for the future. They seemed to believe that by curating memories, by deploying certain words and symbols, by labeling themselves "Ole Miss," they could buttress the cause of white supremacy and overcome the horrors (from their perspective) of Reconstruction.

While much of the first *Ole Miss* annual was intended to be a highbrow literary production, complete with metered verse in the style of English poets, the page labeled "Negro Philosophy" and the title *Ole Miss* were as lowbrow as possible. This contradiction is worth considering. Overall, Standard English dominates the pages of the yearbook, which strikes a consistently educated, even scholarly tone. University of Mississippi students may have been provincial in many ways, but they also had erudite aspirations. The students composing the 1897 yearbook were creating an ode to the Confederate past, but they were also showcasing their own academic prowess and contemporary literary tastes. Alongside juvenile jokes and doggerel stand serious attempts at stories and poems. The lowbrow title seems contradictory to these kinds of highbrow aims. As a term borrowed from uneducated enslaved people, "Ole Miss" may have reminded students of a previous (and for them glorious) social and racial order, but did it not also undercut their vaulted notions of learning and intellectual achievement?

Perhaps the resolution of this tension can be found in the term's comedic function. During this era and beyond, African Americans were often parodied to the great delight of white audiences (figs. 9 and 10). Across the region and indeed country, minstrel shows proved wildly popular, and exaggerated African American features (large lips, white eyes) were key to such comedic modes. In a localized example of such mockery, the student editors obviously drew on such elements for the "Negro Philosophy" section of the yearbook, but they also imported such exaggerations into their choice to title the publication *Ole Miss*. For white students schooled in Standard English, "Ole Miss" was linguistic exaggeration, a disguise of self-deprecating wordplay that would have certainly generated chuckles in 1897.

Figure 9. Opening page of the "Jokes" section from the 1914 University of Georgia yearbook. Racial caricatures and derisive humor were ubiquitous in southern university annuals throughout this period. (University of Georgia, *Pandora, 1914*, 262. Courtesy of Hargett Rare Book and Manuscript Library/University of Georgia Libraries.)

FIGURE 10. Blackface performance at the University of Mississippi during the 1949/50 school year. Such performances were a regular part of southern university life throughout the first half of the twentieth century. Fully tracing this tradition is beyond the scope of this book, but it is clearly traceable through southern university yearbooks and other primary source documents. The tradition suggests that modern incidents of blackface at universities are not outliers or racist innovations but parts of a continuum of confederate rhetoric on these campuses. (University of Mississippi, *Ole Miss, 1950*, 198. Special Collections, University of Mississippi Libraries.)

In minstrelsy, white people dressed as Black people to clown, to jest, and often to poke fun at their own culture by looking through a foreign (if familiar) lens. In their linguistic adoption of the Black term "Ole Miss," white students were painting blackface on their own literary production, simultaneously dressing up and dressing down the yearbook, humbly undercutting some of the highbrow elements and having a laugh at the expense of the other. This wordplay might have been a reassuring way to laugh off the threat of social and racial upheaval, but as Grace Elizabeth Hale has said of minstrelsy, "Minstrelsy entertained not just through ridicule but also through nostalgia."[15] If the term "Ole Miss" was partially lighthearted and self-deprecating code in these early years, it also performed immediate cultural work for Meek and her fellow white students by turning their gaze backward to what was in their minds a better "ole" time—one that was not to be forgotten.

By co-opting the term "Ole Miss" from African American Vernacular English, this white college community was also drawing a direct parallel between their own devotion to the university and the supposed devotion of enslaved people to their enslavers in the antebellum period. Meek and the student editors were thus forwarding a sincere defense of the old order. After all, "Ole Miss" was a term created and used by enslaved people in an exclusively positive way, at least as far as white students knew or cared to admit. Long before the 1848 founding of the University of Mississippi, at plantations throughout the Deep South, enslaved people used "Ole Miss" and its derivatives to label the wife of the plantation owner. Within earshot of white people, enslaved people would have used "Ole Miss" in a friendly, even reverential way. When Elma Meek and others remembered Black usage of the term, they remembered only fealty, love, and devotion. Thus, for white people, "Ole Miss" was a semiotic marker of respect and affection: clear and (seemingly) voluntary linguistic evidence of the terrible myth that enslaved people were happy and content in their enslavement and loved those whom they were forced to serve.

Even today, the most common adjective connected to "Ole Miss" is "affectionate." For example, on its official website in 2019, University Marketing and Communications endorsed the use of "Ole Miss" by stating that "the vast majority of all races embraces the name and does not attach any meaning to it other than an affectionate name for the university." Or consider the official "About UM" webpage, the text of which in 2019 and the time of this writing stated, "Founded in 1848, the University of Mississippi, affectionately known to alumni, students and friends as Ole Miss, is Mississippi's flagship university." Again and again, insiders within the community refer to the nickname "Ole Miss" as "affectionate." This is a well-established adjectival and adverbial tradition at UM. It is also, I argue, a tradition with an emotional lineage extending directly to 1897 and before. It is a tradition with a traceable, if often hidden or unwitting, connection to the idealized "affectionate" relationship between enslaved person and enslaver. Students adore their alma mater just as enslaved people (supposedly) adored the women who enslaved them. Of course, this is a purely white trope, one that becomes deeply problematic and offensive when exposed and analyzed. When left in place and unexamined, however, when repeated across generations, as has been the case with "Ole Miss" and with its accompanying adjective "affectionate" or adverb "affectionately," such tropes—such confederate rhetoric—serve to preserve and support underlying systems of power and exclusion. Certainly most white insiders of the modern era do not consciously support this kind of rhetorical buttressing. They are not active racists in most senses of that concept. They do not condone slavery. They do not promulgate hate. But that is not the point. Their inherited words and symbols, which they continue to embrace and defend, deliver discriminatory legacies of the past into the present.

There can be no doubt that the luxury of self-delusion has been an important ingredient in the success and resilience of white domination in the Deep South. As humans, we routinely delude ourselves through language, either by avoiding painful words or by deploying salubrious ones. By integrating the term "Ole Miss" into their privileged institution, young white Mississippians were strengthening their own deluded rationalizations. For them, "Ole Miss" became reinforcing rhetoric for the argument that colored their generation's entire past, present, and future: Slavery wasn't so bad. The system wasn't so bad. Black people were happier and better off back then, before the lost war and before Reconstruction. In this context, "Ole Miss" became a glorious and worthy container for the love and respect that enslaved people felt for those who held them in slavery and similarly for the love and respect that University of Mississippi students felt for their alma mater. Who could argue with affection?

Precisely because it was so rich with meaning, emotion, and ideological utility, the term soon expanded its territory. Within two years of Meek's suggestion, "Ole Miss" came to signify not simply the yearbook but the university itself. In his *History of the Alumni Association of the University of Mississippi*, Franklin E. Moak described this linguistic leap:

> The year 1896–97 represents a milestone in the history of the University. A student yearbook was published for the first time. The yearbook was edited and published under the auspices of the fraternities. . . . Following an invitation for suggested names, Miss Elma Meek submitted the name, Ole Miss, which conveyed a feeling of respect for the wife of the master of the plantation. She won the prize and henceforth the name of the annual has been known as The Ole Miss. . . . Shortly afterward, the University also underwent a name change. Apparently the change was not deliberated upon in advance, nor was the Chancellor ever asked if he wanted to change the name. The Trustees were not consulted, neither was the charter amended by the Legislature. The name change actually represented more the adoption of the nickname, Ole Miss, because the official name, The University of Mississippi, remains eternally the same. The name, Ole Miss, however, caught on and almost imperceptibly students used it synonymously to refer to their alma mater.[16]

While firsthand accounts and historical artifacts relating to the genesis of the term "Ole Miss" in relation to the yearbook exist, much less is known about this subsequent expansion in usage. During the 1898/99 academic year, the student body consisted of 287 people, and it was within this small network of students that "Ole Miss" went viral, jumping across contexts and broadening its influence.[17] However the term's usage evolved, it happened very quickly and was seemingly an organic, grassroots process.

Thus "Ole Miss" can be viewed as a remarkable homegrown brand, one that took root and flourished without marketing studies, media campaigns, or any planning at all. Despite the haziness of this early history, what is certain is that the term had immediate appeal for the student body. These young people, who were born into the tumult of Reconstruction, rallied around "Ole Miss," energetically adopting it as an integral part of their communal identity. The young people of the day decided to make it not only the name of their student yearbook but the name of their entire community. This rhetorical choice would have powerful consequences, reverberating far beyond the lifespans of the original student rhetors. As Laurie Gries has argued so cogently, rhetoric is often "an ongoing activation . . . a distributed event."[18] The term "Ole Miss" was chosen by students—and then went viral within their community—because it reflected and enacted certain desires, feelings, and ideas. They chose this identifier for particular reasons, some conscious and some unconscious, and then they spread it actively and communally, not for a few days or a few weeks or a few years, but across decades, generations, and an entire century.

"Ole Miss" as Representative Example of Confederate Rhetoric

Viewed from a marketing perspective, the students' selection of "Ole Miss" fits nicely into a well-documented regional pattern. Mississippians and southerners were, in 1897, aggressively nostalgic for the Lost Cause. As consumers, they were anxious to materialize their romanticized memories of antebellum times. Terms and images related to the South were popping up everywhere in the 1890s. White consumers could purchase antebellum references on products as diverse as flour, tea, chewing tobacco, train routes, and colas. Anthony Stanonis has pointed out that "the South became as much an evolving set of images as an actual place. Transformed into such symbols as a stately plantation or a devoted mammy, the South could easily be marketed, a process that accelerated with the rise of advertising agencies, consumer branding, and railroad (and subsequently automobile) travel during the late nineteenth and early twentieth centuries."[19] It was within this market economy that Elma Meek suggested "Ole Miss" to the editors of the university's new yearbook, and it was within this market economy that the term went viral, resonating with the student body and deepening its appeal across the next several decades. As a brand, "Ole Miss" has continued to grow in economic value to this very day. It turns out that Meek's suggestion was, among other things, a stroke of marketing genius.

If white consumers across the South were hungry for references to the "good ole days" of antebellum life, white college students in Mississippi were downright starving for such reassurances. For them, the Civil War and Reconstruction had not been merely an interruption to normal life, but an existential crisis. These historical events had stripped this particular southern generation of many of their birthrights before they were even born. The children of Mississippi's planters and aristocrats who made up the student body in these years had been raised during an era of reverberating defeat. Their familial, moral, racial, and social inheritance had been violently devalued, and they must have felt battered and confused, if not traumatized. As UM student J. B. Webb wrote in a 1905 poem, "For Reconstruction days were to be passed / With rule of Blacks and those of despot caste." Or, as Mississippi congressman John Sharp Williams wrote in 1904, "The ten long years of so-called reconstruction . . . made the four long years of war itself seem tolerable by comparison."[20] The naming of the annual and the subsequent virality of the name provide one localized example of backlash to Reconstruction: young white people making substantial investments in confederate rhetoric.

Working through the changes that come with social progress is difficult; it is much easier to long for better times. By 1897, young white Mississippians were primed for what Karen Cox has called "the marketing and consumption of a Dixie that incorporated the mythology and traditions of the southern past." When Elma Meek suggested the name "Ole Miss" for the yearbook, she tapped directly into many of these longings, and her student peers responded by enthusiastically adopting and cultivating the term. To state the obvious, the student body was in most ways uniform during this period. Students shared a history, a worldview, and a common whiteness. Quoting from an official university catalog, Nadine Cohodas points out that after the Civil War, students at the University of Mississippi were "the sons of parents who had been wealthy but whose wealth had been entirely swept away." Throughout much of its history, "Ole Miss had the aura of an exclusive club for the planter class," a club that Curtis Wilkie has called "a clearinghouse for the state's political power structure as well as a finishing school for the young women who would marry the elite and preside over their mansions."[21] For these white students, whose families were trying to recover from the traumas of the Civil War and Reconstruction, the term "Ole Miss" had profound resonance as a new semiotic resource for summarizing, showcasing, and preserving aristocratic ideals lost to an unjust and undeserved history. The term registered an ideology in which these students had always been immersed; it reified communal longings that were deeply felt and shared.

During the 1898/99 academic year, the students at the University of Mississippi rallied enthusiastically around "Ole Miss." They used it to name their university and their community, thereby making a significant "ideological investment" in this small packet of language.[22] Their investment would grow across much of the twentieth century. While other symbols of the Old South would be lost over time—the racial purity of the school, the rebel flag, the song "Dixie,"—"Ole Miss" would remain, growing stronger and larger as a protective vessel for a cherished ideology.

The Solidification of a Term

In calling on rhetoricians to "actually take time to trace things as they circulate and enter into various relations," Laurie Gries urges them to look beyond rhetorical intent and into the futurity of rhetorical inventions.[23] As she showed with her circulation study of the Obama Hope image, this methodology can open up interdisciplinary pathways to understanding words, symbols, and visual images as they move through the world and transform over time. While Gries's case study is notable for its transformations and mutations, "Ole Miss" is notable for its vital stability. In other words, the term grew in vitality and consequentiality throughout most of the twentieth century, but it did not transform in any substantial sense. Instead, after being appropriated and going viral in the late nineteenth century, "Ole Miss" became and still remains a force for ideological stabilization and stasis.

Across the twentieth century, the term grew into a defining brand name that held enormous resonance and ideological value for the people associated with the University of Mississippi. By 1911, it had solidified and matured, gaining nearly divine powers in the localized mythology of the Lost Cause:

> Beloved "Ole Miss" thou hast been
> A true helper to struggling men;
> E'en in the sixties far away,
> Thou didst help those who wore the gray.
> . . . .
> Long may you live and ever be
> A true emblem of purity
> To all the sons and daughters true
> Who ever wore the red and blue.[24]

This loving ode from the 1911 annual demonstrates the term's growth in influence and status. By this time, it was more than a decade old, no longer new either in its application to the yearbook or to the university. "Ole Miss" had already become "beloved" and apocryphally eternal, a goddess-like figure who could be invoked as "a true helper to struggling men." More than ever, the term facilitated the imaginary act of nostalgia: "E'en in the sixties far away, / Thou didst help those who wore the gray." As a personification of the university, "Ole Miss" now had the power to intercede even in the past—even long before its own inception—to console ancestors, to soothe the loss of a bygone Confederacy. No longer was "Ole Miss" just a label or title. It was, by 1911, "a true emblem of purity / To all the sons and daughters true / Who ever wore the red and blue." This mawkish but deeply felt and earnest poem reflected and contributed to an early foundation for the term's treatment and usage across the following decades. "Ole Miss" was already much more than a nickname. It was revered. If there had been comedic implications in its early usage, such lightheartedness was overshadowed by 1911. The term was growing in sentimentality and seriousness.

In 1913, an editorial in the campus newspaper reflected this elevation of regard and tone, calling "Ole Miss" "a gem which pleased all," a name that suggested "all that was beautiful and sacred and proud in the great state [of Mississippi]." Such sappiness characterized student usage for the next several decades, as the term matured into a cherished and protected linguistic container for Old South sentiments. The 1925 annual, which begins with a mournful narrative entitled "The Lost Cause," is dedicated to Thomas Kimbrough, "Commander of the Mississippi Division of the United Sons of Confederate Veterans . . . Dean on the School of Law . . . true Southern gentleman." Beside the textual dedication, there is a beautifully rendered engraving of the Tiffany stained glass window (still on campus today) that honors the University Grays and, by extension, the Confederacy. The foreword of this annual reflects the reverential way in which the students of the time were using "Ole Miss": "We at Ole Miss have as an heritage the grand and glorious traditions of the Old South, with its slumberous atmosphere and its jovial life . . . but out of the shadows there came the rumblings of war, and from the fields and hamlets of our sunny Dixie our heroes came . . . Ole Miss, with its University Grays, made its contribution to this, our cause."[25] The students of 1925 embraced the name more fervently than ever, again forwarding and celebrating its associations with the ideology of the Old South.

In this post–World War I moment—the year of the Scopes Trial and in the midst of what some have labeled a renaissance in southern art and culture—the students of the University of Mississippi were busy looking backward to an idealized past. It was a defensive posture, and their adopted and cherished name for themselves, "Ole Miss," was a primary guardian of their ideational and affective redoubt. UM students in this era were proudly and consciously becoming what James C. Cobb has called "southern cultural supremacists," southerners who covered over the difficulties and defects of their current system by glorifying selectively chosen supposed strengths of the system lost by their forefathers.[26] The editors of the 1925 annual ended their publication just as they had begun it: by indulging sentiments of nostalgia. The yearbook closes with an engraving of the Confederate cemetery that had by this time existed on campus for some sixty years. The cemetery may have been a quiet spot on the edge of campus, but the old, shady enclave was not ancient history to the students of the era, who saw in it a relevant and fitting conclusion to their annual. These students remained committed to the Lost Cause and to their self-identifier "Ole Miss," which linked them linguistically to a desirable and shared past. For students who revered Confederate monuments, cemeteries, and heroes, the term had become a portable, all-encompassing, and unifying marker, one that by 1925 was as commonsensical and ingrained as a birth name. "Ole Miss" as confederate rhetoric had become a signifier both stable and fully institutionalized.

During these years, and through their yearbooks, successive UM students used words and symbols to create and strengthen a communal memory. Historian W. Fitzhugh Brundage has shown how "collective remembering forges identity, justifies privilege, and sustains cultural norms. For individuals and groups memory provides a genealogy of social identity."[27] Thus, looking through university yearbooks—doing the work of tracing rhetorical artifacts across time, to paraphrase Gries—is equal to looking through a longitudinal family archive. Photos, poems, letters, stories: yearbooks contain all kinds of words, symbols, and images gathered consciously from year to year to offer a scrapbook of self-representation, a carefully curated portfolio of a student body's common identity and values.

After graduation, university alumni no longer receive or pay much attention to yearbooks. They save and cherish the annuals of their time, but they rarely dip into those of subsequent generations. This is largely because yearbooks are insular, aimed at the small audience of classmates and current faculty. It is also because they are produced in very small batches and distributed to current students only. After graduation, alumni gather together around publications like alumni magazines and newsletters. In what is perhaps the first published reflection of the history and origins of the term "Ole Miss," L. A. Smith, writing for the *Ole Miss Alumni News* in 1932, offered this earnest explanation of the orthodox view:

> The slaves on the plantations of the old South called the head of the family "Ole Marster" and his good wife "Ole Miss." . . . The beauty of the tender affection of the slaves for their owners breathes from the very sound of these terms, and it is easy in fancy to transport oneself back to the glamorous days when the lovely lady who was not only the mistress of the home but also each humble cabin on the plantation and in the slaves quarters, gently ministering to the wants and the suffering, and furnishing sympathy and consolation to the sorrowing, furnishing cheer and brightness to the hearts and lives of all the people within the sphere of her domain reigned supreme. Therefore, the term "Ole Miss" is one which is redolent of the romance, the chivalry, the beauty, the culture, the graciousness and the finest traditions of the Southland.[28]

Here, at the height of the Jim Crow era, during which Mississippi saw more lynchings than any other state, the white elites of the university community were using the term "Ole Miss"—their beloved name for themselves—as a vehicle for escaping the vulgar realities of the day. In ever deepening grooves, they were etching communal memories into a shared identity that was incomplete, fantastical, and, by today's standards, sickeningly racist.

From 1877 to 1950, 614 African Americans were lynched in the state of Mississippi, many in broad daylight during what the Equal Justice Initiative has called "terror lynchings . . . attended by the entire white community and conducted as celebratory acts." Local newspapers would promote these events, and huge crowds of white citizens would gather—sometimes with picnic baskets and lemonade—to view the lynchings, which would often "feature prolonged torture, mutilation, dismemberment, and/or burning of the victim."[29] For those white people in the UM community who endorsed or accepted such terror, "Ole Miss" was reifying, ideological language. For complicit others who wished to avert their eyes from the baseness of such horrors, the term delivered a salubrious (if delusional) vision of a simpler and more genteel era. For all white people living within this system, such language carried benefits and protections. Like all confederate rhetoric, "Ole Miss" is a rhetorical artifact of whiteness. Also like all confederate rhetoric, it offers encouragement and shelter to all white people, even to those who reject outwardly racist practices. "Ole Miss" has been (and remains) a preservative of privilege and a complement to racial violence.

By 1932, part of the term's ideological function was as a guardian for white gentility. As the above passage demonstrates, the words "Ole Miss" empowered L. A. Smith to write about enslaved loyalty and white graciousness, even during a time when white communities throughout Mississippi were terrorizing and killing African Americans. In his imaginative reverie, Smith glorified the literal "Ole Misses" of slavery—white women—by depicting them ministering "to the wants and the suffering" of Black people and furnishing them with benevolent "sympathy and consolation." It is nauseating to try to reconcile Smith's published idealization of tenderness with the horrible and terroristic acts pervasive in the Mississippi of his era. Such reconciliation is beyond the scope of this book, but it is certainly deserving of further study. How and why could highly educated white people be so blind to the suffering, to the violence? One part of the answer lies in the rhetoric of the day.

White discourse, including imaginative rhetoric like the term "Ole Miss," gave Smith and other educated white people an escape. Perhaps like modern families who visit Disney World during times of war, white southerners used confederate rhetoric and the false but reassuring perspectives it created to escape the ugliness of their present. But that metaphor needs work, for white southerners were more active than mere visitors. They were perhaps more like misguided Disney imagineers, designing and constructing a perverted world of fantasy, using confederate rhetoric to build their incomplete and destructive visions. For white southerners who wished to consider themselves above violence, confederate rhetoric provided a more genteel tool than lynching to emphasize, preserve, and reify the ideology of the Old South. I doubt that L. A. Smith would have ever written a glorious account of a celebratory lynching for the *Ole Miss Alumni News*. Such baseness would have been untoward and out of place. But his apocryphal reverie of "happy slaves" and "attentive southern belles" was perfect for the publication, the audience, and the era. His narrative was more palatable for white elites who wished to regard "Ole Miss"—the campus, the community, the term—as being above it all, an aristocratic safe haven from Blackness but also from the unseemly racial violence of Jim Crow.

If "Ole Miss" empowered reverie and escape for white people who regarded racial violence as debased or unseemly, it simultaneously enforced the values of the lynch mobs. Like the beautiful campus it names, the term had become a linguistic enclave, a peaceful site of respite (and order) during a tumultuous, chaotic period. In the imagination of Smith, "Ole Miss" was a place where transgressions were not possible—where Black people were presently as happy and as orderly they had been during slavery. Mississippi in 1932 was a violent and repressive place, but "Ole Miss" was a preserve of peace and order. Most college graduates romanticize their alma maters, but in this case, the romanticizing was also in service to a dark and disturbing ideology. For its white students and alumni during the Jim Crow era, more than ever, the term "Ole Miss" was unquestionably good, ideologically useful, and deeply revered.

Similar sentiments were expressed in the article "Elma Meek Gave University Its Name, 'Ole Miss,' Long Probe of Students Reveals," which was published in the campus newspaper and in the *Memphis Commercial Appeal* on October 11, 1936. For this piece, Maurice Fulton and his classmates (G. G. Lyell and V. A. Griffith) reflected on their days as editors of the *Ole Miss* annual in 1897, and Elma Meek recounted her racist logic, which the writer summarized, "Miss Meek, who today resides at Oxford, modestly tells how she took the name [Ole Miss] from the language of the antebellum 'darky,' who knew the wife of his owner by no other title than 'Ole Miss,' and of how she suggested it because she thought it connoted all the admiration and reverence accorded the womanhood of the Old South." The same writer described the term "Ole Miss" as "the valued possession of the University of Mississippi . . . [one] used erroneously in distant places to refer to the whole state of Mississippi in a manner which is resented by supporters of the institution." The university community at this time not only loved and revered the term; they communicated a strong sense of ownership and fealty toward it.

By 1945, nine years later, "Ole Miss" and the public story of its genesis were fully cemented in university lore. The editors of the annual that year (still titled *Ole Miss*) dedicated their volume to Elma Meek: "Through her origin of the name Ole Miss, Miss Elma Meek has won a merited place in the hearts of all who have been in any way connected with the University of Mississippi. . . . Ole Miss has become a traditional symbolism in the minds of the students of the University."[30] Published near the end of World War II and under difficult conditions that included rationing of supplies, editor Frances Moore's 1945 yearbook was—from an editorial perspective—polished and elegant. She and her team made conservative choices throughout their annual, and their decision to dedicate it to Elma Meek was equally conservative. At this moment in the life of the term, "Ole Miss" was neither controversial nor questionable. It was a beloved, safe, and reassuring university tradition.

Perhaps the clearest evidence of the term's stability during this period is an official university document prepared by the Department of Public Relations on October 29, 1947.[31] Without attribution, it reprints nearly verbatim the story that had appeared in the 1936 *Memphis Commercial Appeal* about the origins of "Ole Miss." The unnamed PR employee who updated what was then an eleven-year-old story made only light revisions. For example, "four decades" in the original story became "five decades" in the new version. Extra emphasis was placed on the prominence of the original students involved in the historic decision to adopt *Ole Miss* as the title of the yearbook: namely, editors Lyell and Griffith were labeled as prominent Jackson attorney and Mississippi Supreme Court justice, respectively. The unnamed PR official made no other substantial changes, sidestepping the opportunity to soften or purge Miss Meek's honest recollections about the racist roots of the term. The university community seemingly still had no qualms, and its official, published position—the orthodox view—remained that the term "Ole Miss" was unquestionably good, in large part because it reflected an antebellum and racist fantasy.

Indeed, the term would occupy this stable and beloved position for a long time to come. After more than fifty years of use, the words stood central to the identity of the white elites who attended the University of Mississippi. Across generations, they had imported, cultivated, and reinforced this label for themselves. The beloved self-identifier would not come into question until the civil rights movement began to infringe on the "Ole Miss" majority. When that happened, members of that majority rallied fervently to defend their name.

Buttressing and Defending "Ole Miss"

In the late 1940s and early 1950s, as if in fearful anticipation of the impending civil rights movement, white students at the University of Mississippi increased their investments in Old South words and symbols. Jackie Robinson had integrated major league baseball in 1947, but most of the other tectonic shifts in American race relations—the 1954 *Brown v. Board of Education* decision, for example, and the 1955 beating and lynching of young Emmett Till just seventy-five miles from the UM campus—were yet to come. In 1950, before the civil rights turmoil began in earnest, UM students organized Dixie Week, which would become a treasured annual tradition, an impenitent campus festival of confederate rhetoric. As historian Charles Eagles has detailed, Dixie Week "festivities included replacing the US flag with the Confederate flag, reading the state's Ordinance of Secession, honoring a surviving Confederate veteran from Alabama, a memorial service for confederate soldiers . . . the chancellor's wreath-laying at the Confederate monument . . . the assassination of Lincoln in the student grill, the sale of cheerleaders in a 'slave' auction, and the appearance of the Ku Klux Klan."[32]

Dixie Week was an overt and officially sanctioned celebration of the Lost Cause—and of the inextricable racism central to its mythology. The students of the time accepted and embraced the events as fun, harmless, spirit-building activities. Even as the civil rights movement was beginning to percolate around them, the white students of the 1950s renewed their commitments to the ideology of the Old South. Here began the waning days of prominence for the old order, but most white southerners did not yet see it coming. Instead, in the 1950s, most chose to remain peacefully unaware of the cancerous complexities of their inherited and embraced system. Confederate rhetoric provided some of the shelter necessary for such elective and collective ignorance.

Even future progressives—white people who would later fight racism in its institutions and forms—were students at the University of Mississippi during this era and were complicit or active in the veneration of Old South words and symbols. William Winter is one prominent example. Winter graduated from UM in 1949 and has remembered that his school was "an authentic product of the Old South, and we who are its alumni take nostalgic pride in its Confederate heritage."[33] It is a striking statement, spoken many years later but in the present tense, by a man who has done more to further race relations in Mississippi than any other white person. As governor, Winter took strong stands and implemented lasting policies to gain and sustain racial progress. His public service record is marked by critical thinking, bravery, and compassion. Yet as a young person at UM, Winter and other future progressives celebrated Dixie Week without any qualms and embraced Old South symbols with enthusiasm. Even within their own memories, there is little evidence of dissent during the 1940s and 1950s. Confederate rhetoric had subsumed the identity of the community and was fully, unquestionably, in control.

And here lies one aspect of confederate rhetoric's tremendous power. At UM, such rhetoric had catalyzed a fusion of ideology with school spirit, a fusion invisible to some white people for its completeness and seamlessness. Old South rituals and symbols were simply part of the college atmosphere, part of what gave the university uniqueness and character. As one accomplished 1959 alumnus said to me recently, "Some of us probably thought of the name Ole Miss as racist, and some of us probably didn't." Students could be ambivalent or indifferent because the term "Ole Miss," like the set of symbols it oversaw, was ingrained, commonsensical, and therefore hidden in plain sight.

When hidden in plain sight, ideological language is at its most effective. Fairclough (building on Althusser and Gramsci) has pointed out that "ideology works . . . by disguising its ideological nature. It becomes naturalized, automatized."[34] Thus, it creates (and depends on) a field of words and activities that envelop even those individuals who, under different circumstances, might wish to rebel or resist. "Ole Miss" and the southern symbols gathered beneath its titular banner grew overpowering during the 1950s. The white students of the day—some of whom would prove racist during adulthood and some of whom would prove antiracist—were all willing to define themselves through inherited language that was deeply ideological and problematic by any objective, modern measure. It was language that could go unquestioned because it had become thoroughly ingrained and institutionalized. In the dawn before the civil rights movement, "Ole Miss" was growing stronger. As confederate rhetoric, the term was overcoming and subsuming the University of Mississippi.

Take as another example the final page from the 1953 *Ole Miss* (fig. 11). The textual acknowledgments are gracious and banal; in form and language one might find such sentences in any yearbook of any school in the country. The editors are reflecting on the hard work of putting together the annual, and they are thanking the people who have helped them assemble the publication. The visual image above these routine words, however, stands in stark contrast: a large rebel flag flying prominently above everything else, an overpowering symbol within the totality of the page. Indeed, nothing communicates the ideology of the Old South better than the Confederate battle flag, which connotes an entire system of values, beliefs, and practices. The student editors in 1953 were, on one hand, making a strong closing statement. On the other hand, they were doing so quite casually, plopping the flag down amid unrelated text without feeling the need to explain or caption its presence. By this time in history, the flag had become commonplace and unremarkable. As a symbol, the flag at UM was doing its ideological work in the openness of the foreground without standing out as remarkable or conspicuous.

The words "Ole Miss" offered similar affordances during this era and were directly incorporated into the Confederate flag depicted at the end of the 1953 yearbook. Under normal circumstances, flags speak for themselves. In this case, the semiotic function of the flag is underscored and enhanced by the words "Ole Miss" and the year '53 inscribed directly between the stars and bars. This editorial choice serves as a permanent reminder that the students of 1953 understood their "Ole Miss" as something inseparable from their Old South. In the decades to come, the community would seek to better disguise the words "Ole Miss," usually separating the phrase from the flag, at least in official publications. For now, student leaders were comfortable with the emphatic and conspicuous associations similar to those they had inherited in a clear lineage dating back to Elma Meek.

As the civil rights era simmered around them, UM students strengthened their investments in confederate rhetoric. They not only accepted their linguistic and semiotic inheritances from the Old South, but they cherished and built on those gifts. In the example above, the student editors of 1953 endorsed and underscored the orthodox view of "Ole Miss" that had been hardening for half a century. The ideology of the Old South at UM had become such a prominent part of the community's language system that it could go unrecognized and unnoticed. Through the term "Ole Miss," which named everything and everyone associated with the university, that ideology remained fundamental, pervasive, and governing.

It Certainly Has Been . . .

GREAT—this year of preparing the 1953 OLE MISS for publication. Now that it is completed, we look back and wonder that the year could pass so fleetingly. But, it has been a wonderful experience. There has been the pleasant task of working with the finest staff in OLE MISS history; and then of great personal value were the contacts with those who inspired us in fulfilling our ideas.

GREAT—the cooperation and assistance rendered by Buddy Shaw—his supervision of the printing of our 1953 OLE MISS; Jimmy Cobb and Ed Birchett—the engravings made by Shreveport Engraving Company speak for themselves; and George Ambrester—the beauty pictures were outstanding.

GREAT—the many tedious hours spent, the excellent photographs, and very personal interest of Colonel and Mrs. Cofield; the many services rendered by Billy Gates; the help in directing the Parade of Favorites given by Dr. C. M. Getchell; the photos supplied by "The Arkansas Democrat," "The Times Picayune," "The Courier-Journal," "The Nashville Banner," and especially David Bloom of "The Commercial Appeal."

GREAT—creating a yearbook which we hope you will like. We used an informal theme, for that is essentially the way we thought of Ole Miss students. To a great student body and to a greater and expanding Ole Miss, we made our dedication and though this, our contribution, is of but a temporary nature, we sincerely believe that each of you will find a part which will apply to you. And so, we anticipate that now and in future years you will turn to your record of the year 1952-53 at Ole Miss and stop . . . and revel in memories . . . and find enjoyment.

T. E. MORTIMER, Editor
JIMMIE SHOEMAKER, Business Manager

FIGURE 11. Final page of the 1953 University of Mississippi yearbook. The rebel flag, inscribed with the words "Ole Miss," stands dominant over the text but goes without comment from the writers, illustrating how the defiance of the rhetoric had become commonplace and commonsensical. (University of Mississippi, *Ole Miss, 1953*. Special Collections, University of Mississippi Libraries.)

It seems that no one questioned the term throughout this period. Of course, there were isolated examples of liberal thinking in a broader sense. In her excellent book *The Band Played Dixie: Race and the Liberal Conscience at Ole Miss*, Nadine Cohodas documented students like Alvin Krebs, the editor of the campus newspaper who wrote columns in favor of moderate progress on issues of race. Krebs was threatened, bullied, and eventually run out of Mississippi. Even as she noted outliers like Krebs—white students or faculty who questioned racism in the years before, during, and after the civil rights movement—Cohodas acknowledged the dominant, nearly monolithic culture of the campus, a place where "it was crucial that the young minds of Ole Miss be rigorously trained to preserve the status quo, and most of them were."[35]

In the absence of dissent, the term "Ole Miss" came to define the institution and its character, becoming the banner of identity that flew above every aspect of daily life. As the university's name for itself, "Ole Miss" was overarching confederate rhetoric. It was governing and omnipresent. More effectively even than the Confederate battle flag, the term could perform its ideological work in many contexts (conversations, print, songs, signs) while hiding in plain sight. It became what Laurie Gries has called a "multiple single image" that could pass as a harmless nickname but that contained deeply ideological and racist affordances.[36]

Evidence of dissent or even discomfort with the term is hard to find during the first fifty years of the twentieth century. In my research, I found none. There are some obvious and simple reasons for this absence. For example, African Americans, who had been present on campus from the beginning of the institution's history, first as enslaved people and later as workers, were almost always paternalistically "appreciated" but were never given agency or voice. Indeed, oftentimes, they were not even given names, at least not in the record.

The yearbooks would quite regularly include a page devoted to a few of the African Americans living and working on campus. Figure 12 depicts a representative example from the 1921 yearbook. Presumably the students of the day would have remembered some or all of the workers pictured by name or at least nickname. Yet the editors saw no need to offer those names in the text. One overarching, reductive label sufficed: "Our Life-Savers." Such paternalistic acknowledgment of African American laborers continued into the 1950s. John Cossar, who attended the University of Mississippi from 1956 to 1961, recounted a story about one of his friends, Harper Myers: "He [Harper] lived in the dorm next to us and a lot of people think that James Meredith was the first black man at Ole Miss but that's wrong. Harper's daddy gave him a black man on his eighteenth birthday and the man's name was 'Man.' He lived in Harper's dorm room in the closet, at LaBauve [dormitory]. So Harper would say 'It's time to come on over and have a little drink,' so we go over there and Man would be the bartender. He'd have his little white coat on."[37] Indeed, for decades, Black workers were fixtures at UM, but they were usually nameless or purposefully misnamed, and they were always denied voice or agency. They were, to many white people, personifications of the Old South, reminders of better times and of a less problematic social order. Black workers

FIGURE 12. Photomontage from the 1921 University of Mississippi yearbook featuring unnamed African American women. On southern university campuses, African Americans were commonly presented in yearbooks as unnamed but paternalistically appreciated symbols of faithfulness and loyalty, thus becoming confederate rhetoric themselves. (University of Mississippi, *Ole Miss, 1921*, 174. Special Collections, University of Mississippi Libraries.)

were, when reduced to nameless symbols within the minds of white people, ubiquitous examples of reassuring confederate rhetoric.

By 1960, however, serious dissent and turmoil began to glow on the horizon. The world was turning, and the sunshine of history would soon beam harshly on UM. Mississippi and the university were about to become a sizzling focal point in American history. A young Black man from Kosciusko, Mississippi, a Korean War veteran, decided that he wanted to attend the best school in his home state. He wanted to come to the University of Mississippi—not as a janitor, cook, or bartender—but as a political science major. Soon, every student at the university, then and forevermore, would know his name: James Meredith.

As has been documented in many articles and books, the best of which is *The Price of Defiance* by Charles Eagles, the integration of the university was traumatic on nearly every level for devotees of the old order. In terms of symbols and language, the events of 1962 catalyzed (and continue to catalyze) monumental change. Over the ensuing decades, Dixie Week with its outward displays of nostalgia and racism was discontinued, the rebel flag surged in prominence before it was banned at football games in 1998, and the song "Dixie" was played by the school's "Pride of the South" marching band until 2016. As these and many other examples of confederate rhetoric were being reconsidered and retired, "Ole Miss" grew stronger and was rarely ever questioned.

Indeed, public examples of resistance to the use of "Ole Miss"—even after the civil rights movement—are difficult to find. After James Meredith's arrival, there was some nominal, gentle resistance. During the 1960s, Meredith himself seems to have avoided it, preferring instead "The University of Mississippi." And, during the 1970s, liberal professor Allen Cabaniss registered objections to official use of the term, asking in a memo that the Committee on the 125th Anniversary Observance "please . . . discourage the use of it ['Ole Miss']" so that the "125th anniversary occasion could well be employed as an educational opportunity to stress not the sentimental, but the academic, character and quality of THE UNIVERSITY OF MISSISSIPPI."[38] These two moments of resistance were neither particularly conspicuous nor successful. As calls for change, they were muted, marginal, and wholly ineffective. Many things did change at the University of Mississippi during the 1960s and 1970s, but "Ole Miss" remained a semiotic staple, one that grew in ideological usefulness even as other Old South symbols were gradually weakening.

Supercharging "Ole Miss"

In 1971, it was an ally, not an enemy, who brought the term "Ole Miss" into the spotlight. During a speech delivered to the Ole Miss Alumni Club of

Vicksburg, Frank E. Everett Jr. dwelled on and reconsidered "Ole Miss." His interpretation was at once reflective and formative and established semiotic parameters that would govern the term's definition and usage for the next half century or more.

Everett had been a legendary student at the university in the 1930s. He was elected both student body president and Colonel Rebel (a southernized honorific for homecoming king). He graduated in 1934 with both bachelor's and law degrees and married his college sweetheart, who had been named Miss Ole Miss (a southernized honorific for school favorite). Everett became a successful lawyer in Vicksburg, the founding director of the Mississippi Historical Society, and the author of a book about the Confederate president Jefferson Davis's home. Throughout his life, Everett was devoted to his alma mater, serving in many roles, including president of the Ole Miss Alumni Association. He was eventually inducted into the Ole Miss Alumni Hall of Fame.[39] In other words, by 1971, Everett was UM royalty, a highly respected and accomplished elder of the community. With the speech he gave on May 20, 1971, he secured his place in university history—and supercharged the term "Ole Miss" for decades to come.

Everett was an intellectual person who was devoted to language and who had great rhetorical skill. His 1971 speech has become iconic within the UM community, but it has never been fully explicated. It is rhetorically rich and dense, and it deserves great attention for its consequentiality and influence. According to Joan Bailey, who wrote about the event for the *Ole Miss Alumni Review* in 2006, Everett's speech was delivered to "a large crowd of the Rebel faithful gathered at the Rivertown Club in Vicksburg." It was Everett's task to introduce Chancellor Fortune to the audience, but Everett was inspired to do much more with his remarks. No one seems to remember what the chancellor said that night, but Everett's words thrilled the audience and soon became legendary prose within the university community. "The audience sat spellbound with what some lauded as 'one of the great orations of our time,'" reported Bailey. The speech resonated immediately and has since been printed or excerpted in newspapers, *Ole Miss* annuals, fundraising letters, alumni publications, plaques, certificates, the textbook for the UM orientation course, and countless other venues. Attorney Bobby Bailess, a friend of Everett's and fellow alumnus, later described the speech's popularity within the community: "It rattles off the tongues of Ole Miss graduates like Americans recite the Pledge of Allegiance."[40] Perhaps most prominently, an excerpt of Everett's speech was affixed in bronze letters above the central stairway of the Ole Miss Student Union, where it has towered above thousands of students across many decades. In other words, Everett's speech became a canonical text (perhaps the canonical text) in popular university history. His subject? The term "Ole Miss."

Everett began with the thesis that "Ole Miss" and the University of Mississippi are separable entities, related but distinct: "There is a valid distinction between 'The University' and 'Ole Miss' even though the separate threads are closely interwoven." In Everett's view, the university is "tangible" and temporal, a "physical" place subject to deterioration and change. "Ole Miss," on the other hand, is "intangible" and eternal, a "spiritual" entity that resembles "mood, emotion and personality." The bulk of Everett's speech dwelled on the simple question: "What then is Ole Miss?" Avoiding literal language, Everett used more than twenty metaphors, one after another, to encircle a vague definition of "Ole Miss," to elaborate on its meaning while simultaneously preserving (and promoting) a feeling of mystery. Included in his catalog of metaphors are the following:

> Ole Miss is the citadel where beauty dwells.
> Ole Miss is lacy moon shadows on the great white columns of the Lyceum.
> Ole Miss is a lonely white cross in an endless row of crosses on a remote and rocky mountainside at Cassino.
> Ole Miss is a smile of recognition, an excited embrace, a warm handshake, a friend in every town.
> Ole Miss is an ocean of waving crimson flags with white stars on blue bars—the deep throb of music that beats a battle song.
> Ole Miss is Bourbon Street, at its best, or at its worst.
> Ole Miss, too, is a quiet meditation under blue skies at Sardis Lake or in an ancient country church.
> Ole Miss is an unbreakable unity, a lasting living bond between those past and those present.[41]

These are metaphors of combat, nature, hospitality, sports, Confederate nationalism, alcohol, religion, family, and history. Everett structured his rhetoric to achieve authority and gravity. He framed his meditation not as a credo. (Statements of "I believe" can be moving and sincere, but they are ultimately individual and voluntary.) Instead, Everett repeated the declarative structure "Ole Miss is," which through passive voice communicated a feeling of commandment and permanence. His metaphors became presupposed facts, examples pulled from across history that were communal, recognizable, and revered.

Much of the imagery throughout Everett's speech is southern and obviously replete with nostalgia. It is easy to recognize a longing for the Lost

Cause as well as the moonlights and magnolias of the imagined Mississippi ("Ole Miss is lacy moon shadows on the great white columns of the Lyceum"). The rebel flag makes a prominent appearance in Everett's speech, as does the song "Dixie." This is, of course, deeply ideological content. When read in context, coming immediately after the tumultuous 1960s, it is also transparently defensive. In Everett's conception of "Ole Miss," there is no acknowledgment of racial progress or substantial change of any kind. In fact, the dichotomy that Everett forwarded can be read as a mechanism for making the most beloved parts of "Ole Miss" inaccessible to outsiders. More than a school, "Ole Miss" became a family, "an unbreakable unity, a lasting living bond between those past and those present." Upon first reading, Everett's speech—and his eloquently constructed dichotomous definition of "Ole Miss"—seems all encompassing. Comprehensiveness of this kind is comforting, nearly religious in its appeal, and in his short speech, Everett seemingly gave his audience a universal set of elaborations. In his rich catalog of metaphors and wide-ranging references, there was something familiar and comforting for everyone, or for almost everyone.

What's missing from Everett's 1971 conceit is any direct reference to race. Although it was the consuming conflict at the university during the previous, raging decade, Everett tacks carefully away from the subject, avoiding the shadow of this ongoing problem in order to promote his imaginative vision of white unity. In and of itself, this creative avoidance took some substantial rhetorical skill, as Everett's nominal task was to introduce the chancellor. Just the previous fall, under Chancellor Fortune's leadership, almost half of all Black students on campus had been admonished for peaceful protests aimed at improving conditions and accelerating the hiring of Black faculty. Some ninety Black students had been arrested; most spent the night in the local jail; some were transported to the notorious state penitentiary at Parchman. Following that public episode, Fortune condemned the Black students and promised to punish their leaders. It was a nasty and public event, one that would have been fresh and familiar to the (presumably) all-white audience at this formal gathering at the club in Vicksburg.[42]

So, in other words, the conflict around issues of race at UM was raging, as it had been since Meredith's arrival in 1962. Yet Everett made no direct references to race in his speech. Through his catalog of metaphors, he presented "Ole Miss" as inclusive and unifying, aiming his vision toward a limited, internal audience of the white majority. It seems obvious now—and it would have been obvious to Everett's listeners in Vicksburg in 1971—that his idyllic vision of "Ole Miss" is rooted firmly in the past. Through his adept act of public rhetoric, Everett was forwarding a loving ode to a less contentious time of whiteness and purity. He was breathing new life into his own community's complex of active and resistant confederate rhetoric.

Everett brought to the podium the pedigree of an incomparable southern gentleman: Colonel Rebel, historical expert on Jefferson Davis, witness in the defense of UM administrators during the Meredith upheaval, lawyer, judge, and veteran president of the nationwide Ole Miss Alumni Association.[43] In his speech are references to Confederate glory, a repetitive motif of whiteness, and the equation of "Ole Miss" to the rebel flag and the song "Dixie." All of this is clearly ideological and exclusive, pointing back to the so-called glorious past of the Lost Cause. Often over the years, when Everett's words have been reprinted, a photograph or watercolor of the Lyceum building serves as a picturesque backdrop to the text "lacy moon shadows on the great white columns of the Lyceum." The Lyceum was and remains the centerpiece of a beautifully landscaped campus. It is the oldest building, the architectural foundation of the university, and it was also the epicenter of violence during the Meredith crisis of 1962. Everett must have been intentional, as he looked back beyond that violence, to frame the iconic Lyceum as it once was, pure white amid pure white moonbeams, rather than as a symbol sullied the decade before by tear gas, bullet holes, blood, and violence. Through such nostalgic images and references, Everett was communicating a clear longing for a distant and peaceful past. In thinly veiled code, he was making a strong ideological argument.

More subtly, Everett offered this passage: "Ole Miss is a smile of recognition, an excited embrace, a warm handshake, a friend in every town, village and hamlet from Tunica to Tylertown and Pontotoc to Pascagoula."[44] These ideas were not hyperbole. For Everett and his audience of insiders in 1971, one major benefit of being an alumnus would have been a statewide network of friends and allies. In a small state like Mississippi, one comprised of rural towns networked by country highways and roads, it can still today feel like everyone knows everyone else, at least within certain circles. There are alumni in every town, and hospitality has always been a university tradition. Of course, this particular privilege of membership did not apply to James Meredith or to the small number of other Black alumni who had attended the University of Mississippi by 1971. If white alumni during this period could depend on warm handshakes and friendly smiles in small towns across Mississippi, Black alumni could depend on fear and rejection in equal measure.

In his book *Three Years in Mississippi*, published just five years before Everett's famous speech, James Meredith, UM's first African American alumnus, told many stories of experiencing fear on Mississippi roads. Meredith planned his drives carefully to avoid small towns. He was especially concerned about gas stations, where white "rednecks" often presided. Instead of risking confrontations, Meredith would stop for rest alongside the road, trying to find inconspicuous spots away from population centers. What's more, during his time as a student, Meredith's white classmates mistreated his car whenever possible, once filling the engine with sugar just before his departure for Christmas break. Meredith was forced to drive the car anyway, eventually making it home but ruining the engine forever.[45]

A few years later in 1966, after graduating from UM, James Meredith embarked on the March Against Fear across northern and central Mississippi. Before he could get very far, he was ambushed by a white man with a shotgun, somewhere on the roadside near the town of Hernando. Meredith was shot and bloodied, but he survived. If Frank Everett and other "Ole Miss" insiders enjoyed the hospitality and safety of Mississippi's small towns and roads, Meredith and other Black people were not extended the same protection. It is just one example of how Meredith and other Black students might attend—and even graduate from—the University of Mississippi but were not yet allowed to access the membership privileges associated with attending "Ole Miss." The hospitality of every Mississippi "town and hamlet" was not available to them. Everett's famous and celebrated vision of "Ole Miss" was appealing to the UM majority for many reasons, one of which was the ideology and racism it so concisely and eloquently fortified. It was a linguistic dichotomy that strengthened an experiential one. It was confederate rhetoric in poetic and potent form.

The divisible "Ole Miss"/"University of Mississippi" paradigm forwarded by Everett would carry tremendous ideological utility into the future. If earlier generations saw the two terms as interchangeable and indivisible, Everett separated the terms and placed "Ole Miss" on higher ground. For Everett, the university is physical and temporal, subject to decay, while "Ole Miss" is spiritual and timeless, "a lasting living bond." The conclusion of his speech emphasizes this difference: "The University gives a diploma and regretfully terminates tenure, but one never graduates from Ole Miss. The only grade is 'A,' and the sole basis for expulsion is for loyalty to die. In short, Ole Miss is us."[46] In this conception, someone might earn a degree from the University of Mississippi—as had Meredith and a small number of other Black alumni by this time—but not be included in "Ole Miss," not be part of Everett's "us." Membership in "Ole Miss" required lifelong loyalty, a willingness to embrace that "ocean" of rebel flags, the song "Dixie," and all the other traditions that were distinctly southern—and, of course, distinctly white.

It is difficult to overstate the influence of Everett's speech within the UM community. For the majority of alumni and students, Everett's eloquent and reassuring elaboration on the term "Ole Miss" became revered as gospel, and that reverence continues today. Everett was not simply mirroring sentiments and ideas, he was offering a new defense of a cherished "family" heirloom. He did so by offering insightful associations into what for many felt like an ineffable mystery. He guided the community's understanding by being the first to attempt a detailed definition of the cherished term. At the same time, he was supercharging this beloved name, giving voice to how most people felt, offering words for their inexplicable emotions and their reverential affection for something deeper than a university. Everett was elucidating and elevating the ideals of southern whiteness, concentrating those ideals into a single but powerful term: "Ole Miss."

Since Everett's speech, the majority has seemed incapable of questioning their beloved moniker. Its complexity and problematic history have never been interrogated in any sustained or communal way. Instead, left undisturbed, the term has continued to effectively unite the white majority. Through Everett's public act of rhetoric in 1971, "Ole Miss" was reappointed and recharged as the official label of the orthodoxy. In the context of imposed racial integration and ongoing racial conflict, the term deepened its affordances for white people, who could now keep "Ole Miss" to themselves, even if they had lost the University of Mississippi to others.

But the supercharged "Ole Miss" was not merely serving a palliative function. White people could now better deploy the term to keep Black people at bay. Black students might have access to the university experience through official admission and attendance, but they could still be prevented from accessing the broader, more profound initiations and benefits that defined "Ole Miss." In this way, the term was serving a newly aggressive function, becoming a disguised citadel for the old, all-white conception of this traditional community.

Over the decades that followed, Everett's sentiments were reiterated and reinscribed by the school's majority. Used over and over again, in speeches, letters, plaques, and books, his words became "some of the most beloved and recognizable words ever penned about the university."[47] Increasingly, however, Everett's speech was selectively excerpted in such a way as to highlight not the Old South connections but the deep positive emotions and the laudable sense of unity promoted in his words. For many, the speech was reduced to this somewhat vague and mysterious phrase from its closing paragraph: "The University gives a diploma and regretfully terminates tenure, but one never graduates from Ole Miss." In this reduced form, the speech seems charming and harmless—presenting the term "Ole Miss" through a cloudy and glamorous filter. The ideology and resulting tensions, however, are all still there, loaded into Everett's definition and ready to be discharged. Within the imagination of the majority, an imagination realized through confederate rhetoric, "Ole

Miss" and the University of Mississippi are now separate, tiered terms capable of describing different experiences on a single campus.

For those aligned with the Old South, Everett's terminological split made possible a new inference: Black and white people might all attend the University of Mississippi, but only the privileged (white people) could attend "Ole Miss." Now clearly differentiated from the university, the term "Ole Miss" could protect and preserve traditions incompatible with the perceived trespassers of the civil rights era. One's time at the University of Mississippi was terminal, something that came to an end upon graduation. One's time at "Ole Miss," however, was never ending, a membership that dated back to the university's founding in 1848 and that could be renewed endlessly into the future, as long as one remained "loyal." And so during an era when the university was being integrated—when racial progress was being realized—"Ole Miss" became a linguistic retreat for white people feeling threatened, concerned, or just vaguely ambivalent, a term through which opponents of integration could continue to imagine their alma mater as something pure and uncorrupted. Within the imaginations of the nostalgic majority, perhaps the university had been invaded, but "Ole Miss" could remain inviolable and unchanging. As a term, "Ole Miss" was reaching the apex of its ideological usefulness.

The "Ole Miss" of the Past, Present, and Future

The University of Mississippi is a thriving, flagship, research university with a rich and complicated history. Over the decades since James Meredith integrated the school, the university has made tremendous strides toward inclusion and diversity. University officials and stakeholders deserve to celebrate this progress, which in many ways has exceeded expectations. At the same time, profound problems remain, and linguistic inheritances play a significant role in this lingering tension. University officials continue to promulgate the term "Ole Miss" as "friendly," a valuable brand name that should be defended and embraced by all. In so doing, they are wittingly or unwittingly eliding the historical and ideological nature of this central self-identifier. They are alienating some within the university community who harbor deep reservations, disgust, and/or feelings of fear regarding the term.

These dissenters come from every race and are, of course, marginalized and minority voices on campus and beyond. They often keep their feelings to themselves. Some speak out openly. When Professor Charles Eagles said, "If I could do one thing, the place would never be called Ole Miss again," he was not speaking only for himself. A handful of other professors have expressed similar sentiments over the years. Dr. Charles K. Ross, for example, has gone on the record with several journalists, consistently voicing his opposition to the term. Most opponents, however, are reticent, registering their opposition not by speaking out against the beloved name but by simply refusing to use it. This unorganized form of silent protest is more widespread than most would imagine. Although it has never been studied or documented, this resistance is real and probably growing. If "Ole Miss" can be renewed as a unifying identifier for the quiet minority and for everyone else within this modern university community, if it can win the current naming contest of history, if it can evolve into a "name so beautiful and appropriate" for every member of the present-day university, then it can and will survive for a second century.

For this to happen, however, the term's history and deeply ideological nature needs to be publicly acknowledged, considered, and processed. Reconciliation begins with recognition. Rather than ignoring or confusing the less palatable aspects of the term, those in power today should join with those in the minority to honestly assess and publicly redefine the meaning of "Ole Miss." Can the term be redeemed and refreshed? Can it be disentangled from an Old South ideology that is no longer desirable or representative? I doubt it, but these questions are difficult and communal. Ultimately, I argue not for the rehabilitation of confederate rhetoric but for its retirement. An example like the term "Ole Miss" is a living, vibrant, all-encompassing label for a community. It quite literally defines and names the place and people of the university. It is inescapable and generative, as long as it is in use. As such, full contextualization and transformation seem difficult, if not impossible, given its clearly racist origins and its history of prosecuting such prejudicial damage. Can the term become as unifying for the University of Mississippi of today as it was for the University of Mississippi of 1900, 1930, or 1960? The answers, of course, lie in the "Ole Miss" of the future.

CHAPTER 2

What Is a Hotty Toddy?

From School Cheer to Racist Jeer

> Hotty Toddy is a symbol of the simple authenticity of Ole Miss. It's the heart of the Southland, and it's part of our heritage.
>
> Ole Miss Fan, 2010

In June 1913 at the University of North Carolina at Chapel Hill (UNC), several hundred students, faculty, and alumni gathered on campus in formal attire to unveil and celebrate the new Confederate monument. Governor Locke Craig spoke to the crowd, as did Julian Shakespeare Carr. General Carr, as he was known, was familiar to the crowd for many reasons: he was a revered alumnus, the father of three UNC graduates and one current student, an industrialist, a donor, a semi-successful politician, a vocal supporter of the Ku Klux Klan, and a proud white supremacist. In a long speech full of classical references, poetry, and thick nostalgia for the Confederacy, Carr praised Confederate veterans for defending "the Anglo Saxon race during the four years immediately succeeding the war, when the facts are, that their courage and steadfastness saved the very life of the Anglo Saxon race in the South . . . and to-day, as a consequence, the purest strain of the Anglo Saxon is to be found in the 13 Southern States—Praise God." Speaking at the base of the new monument, a project organized by the North Carolina chapter of the United Daughters of the Confederacy, Carr also showered considerable praise on the (white) women of the South, detailing the wonders of their honor, fealty, and purity. It was in this sentimental vein that Carr delivered the following aside:

> I trust I may be pardoned for one allusion, howbeit it is rather personal. One hundred yards from where we stand, less than ninety days perhaps after my return from Appomattox, I horse-whipped a negro wench until her skirts hung in shreds, because upon the streets of this quiet village she had publicly insulted and maligned a Southern lady, and then rushed for

> protection to these University buildings where was stationed a garrison of 100 Federal soldiers. I performed the pleasing duty in the immediate presence of the entire garrison, and for thirty nights afterwards slept with a double-barrel shot gun under my head.[1]

With this story, Carr delivered several messages. First, he delivered a message about the defense of southern white womanhood: he emphasized his guardianship of white southern women from the perceived threat posed by African Americans, bragging that he "horse-whipped a negro wench until her skirts hung in shreds, because . . . she had publicly insulted and maligned a Southern lady." Second, Carr delivered a message about defiance and resistance: he thumbed his nose at the federal occupation and the entire cause of Reconstruction. Third, he delivered a message about the impotence of the US government: he joked to get a chuckle, ending his story with a memory of sleeping with a shotgun at the ready for the next month, prepared for any unwelcome federal visitors. The federal troops did not stop Carr from his "pleasing duty," nor did they later dare to punish him for carrying out the racial beating. In Carr's public retelling, the federal troops were idle and hesitant, while Carr himself was active and assertive.

Overall, the story enacts a rhetoric of obstinacy and resistance, a rhetoric of violence toward African Americans and of aggression toward the US government. In dedicating the monument in this way, Carr left little doubt as to its purpose. This statue and the many others like it across the South were rhetorical rebukes of "Yankee" insolence. They were memorials to the old southern way of life, and they were white marble shrines to white supremacy.

The statue that Carr celebrated at UNC would come to be known as Silent Sam. Throughout the next century, Silent Sam served Carr's cause valiantly as overt and obvious confederate rhetoric and as a rallying point for the cause of white domination. In 1940, UNC students burned crosses around the monument. In 1953, members of the Kappa Alpha fraternity gathered around Silent Sam to commemorate the birthday of Robert E. Lee. In 1968, after the assassination of Martin Luther King, unknown activists (presumably Black activists) sprayed graffiti on Silent Sam; the next day, white volunteers cleaned the statue and adorned it with Confederate flags.[2] As detailed by UNC Libraries in its rich and multimodal online guide to resources about the Confederate monument, Silent Sam was far from silent across the history of the twentieth century. Instead, the statue was evocative and provocative, serving as a powerful rhetorical actant within the campus community. To return to a concept from rhetorician Laurie Gries, Silent Sam was an unfolding event, a reliable catalyst for emotions, debates, and eventually violence.

By 2018, progressive students at UNC were no longer willing to simply argue about the obvious racism and Confederate nostalgia personified by Silent Sam. Instead, inspired in part by the publication of some of Carr's repulsive speech in the campus newspaper, they took action. They defied administrators, state lawmakers, vocal alumni, and others, and tore down Silent Sam, "yanking the eight-foot bronze statue down from its nine-foot-high pedestal," then cheering and chanting before "smearing dirt on the head of the statue as it lay on the ground." Writing for the *New York Times*, Jesse Deconto and Alan Blinder described the 2018 student action at UNC as a "guerrilla demolition of the statue on the night before fall classes began." It "provoked a crush of official outrage that may reverberate for months in Chapel Hill and in Raleigh, the state capital."[3] Indeed, there was reverberating outrage because the monument still had powerful defenders. Since being erected and unveiled in 1913, Silent Sam had shaped the communal identity of UNC across more than a century. Silent Sam had convinced some UNC stakeholders to value his presence and, to some extent, the history of his cause.

As of this writing, the story of Silent Sam continues to unfold. By late 2019, the public arguments over the monument's meaning and legacy had taken an unusual turn. The North Carolina Division of the Sons of Confederate Veterans sued the UNC System over the status of the statue, which had been hidden away in storage since being torn down by the campus protesters. After some negotiations, the UNC Board of Governors agreed to settle the lawsuit by transferring control of Silent Sam to the Sons of Confederate Veterans and, most unbelievably, arranging for the transfer of $2.5 million into a trust for the statue's maintenance and care. The Sons of the Confederate Veterans saw the settlement as a great victory. R. Kevin Stone, the commander of the Confederate group, described his emotions as "ecstatic" and pledged that his organization would continue "to preserve the honor of our ancestors and to make sure the true history of the South is presented to future generations."[4] If system administrators and lawyers saw this settlement as a way to resolve the Silent Sam controversy and distance UNC from the statue and its legacy, many campus stakeholders disagreed. They pointed out, quite accurately, that the settlement was a financial and symbolic boon to the neo-Confederate cause in North Carolina and would ensure that Silent Sam would rise again in another location.

As the debate continues over this example of confederate rhetoric, I think back to General Carr and to the hundreds of other white North Carolinians who dedicated Silent Sam on that summer day in 1913. They were attempting, in part, to activate and project an argument into the future, one intended to protect and promulgate a racist worldview, to keep white and Black people apart and to preserve a longitudinal message of white supremacy. Could they have imagined such success? More than one hundred years later, Silent Sam—their own local composition of confederate rhetoric—is still successfully sowing racial discord and communicating, quite loudly, white defiance.

Even as modern universities grapple with inherited confederate rhetoric like Silent Sam, new examples of confederate rhetoric are being born, offering the unsettling promise of future unrest. In the modern US South, some white people continue to use Old South words and symbols to enact identity, communicate pride, and forward public and private arguments for racism. Often now these expressions occur on relatively new social platforms like Instagram and Twitter, but these expressions are part of an old rhetorical tradition with deep roots, standing along a continuum that includes other public moments like Carr's racist dedication of Silent Sam in 1913. That this rhetorical tradition remains vibrant into the present is shameful but true. Examples from recent years are plentiful: white students costumed in blackface at an Auburn University party, Black students being called the n-word at the University of Missouri, white fraternity brothers sharing racist videos at the University of Georgia, white students mocking Black Lives Matter on Snapchat at the University of Tennessee, and racial slurs written on the outside of the Center for Black Culture at Duke University.[5] Often university leaders condemn these episodes as isolated and surprising moments that stand apart from institutional identities and traditions. Scholars of rhetoric, however, know that such consequential utterances—such performative compositions—are rarely isolated. Indeed, they are communicative and thus primarily social in nature. Such performances, as Richard Bauman has said, "represent for participants an arena for the display, contemplation, and manipulation of salient elements, practices, and relationships that allow language to serve as a resource for the expression of identity."[6] Racist eruptions on campuses, then, warrant not dismissals or minimizations but sustained consideration and stubborn contextualization. Particularly when rhetoricians perceive patterns of such performances, they can use their interpretative and analytical tools to highlight the full scale and impact of these performances. Persistent performances, no matter how unpalatable, are often not divergent from institutional identities. They are, instead, consistent with some key part of those identities. They are a long-standing and defining tradition.

The University of Mississippi has suffered its own series of racist performances like those cited above. In a very public example from 2019, three white men, all UM students, posed with guns in front of the bullet-riddled historical marker at the site where Emmett Till's dead and disfigured body was pulled from the Tallahatchie River in 1955 (fig. 13). These students went to considerable trouble to compose this particular Old South tableau. They

FIGURE 13. Three University of Mississippi students posing with guns next to the bullet-riddled Emmett Till historical marker. This photograph was posted on Instagram, where it received several hundred likes, and was later brought to national attention by investigative journalist Jerry Mitchell of the Mississippi Center for Investigative Reporting. (Photographer unknown.)

traveled to the remote Emmett Till marker, some eighty miles from campus. They (perhaps) shot the sign themselves. At the very least, they uncased their shotgun and assault rifle as props. They arranged the photograph. They used automobile headlights to improve the lighting conditions. They posed. They smiled. One of them later distributed the image on social media, where it received several hundred likes from friends and followers. A few months later, after the image had circulated for a time within the young men's semiprivate social networks, the Mississippi journalist Jerry Mitchell exposed the image to the outside world.[7] The broad harm of the image and of the resulting discourse began to gain momentum. The racist performance of these three students—and the institution's slow response—reopened racial wounds and created pain and shame within the community. The episode invoked and refreshed the racism that has partially defined Mississippi and UM from their beginnings. Soon, the national media picked up and expanded the story. Reporters from National Public Radio, the *New York Times*, and the *Washington Post* covered the photo and its aftermath. The headlines reminded the world that racism was still alive and well in Mississippi.

RACIST RESIDUES IN THE HOTTY TODDY

Along the spectrum of hateful performances, the staged scene at the Emmett Till marker and the other examples cited above are overt and obvious. But deployments of confederate rhetoric can be influential and powerful even when the delivery is more obscure, more difficult to interpret or condemn. Sometimes, seemingly harmless words or symbols, which on the surface merely express communal pride, can also invoke the South's dark and troubling history. This chapter explores one such example of less glaring confederate rhetoric: the Hotty Toddy athletic cheer at the University of Mississippi.

In examining the Hotty Toddy, this chapter contributes to the literature on rhetoric and identity by showing how seemingly neutral or benign discourse may—like the more obvious performances cited above—invoke dark historical associations and create unintended or unanticipated harm. This case study raises questions about a community's ability to purge discourse of its racist associations, and demonstrates how a seemingly harmless expression like an athletic cheer can retain and thus preserve residues of racism. While statues like Silent Sam can be torn down and removed to museums, how should southern university communities (and other institutions) handle expressions or symbols less glaring than Confederate statuary but perhaps just as troubling? Although this chapter provides an extended, close reading of a particular rhetorical artifact, it also offers a template for interrogating subdued words and symbols that may retain racist residues across time.

The Hotty Toddy is a prominent linguistic and performative artifact in Mississippi and throughout the US South, at least whenever and wherever UM sports fans are present. Unlike other artifacts with problematic histories, however, the Hotty Toddy cheer has yet to become publicly controversial. As I reveal in the following pages, the Hotty Toddy is confederate rhetoric in disguise, rhetoric that often serves positive and unifying roles, but rhetoric that also regularly performs distasteful cultural work and that has, on no fewer than six significant occasions, been weaponized as a racial taunt.

Since at least the 1940s, students at the University of Mississippi have used the Hotty Toddy cheer to communicate their school spirit.[8]

CALL

Are You Ready?

RESPONSE

Hell Yeah! Damn Right!
Hotty Toddy, Gosh Almighty,
Who the Hell Are We? Hey!
Flim, Flam, Bim Bam
Ole Miss, By Damn!

Popular upon its introduction, the cheer has become a school staple over time, outlasting or displacing other cheers that have waxed and waned in popularity.

For many generations now, students matriculating at UM have memorized and performed the Hotty Toddy as a rite of passage. Its usage as a performative expression of communal pride and identity has remained prominent at sporting events and has also grown beyond athletic contexts into realms as various as commencement exercises and wedding receptions. Whenever groups of students, alumni, and friends wish to celebrate their affiliation with UM, they are likely to perform the Hotty Toddy cheer.

This resilient tradition seems to be growing in importance. The 2017 senior class decided to commemorate the Hotty Toddy by donating—as their class gift to the university—a historical marker explaining and celebrating the cheer's usage and vitality. The plaque will read, in part, "Universities have cheers, Ole Miss has Hotty Toddy. It's a feeling, ideal, fight song, prayer, verbal handshake and way of life, all rolled into one."[9]

The Hotty Toddy has regularly jumped contexts, expanding its usage beyond athletic settings. For instance, it has been put to benign use in wedding celebrations, examples of which can be found on YouTube.[10] The cheer seems joyous and unifying in such familial moments. But the Hotty Toddy has also been racialized and rhetorically weaponized. At several points during school history, white students have used the Hotty Toddy as hate speech to exclude and punish their Black peers. And so, on one hand, the Hotty Toddy is a school cheer celebrated as a unifying tradition. On the other hand, it is a hateful jeer used purposefully to divide the community along racial lines. Documenting and contextualizing this rhetorical duality and explaining the Hotty Toddy's complex relationship to this community's identity are among the goals of this chapter.

It is worth noting that other cheers at other southern universities have also jumped context in this way. In 2015, white observers of the homecoming parade at the University of Missouri used their school's most famous football cheer, M-I-Z-Z-O-U, to castigate Black students who were staging a peaceful protest. Also in 2015, Anthony James, an African American student at the University of Alabama, reported being taunted by white students yelling "Roll Tide, Nigger!" from a passing pickup truck. Much earlier in history, in 1956, white University of Alabama students expressed their opposition to the federally ordered admission of Autherine Lucy, who was Black, by chanting after a basketball game, "Two, four, six, eight, we don't wanna integrate!"[11] More research and localized analysis needs to be undertaken within other university contexts, but these examples suggest that there is, indeed, a wider discursive issue at play. School spirit and racism are sometimes intertwined and enacted through athletic cheers, and this rhetorical phenomenon has occurred at multiple universities on multiple occasions.

Nothing is simple or straightforward in Mississippi (or in the US South), not even a celebratory football cheer. The Hotty Toddy is complicated confederate rhetoric that deserves close analysis for many reasons: (1) the Hotty Toddy is a successful, long-lived example of how individuals use language to emerge, preserve, and showcase communal identity; (2) it is a linguistic and poetic ritual that unites generations; (3) it contains, reflects, and reifies feelings and ideas related not only to school spirit but also to regional (southern) pride; (4) it delivers ideological content across time; (5) its mode affords some speakers recurring opportunities to align their emotions or affects with conceptions of a besieged identity; and (6) it has regularly jumped contexts, expanding its usage beyond athletic settings.

Analytical and Theoretical Tools

In seeking to better understand the Hotty Toddy as a linguistic and performative act of identity, I draw on several analytical and theoretical interpretative tools from scholars of linguistics, rhetoric, and critical discourse analysis. Mary Bucholtz and Kira Hall have opened a useful path toward understanding the relationship between linguistic/semiotic practices and identity. Harmonizing many theoretical antecedents, Bucholtz and Hall have shown that identity is "constituted through social action, and especially through language." Identity formation does not occur in isolated, solitary conditions of quietude but relies on performative and dialogic linguistic actions. Identity is not simply reflected through linguistic and semiotic practices, it *emerges* from them and, as such, is "fundamentally a social and cultural phenomenon."[12] This emergence principle is key to my understanding of the Hotty Toddy cheer. Language and its performances shape and determine identity for rhetors, even as language and its performances impact audiences. Rhetors are not simply reflecting and/or communicating identity through language, they are creating (emerging) identity as they speak, perform, or, in the case of the Hotty Toddy, cheer.

Guided by rhetorician John Oddo, I turn also to J. R. Martin and P. R. R. White of the Sydney School, linguists whose engagement system provides several lenses for understanding how rhetors (cheerers, in this case) perceive and manage their putative audiences.[13] This engagement system, when applied to the Hotty Toddy, uncovers a key function of the cheer: its power and ability to alienate and exclude. As a set of partially monoglossic utterances, the Hotty Toddy signals and enforces little tolerance for alternative viewpoints. With each (loud) iteration, the cheer serves as a social reification of the orthodox view of communal identity. Rhetors use the Hotty Toddy to enforce clear parameters and discourage dissenting views. As such, the Hotty Toddy contains the power to punish—to push internal objectors or external intruders beyond the pale. Rhetors at the University of Mississippi have used the Hotty Toddy, with its monoglossic capabilities, against opposing football fans, but they have also used the cheer against "others": namely, African Americans who dared to challenge cherished boundaries and traditions. How are orthodoxies preserved? Sometimes through seemingly innocent and banal language.

Although the darker sides of the Hotty Toddy's capacity are normally hidden, they have revealed themselves intermittently during the cheer's history. Previous writers, including historians, have recorded six performances in which the cheer was repurposed and redeployed as racialized hate speech. In these accounts, the hateful Hotty Toddy cheers were noted but not emphasized or analyzed. They were treated, instead, as incidental semiotic symptoms when compared to the surrounding historical action. Using the concept of indexicality, I offer an alternative perspective, focusing on these hateful performances to draw out, connect, and dwell on their significance. My goal is to explain how and why the Hotty Toddy has been available and effective as a racist taunt.

As a concept, indexicality will be important in this and other chapters. Indexicality is a semiotic phenomenon always at work. Mikhail Bakhtin, Michael Silverstein, Richard Bauman, and Adam Hodges have shown how language can anchor certain messages, thereby limiting interpretative parameters even for future speakers and hearers. Political slogans, for example, index broader campaign messages and serve as reminders of those messages long after the campaign itself has ended. Thus, a simple slogan can become inflated with meaning and can be longitudinally altered. Indexing makes certain meanings always available or, viewed from another angle, always unavoidable. Hodges has detailed this reality for Barack Obama's "Yes, We Can" slogan. Rhetors cannot now use that slogan without indexing certain political ideas.[14] And, after the 2016 election, will anyone ever be able to say "Let's Make America Great Again" without indexing Donald Trump and his polarizing views? These expanded meanings are quite durable and become, in fact, unavoidable, especially within finite discourse communities like southern universities, which define themselves according to their traditions.

All confederate rhetoric is bound to a certain degree by its indexes, by the usages and contexts of its past deployments. When white people at the University of Mississippi hurl a beloved cheer against Black classmates, the cheer itself fuels and performs punitive cultural work and redefines itself in ways that are not easily revised or redacted. Neither marginal nor incidental, the Hotty Toddy thus becomes in its darker deployments not simply a symptom of oppressive tendencies but a motivating and guiding rhetorical tool for the emergence and prosecution of oppression itself.

The Hotty Toddy under Normal Circumstances

Before exploring some of the known moments when this provincial athletic cheer has been used as a racialized jeer, let me first describe the Hotty Toddy under the normal circumstances of its deployment. These are friendlier and more frequent moments when the cheer can be heard and observed on the UM campus before, during, and after athletic events, the most prominent and valued of which are football games. Groups large and small perform the Hotty Toddy loudly and repeatedly throughout the duration of the tailgating festivities and during the football game itself. Many recordings of these performances can be found online. Take, as a representative example, the 2012 performance depicted in figure 14. In the opening seconds of the video, off camera, someone asks, "Are You Ready?" This is the solitary, standard call that begins the collective group response: "Hell Yeah! Damn Right! Hotty Toddy, Gosh Almighty, Who the Hell Are We? Hey! Flim, Flam, Bim Bam, Ole Miss, By Damn!"

When analyzed through the lens of the emergence principle (recall Bucholtz and Hall), several characteristics of the above performance prove conspicuous. First, the Hotty Toddy is an intensely social interaction. The example in figure 14 typifies hundreds of other performances every game day. It takes place in the community's most sacred social space, the Grove, where UM insiders party together, shore up business and political contacts, and consume large quantities of food and alcohol. According to former chancellor Robert

Figure 14. Students chant the Hotty Toddy in the Grove before a 2012 football game at the University of Mississippi. ("Ole Miss Hotty Toddy Chant," posted by Taylor Tailgates, September 19, 2012, YouTube, https://youtu.be/6KPvZWLiwDg. Screenshot by the author.)

Khayat, "On football game weekends, it [the Grove] becomes Mississippi's No. 1 social event."[15] Within this vibrant social space, UM fans perform the Hotty Toddy for each other and for hundreds of their peers standing in close proximity. In other words, the cheer has certain dialogic capabilities. Not only is each enthusiastic performance a call-and-response, but one performance can often trigger another performance, especially within the dense campus crowds of game day. The chant thus serves as an audible unifier, a poetical mechanism for declaring and strengthening communal identity.

Bucholtz and Hall have labeled such moments of discourse—when self-conceptions enter the world through language—as "the social ground on which identity is built, maintained, and altered." UM fans use the Hotty Toddy to continually create and re-create their communal identity. The cheer is not simply a showcase or spectacle; it is, instead, language that facilitates the emergence and display of a unified self-conception. In the framework of Bucholtz and Hall, the Hotty Toddy's call-and-response marks a moment "when identity is emergent in discourse."[16] For the UM community, the Hotty Toddy is truly a collective reply to the existential and embedded question "Who the hell are we?"

If identity is often a hazy or obscure concept—one difficult to pin down, especially for collectives—the Hotty Toddy serves as a concrete artifact for analyzing this particular community's collective identity. In other words, the performative and conspicuous chant provides the means "to locate identity as an intersubjectively achieved social and cultural phenomenon." For UM insiders, it is a rhetorical vehicle for the formative and reflective work of identity creation and reification. For analysts, the cheer becomes an audible artifact that is both catalyst and residue of that identity formation. In uniting to deliver the Hotty Toddy, students like the young men depicted in figure 14 are not simply reflecting identities previously assumed but are reiterating publicly and socially a collective identity that emerges and strengthens again and again with every interactive performance. The cheer illustrates what Bucholtz and Hall have termed "the emergent quality of identity" through language.[17] The authoritative conclusion of the Hotty Toddy underscores this key functionality: "Who the Hell Are We? Ole Miss, By Damn!"

Through the linguistic and semiotic demonstration that is the Hotty Toddy, the young men in the present example (and others like them across time) enact their affiliated identity as "Ole Miss Rebels." By joining together and declaring their unity through this chant—and by repeating the chant on game days and, indeed, throughout their lives—students, alumni, and fans are quite literally forming and solidifying their communal "school spirit" with every performance. The words of the cheer declare the identity, and the concomitant social performance provides a vehicle for that identity's emergence (and continual reemergence) into the world.[18]

The fact that identity emerges and is reified by a symbolic or linguistic performance—in this case an athletic cheer—is not a novel point. Humans in many contexts emerge and reify their individual and communal identities through symbolic or linguistic performances. Consider, for example, national anthems and religious recitations like the Nicene Creed. What is most interesting in the case of the Hotty Toddy, however, is that as an identity performance, the cheer is complicated by residual, problematic, and proximate indexical meanings. Just as Hodges has shown that Obama's "Yes, We Can" slogan cannot be uttered now without indexing certain political ideas, the Hotty Toddy cheer, whenever deployed and regardless of the rhetors' immediate intent, might always bring with it the residues of racist meanings that have sometimes accompanied its usage.

The Hotty Toddy cheer with its irrational but clearly defiant declaration of identity gained traction and prominence during the latter stages of Jim Crow, a time when the all-white UM community adopted a panoply of overtly Confederate and Lost Cause symbols to complement and strengthen existing confederate rhetoric. Recall from chapter 1 how the term "Ole Miss" is, in and of itself, ideological language that has served to punish and exclude Black students and alumni while celebrating and buttressing white students' and alumni's claims to the institution. With this in mind, note how the Hotty Toddy functions (perhaps primarily) as a poetical delivery mechanism for the words "Ole Miss." After all, the entire chant builds up to the culminating declaration of identity: "[We are] Ole Miss, By Damn!" These associations and historical context help explain how the Hotty Toddy has been accessible as a racist taunt, despite not containing any explicitly racist content.

At several points in history, white students at the University of Mississippi have used the Hotty Toddy to express hatred and racism. In 1963, for example, students used the chant to spontaneously celebrate the news of the assassination of John F. Kennedy, who had forced the school to integrate the year before. And, in 2012, white students used it against their Black classmates to protest the reelection of Barack Obama, the country's first Black president. These and other episodes are fully explored later in this chapter. For now, it is enough to say that the Hotty Toddy remains partially tethered to the racist ideology of the Old South. White rhetors with racist intentions have thus been able to repeatedly summon the cheer to express their views and to punish or marginalize African Americans.

When left alone within southern institutions, overt confederate rhetoric can perpetuate problems, including the oversimplification of racial categories, the dominance of white power structures and white frames of reference, and the longitudinal marginalization of Black people and other "others." This is one way in which racism's lifespan has been extended in the US South. What may also be true is that subtle confederate rhetoric like the Hotty Toddy is also pernicious because it can survive and thrive without drawing attention to itself. It can preserve racism surreptitiously. While Old South associations are always present and available within such language, those associations are not always conspicuous. In other words, rhetors can knowingly or unknowingly hide (or deny) the full complexity of such rhetoric.

Indeed, Old South associations have been embedded within the Hotty Toddy cheer. In 2018, among the top results of a Google search for "What is the Hotty Toddy" was an official UM news story from 2014. The story forwards the orthodox view that "the origins of the phrase [Hotty Toddy] remain a mystery," but also emphasizes that "one thing is for certain: Hotty Toddy and Ole Miss are inseparable." Accompanying the story is a promotional video of interviews conducted on campus and in the town of Oxford. Off camera, someone asks, "What does Hotty Toddy mean to you?" A number of UM students and alumni respond with their thoughts. The first respondents offer vague guesses. One international student summarizes a common confusion, "I really don't know. We see that everywhere, but we don't really know the meaning of it." After this, there are some funny responses. One child says that Hotty Toddies are pretty girls and that his mother was once a Hotty Toddy. A middle-aged woman says that Hotty and Toddy are the names of her cats. A male football fan says that Hotty Toddy means "Go to hell, LSU." Near the end of the video, the responses become more substantial. A young, white female student or alumnus says that Hotty Toddy "unites people . . . like we're family." Next, an older white woman gives the penultimate interview, remarking that "Hotty Toddy is a symbol of the simple authenticity of Ole Miss. It's the heart of the Southland, and it's part of our heritage." The video closes with an interview of an African American female student on campus in front of Fulton Chapel. She says, "To me, Hotty Toddy means a welcoming and opening expression by Ole Miss that signifies unity on the Ole Miss campus."[19]

The video, which runs less than two minutes, has attracted more than twenty-five thousand views since being published. It is billed as showing "different perspectives on the meaning of Hotty Toddy." Most interesting for the purposes of the present discussion are the final two perspectives: that of the older white woman and that of the young African American woman. Although they are presented together in this video, side by side in time, their perspectives are neither consistent nor reconcilable when read critically and in context. The video strives to strike a happy and upbeat tone. There is music in the background from the Ole Miss "Pride of the South" Band. There are, as mentioned, funny entries. Everyone interviewed is smiling and positive. But the presence of humor and music betrays real tensions in the substance of the perspectives. While the young African American student sees Hotty Toddy as "a welcoming and opening expression . . . that signifies unity," the older white woman emphasizes the Hotty Toddy's connections to the "authenticity of Ole Miss" and to some vague but emotional "Southland." She concludes by saying that "it's part of our heritage." This is classic and direct nostalgia, clear evidence that for some users, the Hotty Toddy chant—and the shortened phrase, Hotty Toddy—are consciously linked to Old South associations that might be called confederate.

If the Hotty Toddy cheer carries Old South associations, then there are some profound and disruptive implications for the UM community, which currently uses the Hotty Toddy as if it is purely unifying and innocent. If there are active racist affordances within this cheer, if the Hotty Toddy is a preservative of racism in any form, then should the community confront those affordances and/or change or retire this unexamined tradition? Again, for the purposes of this case study, the intention of individual rhetors is far less important than the consequentiality of the rhetoric. Does the Hotty Toddy shape communal identity in ways that are entirely positive, or does it transport and impose remnants of racism into the present?

This is an important question because even today the Hotty Toddy cheer serves certain initiatory functions for students entering the University of Mississippi. Whatever ideas and potentialities it can deliver are being delivered year after year to each successive generation within the community. College is a time of transition, and the Hotty Toddy cheer is one very prominent mechanism for bringing UM newcomers into the communal fold. The cheer is taught to new students at orientation, and it is featured in the textbook for UM's popular orientation course.[20] Before and after matriculation, students learn the cheer from admissions counselors, university officials, and from each other. The Hotty Toddy is a vibrant linguistic and semiotic tradition embraced and cultivated by university leaders and by students themselves. It is a rite of passage into the university.

But, as I have already suggested, the significance of the Hotty Toddy extends far beyond orientation or athletic events and into nearly all stages of student and alumni life. In fact, the chant has been abbreviated into a greeting that is used daily by some members of the community. As Doug Ward of ESPN noted, the phrase "Hotty Toddy has no real meaning, but it means everything in Oxford. For students, fans, and alumni, it is a greeting, cheer, and secret handshake all rolled into one." The words may not denote anything directly, but the Hotty Toddy connotes and encapsulates better than anything else "the spirit of Ole Miss."[21] What are we to make of language that is at once ideationally barren but also deeply meaningful?

Perhaps part of the explanation lies in the universal appeal of mystery. Fraternity slogans and ritualistic passwords are examples of archaic language that sounds to outsiders like gibberish but that contains deep meaning for initiates. Much of the language of the Hotty Toddy serves a similar function. It may not make sense to outsiders, but it has become a localized, club-like marker: a distinct password reserved by and for members of the UM community. As such, the Hotty Toddy relies on and is strengthened by its cryptic nature. In a very real and practical sense, the cheer has become a coded rite of passage, a symbol of community membership. If you are in the UM club, you know and perform the Hotty Toddy. If you are not in the club, you do not. The students of the 2017 senior class underscored this functionality in their proposed plaque, which celebrates the Hotty Toddy as a "verbal handshake" used only by "Ole Miss Rebels." Or, as Stuart Stevens remembered in his memoir of growing up in Mississippi, "On the way to the game, Confederate flags were everywhere, but that was normal. . . . I always loved the way the crowds got bigger the closer we got to the stadium. . . . Not that I was friends with my fellow fans, or even knew more than a handful of them, but they were Rebel fans. We were Rebel fans. Perfect strangers would greet each other with 'Hotty Toddy,' and it was like a powerful password into our special clubhouse."[22]

If the Hotty Toddy initiates and distinguishes members of the UM community, it also serves to maintain a certain continuity of communal identity across generations. It forms solidarity between old and young. Other universities have linguistic traditions that function in similar ways: cheers or chants that connect young people with previous students who in different eras also learned and performed the very same words. Students at the University of Tennessee sing "Rocky Top," students at the University of Georgia bark like "Dawgs" in unison, and students at Texas A&M invent and perform fairly elaborate hand signals. Similarly, for students at UM, the Hotty Toddy is a clear and unique demonstration of allegiance—and an opportunity for newcomers in new generations to promulgate and reproduce an inherited identity. UM student Blaire Jackson reflected on the Hotty Toddy's ability to unite generations in a 2014 article in the student newspaper: "I think we like the fact that it is tradition; 'Hotty Toddy' is not a new thing that somebody came up with a year ago. My parents, grandparents, aunts, uncles all went to Ole Miss, and they've been saying 'Hotty Toddy' since they were in school. It's just a way to associate with the school." In that same article, Jenna Artz, a staff member, agreed and elaborated, "To me, saying or cheering 'Hotty Toddy' means I am a member of the Ole Miss family. Hotty Toddy brings forth a sense of community. We are all united with one common goal—having the utmost spirit for our institution." Even if members of the community know little about the ideational meanings of the words or about the history of the cheer, they all seem to understand its importance as a tradition that promotes continuity of identity across the decades. Bucholtz and Hall posit that identity is not preexisting but is instead "the emergent product" of linguistic practices.[23] The Hotty Toddy is an example of how language can serve to both emerge and stabilize identity. As this utterance is repeated across decades, it creates a constancy that unites multiple generations.

Bucholtz and Hall approach "identity as a relational and sociocultural phenomenon that emerges and circulates in local discourse contexts of interaction rather than as a stable structure located primarily in the individual psyche."[24] Within the Hotty Toddy is ritualistic language through which identity emerges and reemerges across time. The chant itself has become a "stable structure" of "local discourse," one that provides a point of firmly rooted identity across generations. Since the chant remains unchanged (guardedly so), part of the Hotty Toddy's functionality seems to be as a preservative of identity. Repeating the Hotty Toddy across days, years, and decades creates individual and communal stability. Given the cheer's long lifespan, its resistance to modification, and its beloved status, it is obvious that many members of the UM community find such stabilization to be deeply comforting and salubrious. In this sense, the Hotty Toddy is positive and encouraging, a semiotic column of great emotional support.

Context, Evaluation, and Emotion

The Hotty Toddy as a local linguistic ritual holds tremendous power for the particular discourse community of the University of Mississippi. It serves to emerge and preserve traditional and cherished notions of identity, and this function seems harmless, or even admirable. How, then, does one explain its darker deployments? The answer lies in fully considering the substance and context of this particular community's traditional notions of identity, which were established by a white majority during a fervently defensive and racist era in Mississippi. Perhaps no other American hegemonic moment has been as extensively studied as Mississippi during Jim Crow, a time when white people were preoccupied (obsessed) with the construction and buttressing of institutional, economic, social, and linguistic barriers to African American progress, opportunity, and equality. As historian James C. Cobb has said, white southerners "met the long-awaited assault on their racial system with a violent defiance that often seemed totally irrational, if not downright deranged."[25] In Mississippi, and certainly at its flagship university, this "violent defiance" was exuberantly performative and rarely subtle.

Public spectacle and demonstrative outrage played a key role in rallying white resistance and discouraging Black transgressions. The Hotty Toddy cheer, with its irrational but clearly defiant lyrics and vigorous declaration of identity, gained traction and prominence during the latter stages of Jim Crow, a time when the UM community adopted a panoply of Confederate and Lost Cause symbols to illustrate and enact its resistance to racial progress and to distinguish its defiance to the larger, more progressive world. This localized confederate rhetoric included the nickname "Rebels," added in 1936. By 1948, the Confederate battle flag was ubiquitous on campus, and the Ole Miss Band's halftime routine featured the unfurling of "the world's largest Confederate flag to the stirring strains of 'Dixie.'" By 1950, students and school officials were organizing Dixie Week, the first in what would become an annual celebration of southern heritage. This festival of confederate rhetoric included campus speeches praising Robert E. Lee, a public reading of the Ordinance of Secession, and "the auctioning of cheerleaders who served as slaves for the week to their buyers." As historian Charles Eagles has detailed, these activities revealed the dominant campus attitudes about race. The all-white student body was outspoken and demonstrative in its defense of states' rights and in its celebrations of "white supremacy, slavery, and the Lost Cause."[26] Even by the 1960s, when students in other parts of the country were demonstrating against various establishments, most UM students were doing everything possible to defend the Lost Cause, to defend orthodoxies taught to them by their parents, grandparents, and great-grandparents. It was within this conservative and racially defensive environment that the Hotty Toddy became a cherished tradition.

Many of the symbols born and cemented at UM during the 1930s, 1940s, and 1950s have faced criticism in recent years, and some have been nudged aside altogether. Although the progress has been slow, painful, and public, it has been real. For example, the campus community no longer celebrates Dixie Week, no longer displays rebel flags by the thousands, and no longer officially endorses Colonel Rebel as the university mascot. The Ole Miss Band, known as the "Pride of the South," no longer plays "Dixie" as an official university anthem. After a courageous decision by interim chancellor Morris Stocks in 2015, the university stopped flying the Mississippi state flag because its design at the time contained the Confederate battle flag.[27] These struggles over symbols have been heated within the UM community. Each step has included public debates, editorials in the campus newspaper, forums, speeches, arguments of all kinds. The attention and anxiety have been significant and real.

Yet the Hotty Toddy has escaped scrutiny. Whether from those in the community who wish to preserve every UM tradition at any cost or from those in the community who wish to critically evaluate and, if necessary, eliminate traditions, the Hotty Toddy has not yet been a point of contention. Amid all of the recent local, regional, and national debates about Old South symbols, no one has noticed the Hotty Toddy. There it stands, even today, embraced by the 2017 senior class and by the university administration as a wholesome and unsullied tradition. Perhaps modern-day reformers have overlooked the cheer because of its vague language and oblique meanings. The Confederate statue standing near the center of campus is a direct reference to the Old South. The Hotty Toddy is not. Yet, as performative language and through its history of usage, the cheer has done cultural work similar to that of the Confederate statue. The Hotty Toddy may be vague and coded language, but it has also been an active guardian of Old South sensibilities.

Six Hateful Deployments

On November 6, 2012, Barack Obama was elected to a second term as president of the United States. At the University of Mississippi, late that night, African American and white students clashed in what they themselves described on social media as a "riot." By most objective accounts, the event was an intense confrontation or protest. Some four hundred students were participants and/or witnesses. Racial epithets were shouted. Student journalists on the scene described hateful interactions, the smell of alcohol and marijuana, and widespread chaos and fear. The University Police Department made several arrests. At some point in the night, a group of white male students gathered together near a dormitory and burned Obama-Biden campaign signs.[28] Other white students encircled these young men, watching and cheering the ceremonial conflagration. Pictures of this hateful rally, which for some evoked historical images of the Jim Crow South, made national news.

Within the context of this riot or protest—one in which students divided themselves along racial lines—white students repeatedly used the Hotty Toddy cheer to unify themselves and to taunt and exclude their African American peers. The university's official and public report states, "Near the Student Union, it was reported that racial slurs and epithets were heard from passengers in moving vehicles, shouted at African-American students. Students also heard 'Dixie' played from the vehicles and chants of 'the South will rise again.' White students also were reported to have chanted 'Hotty Toddy' periodically as a way to further divide students along racial lines."[29] It is repugnant but not surprising that white students would use racial slurs, the song "Dixie," or the chant "the South will rise again" when seeking to repudiate African Americans and President Obama. These are familiar tools in any southern resurgence of racism and exclusion.

The one rhetorical instrument unique to the University of Mississippi, however, is the Hotty Toddy, a cheer or chant promoted during the light of day as a unifying marker. Presumably, this display of school spirit should bring students, white and Black, together. Indeed, during their matriculation as freshmen, UM students of all races and backgrounds learn and use the Hotty Toddy as a rallying cry, an icon, and a rite of passage. By memorizing the call-and-response and by reciting it on command, students demonstrate—at parties, sporting events, commencement—that they stand in communion with their peers. At such upbeat moments, the cheer seems entirely positive and unsullied. On November 6, 2012, however, the Hotty Toddy showed its dark side, as white students used it defiantly and angrily against their Black classmates.

This hateful, divisive, and racialized repurposing was not lost on the Black students (and sympathetic white students) who received the mob's rhetorical blows. Many were stunned to hear their school chant suddenly hurled at them as repudiating, exclusionary language. As one student witness reported, "The Hotty Toddy chant will never be the same . . . again."[30] What is usually a linguistic and melodic act of community and togetherness—a show of school spirit—became an intonation of hate on this night in 2012. Disturbingly, it was not the first time.

In 1982, at a commemoration of the anniversary of the integration of the University of Mississippi (one designed to showcase the racial progress of the previous twenty years), a large group of white students walked out of the ceremony in protest during James Meredith's remarks. Meredith, who had been the first African American student to attend UM, was speaking critically of southern symbols like the Confederate flag, the Colonel Rebel mascot, and the song "Dixie." These criticisms were too much for many white attendees, who abandoned their seats in protest and gathered together just outside the doors of the venue. Once there, the mob "started to sing 'Dixie' and go through the well-known 'hotty toddy' football cheer that ends 'Who the hell are we . . . Ole Miss by damn.'"[31] Several attuned and alarmed administrators managed to herd the crowd of white students away from Fulton Chapel before the conclusion of the ceremony inside, perhaps preventing an uglier scene.[32] This episode ended peacefully but not before white students had deployed the Hotty Toddy as hate speech. They hurled the cheer in resistance to threats against beloved symbols of white domination. James Meredith was by 1982 a graduate of the University of Mississippi, but he was not, in the eyes of the white student majority, included in the "we" that was the "Ole Miss" of the Hotty Toddy cheer.

If James Meredith heard white students using the Hotty Toddy against him in 1982, the sound must have been familiar. A different generation of white "Ole Miss Rebels" had used the cheer against him twenty years before, in 1962, when the Hotty Toddy was deployed as hate speech during the days and hours leading up to his registration on campus. The government of Mississippi was doing everything in its power to prevent the integration of the university, with Governor Ross Barnett leading the resistance against President Kennedy and the Justice Department. On campus, the students expressed their own opposition to integration through protests that eventually turned deadly. The Hotty Toddy was rhetorical fuel for this white student resistance. On September 20, on one of James Meredith's first attempts to register on campus, white students used the Hotty Toddy at least twice. Historian Charles Eagles described how "in the morning, hundreds of students milled around in front of the Lyceum waiting for Meredith and chanting 'Hotty Toddy,' the school fight song, and various segregation slogans such as 'Glory, glory segregation. The South shall rise again.'" Later in the day, when Meredith arrived on campus, he was "welcomed" with the Hotty Toddy and other jeers. Russell H. Barrett, an eyewitness (and history professor), remembered the evening: "Meredith was brought to the campus just before 5 p.m., accompanied by Department of Justice attorney St. John Barrett, Chief of the Executive Office of U.S. Marshals James P. McShane, and two U.S. deputy marshals. Highway patrolmen escorted them onto the campus and along a road lined with patrolmen to the Continuation Center. As Meredith entered there were some boos and mild epithets, and during his twenty-minute stay the mixed crowd of students and outsiders chanted 'We want Ross' and the Ole Miss 'Hotty Toddy' yell." On this pivotal day in UM (and American) history, James Meredith was refused admission by Governor Barnett, who had been named temporary registrar of the university. Meredith's federal escort rushed him away from campus before the jeers could turn into physical violence.[33] White students had once again deployed the Hotty Toddy against racial progress. More rhetorical, legal, and physical resistance was on the horizon.

After ten days of political and legal wrangling, James Meredith returned to campus on September 30, 1962, this time with five truckloads of armed and helmeted US marshals to protect him. William Doyle has written that "the government of Mississippi was now quickly sliding into a state of rebellion against the United States of America." Watching and recording that rebellion was Ed Meek, a UM public relations employee. Meek recalled that students on this evening used the Hotty Toddy to taunt the federal marshals who had gathered at the university's main administrative building, the Lyceum: "My memory is that it [the riot] started as a pep rally. . . . Hotty toddying and bugles. . . . It was very festive until it got close to dark, and I heard a bottle over my head that hit a marshal—and that was the beginning of it." Meek has recently produced a book of photographs and personal recollections from the time of the riot. The book is a collaboration with the journalist Curtis Wilkie, who was a UM student in 1962 and another eyewitness to the riot. Later in life, Wilkie would become Washington bureau chief for the *Boston Globe*, but on this night in 1962, he was a young student, taking notes and making drawings of the action. Wilkie agreed with Meek that the Hotty Toddy was a rallying cry on that momentous evening. "Yeah. There were a lot of Hotty Toddy chants," said Wilkie. "It had gotten dark in the last fifteen minutes or so, and everything just kind of deteriorated from a pep rally type mood to a very ugly one, and these were all students who were involved." It was from this turning point that the night became terrible, conflagrating into one of the most violent and destructive episodes of the civil rights movement. Two people died, many were badly injured, and President Kennedy was forced to declare martial law in Oxford, deploying some thirty thousand federal troops to restore order and to ensure Meredith's safe matriculation.[34]

Historians Charles Eagles, Taylor Branch, Walter Lord, and others have detailed the events of that horrible night at the University of Mississippi, a night when civil unrest spiraled beyond the control of even the president of the United States. Although some have mentioned the festive atmosphere that precipitated the riot, no writer has yet considered the Hotty Toddy in context as catalyzing language. On the UM campus, in 1962, when the white students wanted to express their anger and resentment, when they needed a rhetorical tool to lash out at their federal "oppressors" and to reject James Meredith and all of the Black people he represented, they rallied from and around the Hotty Toddy cheer.

Figure 15 is a photograph Ed Meek took just moments before the outbreak of violence as students were performing the Hotty Toddy to protest the presence of federal marshals and the arrival of James Meredith, which was rumored to be imminent. The scene is in some ways similar to the image from 2012 analyzed earlier (see fig. 14). UM students are featured in both, chanting the same cheer, emerging and demonstrating a communal identity, and doing so with zeal. In both moments, violence is approaching. In the first, the violence will be contained to the football field. In the second, the violence will be deadly and will change American history.

The Hotty Toddy appeared alongside plenty of other racist rhetoric in the hours preceding the 1962 riot. Doyle and other historians relay other examples of racist jeers and slogans heard that night. One student, for example, confronted the US marshals: "I am just a little fuck. Go ahead and shoot me, you nigger-loving son of a bitch!" The crowd also chanted "We want Meredith," "Get the nigger out," and "Get a rope."[35] What is notable is that the Hotty Toddy cheer was consistently deployed alongside such overtly racist language during this full day and evening of invective, monoglossic rhetoric. Many students in 1962 directly associated their school cheer—and their very affiliation with the university—with racism and Jim Crow. They were using their fight song to emerge and defend a communal identity, one in which segregation was an essential part. Indexing far more than school spirit, the Hotty Toddy was seen by student rhetors as effective hate speech for repudiating Meredith and the federal government, both imminent threats to the sanctity of the South's institutional and social order. On the other side of the civil rights movement, African American leaders used slogans and spirituals like "We Shall Overcome" to great effect. It should not be forgotten, though, that white traditionalists also had slogans and songs. For the UM community,

Figure 15. Students chant the Hotty Toddy and other anti-integration, antifederal slogans in 1962 moments before the outbreak of the riot at the University of Mississippi. Fifty years and a few hundred yards separate the location of this photograph and that of the video depicted in figure 14. (Edwin E. Meek, *Riot: Eyewitness to Anger and Change* [Oxford: Yoknapatawpha Press, 2015], 72. Special Collections, University of Mississippi Libraries.)

the Hotty Toddy functioned as one of these, serving consistently as a rallying cry in the defense and preservation of racial power. Thus, the Hotty Toddy was localized and effective confederate rhetoric.

The cheer certainly worked overtime during the hours preceding the 1962 battle on campus, as the swirl of school spirit and southern racism was overt, confrontational, and inciting. One FBI informant on campus during the evening remembered hearing the following variation: "Hotty Toddy, God A'Mighty, Who in the hell are we? Flim flam, bim bam, white folks, by damn!"[36] This mutation illuminates the normally implicit racism that is always embedded and available within the Hotty Toddy. The unknown cheerer exchanged the words "Ole Miss" for the words "white folks." For some white students of 1962, 1982, and 2012, the Hotty Toddy that marked membership in the UM community was a ritualistic performance reserved exclusively for white people. Whiteness was the prerequisite for membership in this southern club, and the Hotty Toddy was the rhetorical "handshake" that signaled good standing and loyal affiliation. When needed, the cheer could be pressed into service to enforce cherished racial norms. This racist functionality normally lies dormant just beneath the surface of the school cheer. It is quite possible, in fact, to deny this functionality altogether. As noted earlier, the cheer's vocabulary and overt meaning are opaque. And this perhaps explains how the Hotty Toddy has avoided scrutiny within the very community that knows it best, even while other more obviously racist symbols—like the rebel flag—have been criticized and shelved.

Before becoming a journalist, James L. Dickerson attended the University of Mississippi in the early 1960s and witnessed this chilling episode.

> On Friday, November 22, 1963, the Ole Miss campus was relatively quiet. . . . That November afternoon the sky was deep blue. I was in one of the older dorms. . . . The temperature was in the fifties, crisp and cold for Mississippi. That day I was aware of a general increase in noise outside my window. It started out slow and then sort of exploded. . . . Car horns echoed across the campus. Pickup trucks, convertibles, souped-up Corvettes—all sped up and down the streets as students hung out the car windows, their arms outstretched. Rebel yells filled the air.
>
> Suddenly, I heard screams amid the car horns.
>
> "He's dead!" someone screamed. "The son of a bitch is dead!"
>
> I peered out the window. A large rebel flag the size of a bedsheet was unfurled from a dormitory window. Bug-eyed students, their faces flushed with excitement, rushed out into the street, arms waving.
>
> "Kennedy's been shot!"

> Someone began a cheer. "Hoddy toddy, God a'mighty, who in the hell are we?" went the cheer, then ended with, "Ole Miss, by damn!"[37]

In celebrating President Kennedy's assassination with the fervor of the Hotty Toddy, these students were falling back on familiar rhetoric. The scene reminds me of a more recent celebration of patriotism of another sort, when college students, mostly from Georgetown, assembled spontaneously outside the White House to celebrate the killing of Osama Bin Laden. In that moment, young Americans chanted slogans like "USA, USA," asserting their identity in opposition to a hated enemy and reifying their communal connections with one another.[38] In 1963, the students described above viewed Kennedy as an enemy of Mississippi, of the university, and of their own cherished identity. Kennedy had, after all, sent troops to conquer the racism that was integral to their way of life. If this spontaneous and open celebration of Kennedy's assassination now seems repulsive and stomach churning, it must have seemed instinctual and commonsensical to many of the UM students of the day. Kennedy was their clear enemy, and Kennedy was dead. The students did the natural thing: they declared victory by chanting the Hotty Toddy, thereby reminding each other and the world that their identity had survived Kennedy's attacks. Who the hell were they? They were white folks, Mississippians, and "Ole Miss Rebels."

Monoglossic Rhetoric and Racist Affordances

The very attributes that make the Hotty Toddy an effective football cheer also make the it an effective racist jeer. One of those attributes is its ability to emerge and reify communal identity, to bring and hold people together. Another key attribute is the Hotty Toddy's monoglossic ability to exclude and constrain opposing audiences. John Oddo has argued persuasively that scholars of rhetoric should use tools of discourse analysis to better understand speech acts, like the Hotty Toddy, in which "rhetors choose to construe reality and constitute putative audiences." Such speech acts are complicated dialogical moments because rhetors use utterances to simultaneously speak to and silence their hearers. These utterances are intertwined examples of audience engagement and audience discouragement. For analyzing such moments, Oddo points specifically to work by systemic-functional linguists like J. R. Martin and P. R. R. White of the Sydney School. Their engagement system provides a sophisticated tool for analyzing the ways in which rhetors manage relationships with their hearers.[39] Sometimes rhetors seek to invite responses; sometimes they seek to fend them off.

Following Oddo's lead and applying Martin and White's engagement system to the Hotty Toddy cheer reveals that its rhetors, like the young men in the performances discussed above, seek to engage their audiences in a very specific way to ensure a very specific set of outcomes. Fans perform this chant not to invite debate but to dishearten and silence their listeners. It is, indeed, a *fight* song and effective as such because it leaves little room for rebuttal or dissent. Communal identity is declared through the cheer's bare, hostile, and somewhat confusing assertions, through language that is ideationally barren but emotionally charged, through purposefully vulgar words, and through concluding and disorienting rebel yells. It is a cheer or fight song that answers its own questions and that leaves little room for uncertainty or debate. "Who the hell are we?" is the penultimate question of the cheer. "Ole Miss, By Damn!" is the ultimate answer.

Martin and White define such resistant speech acts as monoglossic. Rather than inviting dialogue, monoglossic utterances severely limit opportunities for audience response, thereby enabling rhetors to seize and hold attention while discouraging the voicing of dissenting views. Likewise, the Hotty Toddy silences putative audiences, effectively delegitimizing those enemies and confining them to very limited roles as discoursal "partners." While one or two individual components of the cheer may seem dialogic—such as the question "Who the hell are we?"—those components are not in actuality inviting. When delivered as part of a routinized script, these dialogic gestures do not open genuine possibilities for response. Instead, outsiders, such as visitors to the Grove on game day, are pushed aside or marginalized by the totality of the cheer. Such hearers are placed in a socially awkward position, and their passive role as outsiders is reinforced by this monoglossic utterance, which recognizes no dialogic alternative and which rewards conformity. As rhetoric, the cheer creates and enforces a dramatically unequal relationship. Insiders understand and deploy the cheer. Opponents and outsiders listen and observe, but they are given neither voice nor opportunity for response.

These repellant and punitive effects are key to understanding the rhetorical power of the Hotty Toddy and its great utility as an athletic fight song. Fans can use this linguistic and performative monoglossic utterance to unite themselves and to startle and silence others. What more could rabid football fans wish for? Indeed, if the cheer was merely used in athletic contexts, the Hotty Toddy would be interesting for its effectiveness at emerging school spirit (identity) and for communicating athletic bias, but all in all, it would be a rather one-dimensional phenomenon.

However, identity at the University of Mississippi runs much deeper than a simple, salubrious, and cathartic affiliation with the football team. For some

"Ole Miss Rebels," communal identity—the one emerging from and reified by the Hotty Toddy—encompasses ideological legacies from a racist and deeply problematic past. Proof can be found in the cheer's unsavory history. As shown above, the Hotty Toddy has been deployed in contexts and services far more profound and consequential than game days in the Grove. It has been used regularly not just as an athletic cheer but also as racialized hate speech. It is a tradition deeply intertwined with Old South sentiments.

Rebel Yell and Impropriety as Mechanisms of White Defiance

Before concluding this chapter, I will briefly discuss some characteristics of the Hotty Toddy that seem to have contributed to its cultural functionality. For one, the chant is an ideal vehicle for delivering angry and defiant emotional (or affective) content. One need only inspect figures 14 and 15 in which young men are shown performing the cheer with clenched fists, pointed fingers, and hostile facial expressions. In both instances, they turned directly to their primary audience, a frontal angle that suggests direct, menacing confrontation. Their intense gazes reinforced this impression of hostility, as the young men stared directly into the camera, holding "eye" contact throughout the duration of the vociferous cheer.[40] While the young chanters of today may or may not connect this anger to feelings of southern defiance, the emotional residue of the cheer may come directly from that old, intense source, one rooted in the loss of the Civil War and in the rolling and roiling threats of the civil rights movement. Again, the Hotty Toddy was created and cemented as a tradition in the context of white resistance to racial integration.

The conjured anger of the performance, whether simulated or real during modern deliveries, can best be understood by considering the Hotty Toddy as a fight song or battle cry. Every respectable Hotty Toddy performance ends with a loud and vigorous yell, known regionally as a rebel yell. These rebel yells echo the battle cries used by Confederate soldiers during the American Civil War. Keith Yellin, a scholar of military rhetoric, cites the "dreaded rebel yell" as a prominent historical example of a common warrior trope: "The battle cry is the capstone of battle exhortation, not only because it radiates in all directions but because it comes last sequentially. . . . When nothing more than weapon and lungs separate the individual warrior from his enemy, it is the end of the line for rhetoric and the start of physical brutality."[41] In the case of the Hotty Toddy, this break between rhetoric and physical brutality is normally quite literal: it is a break between cheering and football. At UM, the largest and most enthusiastic Hotty Toddy performances occur just before kickoff in the football stadium, when some sixty thousand fans chant in unison and conclude with independent, echoing rebel yells, just before real human bodies clash violently on the field.

While football fans from other schools often end their own chants with generic yells or screams, the fans at UM do so with particular zeal. Some UM fans also, I am arguing here, consciously connect their vociferous conclusion of the chant—their yell—to the specific historical idea of the rebel yell. My evidence for this comes from the proliferation of references to "rebel yell" within UM athletic culture. For example, Stan Sandroni, a UM radio legend, began and hosted for twenty-one years a popular talk show he called *Rebel Yell Hotline*, "where Rebel fans could hear the good side of Rebel sports." On the loudspeakers at football games, a common song played at full volume is Billy Idol's "Rebel Yell." UM fans often pair the Hotty Toddy with the words "rebel yell," as Emily Howerton Pratt did in this Facebook post from 2013: "Hotty Toddy, Gosh Almighty! I love God, Sweet Tea, and the SEC . . . Pinned, shared and giving a rebel yell to all my . . . ladies." Or, as an article in *Bows & Beaus: A Southern Lifestyle Magazine* said in 2017, "A Hotty Toddy isn't just good for an Ole Miss Rebel yell"—it is also the name of an alcoholic drink good for alleviating cold symptoms.[42] In other words, unlike cheering football fans at other schools, many UM fans clearly affiliate their culminating battle cry with the concept of the Confederate "rebel yell."

While not scripted (nor usually transcripted), the concluding rebel yells are essential components of the Hotty Toddy itself. As Yellin suggests of battle cries in general, the rebel yell at the end of the Hotty Toddy is the capstone to this fight song, the moment that unites its linguistic, social, affective, and ideological purposes. Rhetors (cheerers) give voice to a communal identity deeply rooted in and reliant on (at least in part) the doomed Confederate ideal. The Hotty Toddy with its concluding battle cry taps into a traditional and ongoing affiliation between "Ole Miss" and the Lost Cause of the South. The old southern cause may have been lost long ago, but in and around the football stadium, simulated and satisfying victories are still within reach.

If this association between yell and rebel yell seems tenuous, one need only consider a 2009 controversy over the playing of the song "Dixie" in the University of Mississippi football stadium. Fans had long concluded their singing of "Dixie" in unison by chanting "The South will rise again!"[43] It was an unofficial but orthodox and prevalent tradition, one that animated an appealing fantasy for white people in the UM community. The Hotty Toddy may serve similar purposes for some. During decades when white people in the South were constantly and painfully aware of loss—rituals like the Hotty Toddy gave them concrete and satisfying mechanisms for defending inherited identities and for imagining different outcomes. White fans uttering the Hotty Toddy could chant together, find strength in numbers, and temporarily avoid the painful realities of an increasingly hostile and threatening world. Like other examples of confederate rhetoric, the Hotty Toddy with its culminating rebel yell reassuringly protected the sanctity of the Old South, at least within the gates of the UM campus.

Such connections between the Hotty Toddy and the ideology of the Old South were far more obvious in the early days of the cheer, when it was merely one part of that rich panoply of Confederate imagery, when the Grove and the stadium were full of rebel flags, Confederate uniforms, and the recurring strains of "Dixie." By the second decade of the twenty-first century, when the Hotty Toddy stood as one of the last survivors of this complex of Confederate symbols, it became all the more mysterious—and paradoxically meaningful—to some students, fans, and alumni. Few may understand the ideational meaning of this cheer (the ideas behind the words), but most within the community agree on its resonance and profundity. Yet the cheer has not become a gentle or inactive artifact of nostalgia. Judging from the hundreds of recitations that I have personally witnessed in the last decade or two, rhetors (cheerers) at UM continue to deliver the Hotty Toddy as a fight song, usually completing it with great intensity and sometimes with palpable aggression.

This aggression is reified by the vocabulary of the cheer. The Hotty Toddy contains four curse words in five lines ("hell," "damn," "hell," "damn") plus a thinly veiled heresy in the second line ("Gosh Almighty"). These vulgarities might be considered aggressive language within most pockets of American culture. Within the context of southern American culture, however, such vulgarities and religious incursions are conspicuously transgressive, even downright offensive. Words like "hell" and "damn" uttered aggressively would normally be quite jolting in polite southern company, of the kind that gathers in the Grove, where many rules of etiquette and formality are respected and enforced.[44] Mary Libby Bickerstaff Payne, a female student at UM during the 1950s, remembers changing the words of the Hotty Toddy for this very reason: "I did Hotty Toddy so it was 'Hotty Toddy, gosh amighty, who are we, who are we? Flim flam, bim bam, Ole Miss we am.' I wasn't going to say curse words."[45] Bickerstaff Payne's sense of propriety reveals that some UM insiders believe that offensiveness is, indeed, built into the language of the Hotty Toddy. Even today, there is similar censorship when the children at the UM preschool learn the Hotty Toddy as an informal part of the curriculum. Their sanitized, pre-K version ends not with "Ole Miss, By Damn!" but with "Ole Miss, Yes Ma'am!" (These children are usually in the second or third grade before they learn that they've been tricked or, as their parents might suggest, protected from reciting offensive words.) The point is that vulgar and hostile language within the standard Hotty Toddy is objectionable and aggressive, especially within the linguistic norms of this particular community.

The Hotty Toddy challenges decorum as part of its design. Cheerers, like the young men in the video discussed above, use the Hotty Toddy to violate acceptable linguistic and emotional norms precisely because such transgressions best communicate hostility and disrespect toward their enemies. As Jonathan Hunt has written of swearing in general, "A simple four-letter word . . . can powerfully stage sincerity and spontaneity; it may reveal the ways in which violations of convention are themselves governed by convention. . . . Both reviled and admired, a profanity . . . can divide an audience like no other utterance."[46] Vulgarity in the Hotty Toddy does, indeed, divide. Even as the cheerers transgress, however, they do so publicly and proudly in what has become an acceptable—even celebrated—fashion. The key output of this semiotic and linguistic complexity is a fierce and defiant emotional message that unites most insiders and excludes others.

Conclusion and a Call for Contextualization

In this chapter, I have explicated six hateful deployments of the Hotty Toddy cheer across five decades. Those deployments form a pattern that reveals quite clearly the ideological utility of this beloved tradition. Across generations and contexts, the Hotty Toddy has functioned as exclusionary and punitive language, as confederate rhetoric. White students have defaulted to this rhetorical tool when emerging and asserting their inherited identity, one that is inherently exclusionary. Often in the US South, genteel racism is invisible, covered over consciously by rhetors savvy about their own vulnerabilities and about the potential responses of their detractors. These rhetors find comfort in code. Some of this code—only the opaquest and thus defensible—has survived the reformative tides of the civil rights era. In the case of the Hotty Toddy, the code has avoided scrutiny altogether and has survived within a cherished and unquestioned linguistic tradition. At the University of Mississippi of today, white and Black students learn and value the Hotty Toddy. It is often put to positive uses. The problem, of course, is that as language and symbol, the cheer may preserve outmoded potentialities that most modern UM students would repudiate, forcefully so. Despite conventional wisdom within this community, the Hotty Toddy is not an entirely wholesome tradition. Perhaps it should not be embraced and buttressed without first accounting for its complete history and usage. Otherwise, the Hotty Toddy will simply continue to emerge and protect racist paradigms that are undesirable residues of a previous era.

Like everything else in the US South, language is complicated. The Hotty Toddy is one multilayered example. During moments of reaction and protest, when white "Ole Miss Rebels" have wished to defend and protect their localized orthodoxies, they have deployed this football cheer as a punitive, racist jeer. For them, the Hotty Toddy can give emergence and strength to an exclusionary communal identity. It can preserve white power and protect the status quo. As an extremely effective monoglossic utterance, the Hotty Toddy has served as an apt way to draw a line in the sand. White UM students have used this cheer to affirm a stubborn allegiance not to the ideals of the modern world but to those outmoded ideals of the lost Confederacy. Thus, in these moments, the Hotty Toddy provides white people in the majority with an enthusiastic method of resisting change. White students can and have used this cheer to preserve and defend ideological views that have otherwise been under attack and in decline since Reconstruction. They have done so as recently as 2012.

Perhaps much of the racist functionality was built into the Hotty Toddy from the beginning since it was generated and popularized during Jim Crow. It was, after all, a central symbol within that sea of symbols at UM that were purposefully racist, intentionally ideological. In the 1940s, 1950s, and 1960s, as historians have shown, the university community—like most white southern institutions—was preoccupied with glorifying the Lost Cause and resisting racial progress. At nearly every turn, students were actively defining themselves and their school in racial and regional terms. The Hotty Toddy has largely escaped scrutiny while other, less opaque, traditions like the rebel flag, the anthem "Dixie," and the Colonel Rebel mascot have been accounted for and expelled, at least officially. The Hotty Toddy, on the other hand, with its nonsensical words and ambiguous origins, has never been widely regarded as an affiliate of racism. Yet, as I have shown in this chapter, the cheer has been an active affiliate of racism across many decades.

How do today's students feel about the Hotty Toddy? As mentioned earlier, they revere it. Indeed, the senior class of 2017 plans, as of this writing, to commemorate the Hotty Toddy through a historical marker that will be their lasting gift to the university. It will read in part: "Universities have cheers, Ole Miss has Hotty Toddy. It's a feeling, ideal, fight song, prayer, verbal handshake and way of life, all rolled into one. . . . If institutions and traditions make up the fabric of Ole Miss, the thread of Hotty Toddy holds them together. . . . So yell it. Feel it. And above all, live it. Hotty Toddy."[47] Judging from the proposed language of the plaque, which is entirely celebratory and reverent and which does not acknowledge the Hotty Toddy's complicated history, students in 2017 were unaware that their beloved cheer has a complicated history. Whether conservative or liberal, Black or white, the students at today's University of Mississippi love their university and wish to demonstrate their school spirit. The Hotty Toddy is a particularly effective method for such positive emergence and expression. As language, the cheer is unique, potent, and unifying when used in most contexts. Under normal circumstances, its ideological roots are invisible and submerged. Seemingly innocent, it remains a beloved tradition, a rite of passage, and a proud rhetorical legacy.

The problem, of course, is that this reverence for the Hotty Toddy is passed along without much context or understanding. Most students have no idea that the Hotty Toddy has been deployed as hate speech to exclude African Americans, to taunt James Meredith, to fuel more than one campus disturbance, and to celebrate the assassination of President Kennedy. Just as Confederate monuments need to be contextualized in today's world, the Hotty Toddy may need to be fully contextualized and understood before being promoted as a central mechanism for assent and membership in this modern university community. Before an official campus plaque is erected to celebrate the Hotty Toddy, perhaps an official campus plaque should be erected to contextualize the cheer. If the UM community does not undertake this difficult work, if ignorance is allowed to fester, history suggests that the Hotty Toddy will continue to possess and preserve ideological content from the community's shameful past. The same attributes that make the Hotty Toddy a fantastic fight song in athletic contexts will continue to make it a convenient and effective fight song in racist contexts. As Norman Fairclough has suggested, language scholars have an "auxiliary" role to play in such reexaminations of "problems of language and power."[48] While academics can question cherished orthodoxies, the truly important actors are the people within the "Ole Miss" community itself. The students, alumni, and friends of "Ole Miss" can and should come to terms with the Hotty Toddy's full legacy, or else risk preserving and defending aspects of the university that are unhealthy and undesirable.

Indeed, it seems clear to me (as one member of the community) that the vast majority of today's stakeholders would find the dark side of the Hotty Toddy to be completely repulsive. This evolving and modern institution bears little resemblance to the University of Mississippi of earlier eras. Our student body and faculty is among the most diverse in the Southeastern Conference. Administrators, faculty, students, staff, and alumni are trying hard to move ahead on issues of race and diversity. We have cast aside the rebel flag, the song "Dixie," and other examples of confederate rhetoric. The progress has been real and impressive. It has also been incomplete. There is more to do, of course, including the continued reconciliation of symbols and language from the university's racist past. The Hotty Toddy should be placed into this contextualization queue, so that the community can perhaps reconcile the cheer, expelling those semiotic potentialities that have allowed it to be weaponized during the distant and recent past. Rather than preserving residues of a hateful era, the Hotty Toddy can perhaps be cleansed to become monoglossic rhetoric used only against opposing football fans. Black and white UM fans could then cheer together with words that could never be used for division or oppression.

If the Hotty Toddy could be reconsidered and refreshed, it would become a rhetorical tool to emerge a wholly positive and unifying communal identity, to extirpate certain undesirable traditions. Until then, facile language like that displayed in the proposed plaque will only provide ongoing linguistic shelter to outmoded ideals. Language and identity are intertwined. One cannot be improved without the other. Coming to terms with beloved but problematic language on this very specific and granular level is one localized method of helping the University of Mississippi, the state of Mississippi, and the US South at large, transition fully and successfully from ole to new.

CHAPTER 3

Minimization at Mizzou

Confederate Rhetoric and Interpretative Difference

CONFEDERATE RHETORIC PERVADES UNIVERSITY CAMPUSES in the US South. The legacy of the Old South can be found on flags, on campus buildings, in student yearbooks, in fraternity traditions, in official and unofficial university names, in athletic cheers, and oftentimes in student interactions. Such language and symbols of the Old South have shaped and constrained the communal identities of these universities, which have become depositories for regional traditions of social and cultural stasis over the previous century.

Linguistic traditions can unify people across generations. Indeed, on the whole, unification is the very purpose of tradition. Problematically, though, in the universities of the US South, linguistic and semiotic traditions have often unified white stakeholders around notions of inequality and racism. These roots are difficult to extirpate, especially because university communities are often outwardly protective of their traditions, which are celebrated and cherished. For example, as detailed in the last chapter, students at the University of Mississippi express a high regard for the Hotty Toddy cheer, a rhetorical actant that initiates students and other stakeholders into the UM community. Students learn the cheer during their freshman year or oftentimes earlier (in some cases before kindergarten). They repeat the cheer throughout their lives, in college and beyond, particularly whenever they return to campus for football games. Thus, this linguistic tradition serves to renew memberships and affiliations year after year. More than a simple cheer, the Hotty Toddy is a ritualistic call-and-response that brings people together and that creates and identifies insiders. It is a form of secular (or athletic) communion, and thus it is revered and cherished for its unifying power across time. But, as the previous chapter revealed, the Hotty Toddy has been used in darker moments to divide people within the community, to promote abuses of power, to create a confederacy of first-class citizens, and to discourage and punish second-class citizens. And this type of linguistic ordering and enforcement—this type of tradition—is also present at other southern universities.

Just as confederate rhetoric can serve to reinforce group identity, it can also perpetuate and exacerbate existing community divisions and exclusions. Reuben Faloughi was a graduate student at the University of Missouri (Mizzou or MU) in 2015. When he and other Black students staged a peaceful protest during the homecoming parade, white onlookers used the M-I-Z-Z-O-U cheer to drown them out and to communicate anger and disapproval. White men from the crowd then escalated the confrontation by physically pushing the Black students aside. One person driving in the parade even bumped an African American protester with a car. Finally, the police intervened. Faloughi felt bullied and afraid. He and his Black peers were asking for increased tolerance and attention to issues of race. Instead, they were shouted down by their university's most prominent cheer, one that is central to the Mizzou identity, one that they themselves had (presumably) used at football games to celebrate their school pride and community belonging. According to the University of Missouri website, the word MIZZOU "has many fun uses, such as a call-and-response cheer at athletic games in which people on one side shout 'M-I-Z,' and the other side replies 'Z-O-U.' The cheer has become so popular that you could receive an 'M-I-Z' greeting anywhere in the world. And you know the answer." Somehow in the moment of the parade protest, just as in many moments at UM, a performative utterance intended to unify students (a literal rallying cry) was weaponized and racialized. White people cheered against Black people. M-I-Z-Z-O-U had suddenly been converted (or had revealed its full capacity) and was now being used to punish and expel, to move certain students beyond the pale and out of the way. "I tell people that protest was the modern sit-in," said Faloughi. "You see the level of hatred in people's faces and the level of hate of who you are, and these people don't even know you."[1] In 2015, fueled by the school cheer, the traditional homecoming parade at Mizzou became a fiercely divisive event, one that reanimated and strengthened racial biases within the campus community.

If white people at southern universities can use football cheers to counteract and silence Black students, what other language is being used to draw dividing lines, to enforce (purposefully or inadvertently) traditional racial inequities? To state the obvious, today at the University of Mississippi, the University of Missouri, the University of Alabama, the University of Virginia, the University of Georgia, and many other southern universities, African American people apply, receive admission, attend classes, partake in communal activities, graduate, join the alumni association, and seemingly become full and lifelong members of these university communities. But do African Americans always feel fully included? Do they readily and completely associate with the orthodox identity of "their" schools? Much evidence suggests not. Much evidence suggests that many Black students and alumni at predominantly white southern universities often feel like visitors. They often feel discouraged by the institutionalized rhetoric of their own institutions. Confederate rhetoric is a primary generator of these experiences of alienation, which contradict stated commitments from these educational institutions (in mission statements, strategic plans, presidential speeches, etc.).

In some ways, such stated commitments represent rhetorical progress, and that progress should be marked and celebrated. Fifty or sixty years ago, leaders at predominantly white southern institutions were rarely willing to even gesture toward inclusion and diversity. The discourse has now improved. Yet rhetorical progress remains incomplete. Old oppressive meanings survive on these campuses, sometimes in seemingly innocuous words and symbols, like the Hotty Toddy at UM or the M-I-Z-Z-O-U cheer at MU. My central thesis in this book is that all such confederate rhetoric must be exposed and either reconciled or rooted out if campuses wish to avoid the repeated eruptions of racism that have been ongoing for decades. When there is latent racism in mainstream or orthodox words and symbols, some white students will continue to feel licensed to express racism in explicit and implicit ways, and many students of color will continue to feel discouraged and excluded.

Latent racism and its related eruptions can be found at every predominantly white southern university. This is not simply a problem at UM or MU. In February 2019, white students at the University of Tennessee, Knoxville (UTK), posted blackface images of themselves on Snapchat. Their caption underscored their racist intent: "We for racial equality boys. Bout to get this free college now that I'm black let's goooooo #blacklivesmatter." Of course, the university condemned the social media post through public statements, through a community forum, and through other typical means of response. University leaders were able to manage the immediate public relations crisis, and the chancellor, Wayne T. Davis, made further commitments to no longer ignore racism but to "name it and confront it."[2] Yet this was simply one in a long series of hateful episodes at Tennessee, one in a long series of hateful episodes at major southern universities. When white students at these institutions give energetic voice to hatred, they may be contradicting the wishes of administrators, but they are also tapping into long traditions of exclusionary language and symbols. The 2019 episode at Tennessee happened within the (supposedly) closed and safe network of Snapchat, but it was not long ago when similar blackface images could be found in the (supposedly) closed and safe pages of UTK yearbooks. My point here is that confederate rhetoric is a tradition at places like UM, UTK, and Mizzou. It is one key regulator of status and true membership. Real progress has been achieved and should be celebrated, but these institutions continue to harbor traditions that are exclusionary and oppressive. Oftentimes, these traditions are rhetorical.

This chapter explores how racism has remained latent and available at the University of Missouri. As chapter 2 demonstrated, modern identities at universities are often complicated by confederate rhetoric's capacity to carry residual meanings from the past into the present. Indexicality is not optional. When words and symbols retain connotations to racism, those connotations are not easily abandoned. Instead, they are easily archived and accessed. Because many such words and symbols have accumulated at southern universities, they are, even today, promoting racial divisions and reifying inequities, often overpowering less ingrained efforts to promote diversity. These dynamics can lead to episodes of confusion and chaos, and such episodes remain common.

In order to better understand these powerful rhetorical dynamics, in this chapter I chart deployments of and reactions to confederate rhetoric during a series of events at the University of Missouri that reveal the inflammatory effects of confederate rhetoric over time. Since this is a study of language and culture, my analysis focuses on the linguistic highlights of the period, those salient moments when words perform actions, when communication and interpretation steer historical events. Using critical discourse analysis and sociolinguistic interpretative tools, I unpack an extremely dense and chaotic six-year period at Mizzou. It was a time of active hate speech, student protests, and attempts by university leaders to respond in ways intended to protect the university's reputation and support the community's minority constituents. In the end, this period resulted in chaos and regression. At work, sometimes hidden and sometimes in the open, was confederate rhetoric, which in the end reasserted itself and promoted traditional structures and practices of dominance, power, and discrimination.

The Chaotic Consequences of Inattention

Those who believe that Old South language and symbols don't matter—that they are ancient history—should test their theory against the happenings at the University of Missouri from 2010 to 2016. Indeed, the mishandling of institutional responses to racialized language and symbols during this period had profound and material consequences for this flagship university. At the University of Missouri in Columbia, known as Mizzou or MU, there was (is) a traceable pattern of institutionalized confederate rhetoric. University leaders—and others in positions of power or privilege—failed to recognize this string of utterances and aggressions as interconnected, choosing instead to interpret each one as an isolated episode. As a result, confederate rhetoric at Mizzou was never fully contextualized or confronted by those in power. Frustrations and divisions grew. Eventually, in 2015, the rhetorical conflict triggered a large-scale campus protest that made national news.

The tumult led to the high-profile resignations of both the university chancellor and the Missouri system president. If these resignations were seen as victories by the protesters, they were soon overshadowed by the subsequent repercussions, which included a devastating drop in student enrollment and a concomitant budget crisis. Leaders at Mizzou had misunderstood and misdirected the campus discourse around issues of race, and the results were devastating for the entire community.

Before the culmination of these events, Mizzou was growing steadily, thriving by most metrics. Budgets were healthy. In the aftermath of these events, by 2017, freshman enrollment dropped 35 percent, and a new university administration cut four hundred positions, closed seven residence halls, and slashed operational budgets across campus units. Not only had the university been fractured by words and symbols; it had also been fiscally devastated by them. Most worrying, African American student enrollment dropped precipitously.[3] If the protests had been conceived as an attack on racist speech acts, then it could be argued that those hateful speech acts had ultimately won the day. The events at Mizzou serve as a cautionary story, providing strong evidence that words and symbols have a lasting impact on communities. It is also a story that demonstrates the difficulty of countering embedded campus traditions of confederate rhetoric.

Modern universities spend millions of dollars every year on public relations; they staff robust communications offices with writers, videographers, graphic designers, and photographers. They engage purposefully and energetically in public promotion and advertising to market their preferred image. Beyond these internally driven efforts, universities also hire outside marketing firms to create and distribute advertising. They use athletics, particularly football, to disseminate images of positivity and vibrancy. Such marketing is aimed at prospective students, alumni, government officials, and other constituents. In today's digital world, however, even these coordinated and savvy campaigns can seem impotent when a single, contradictory social media post goes viral. One student can suddenly become the most prominent spokesperson for the university, reaching a broad audience and instantly affecting the public's understanding of the university's identity. Coordinated institutional rhetoric can be overwhelmed by passionate (and oftentimes spontaneous) personal rhetoric.[4]

Such rhetorical leveling happened at Mizzou on September 12, 2015, when the president of the student body, an African American student named Payton Head, voiced his personal reality. Head jarred Mizzou by countering its mainstream narrative through a Facebook post, excerpted here: "I just want to say how extremely hurt and disappointed I am. Last night as I was walking through campus, some guys riding on the back of a pickup truck decided that it would be okay to continuously scream NIGGER at me. I really just want to know why my simple existence is such a threat to society. For those of you who wonder why I'm always talking about the importance of inclusion and respect, it's because I've experienced moments like this multiple times at THIS university, making me not feel included here."[5] His post spread quickly throughout the Mizzou community. It resonated with many minority students, triggering a flood of similar narratives and shared complaints about the broader community's complacency and inattention. Head's post gave voice to a common experience for students of color: Black and other minority students at Mizzou were tired of encountering slurs and symbolic aggressions. By one tally, there had been nine hate crimes reported to the MU Police Department in the previous three years alone.[6] As reactions to Head's Facebook post accumulated in the days that followed, students focused most of their frustrations on the ways in which the Mizzou majority repeatedly reacted or, more precisely, failed to react to such aggressions. Administrative apathy captured the most attention and catalyzed the consequential events that followed.

Head's post was much more than a straightforward report of racial hatred. His careful phrasing reflected an insider's awareness of the campus community and of the prevailing attitudes of skepticism and dismissal. As the president of the student body, he was very much an insider at Mizzou; thus, he understood the orthodox frame through which his community processed such incidents of hatred. He aimed his message not at his minority peers but at the Mizzou majority. With his introduction ("for those of you who wonder why I'm always talking about the importance of inclusion and respect"), Head addressed those who had previously questioned the need to talk about inclusion. He addressed those in positions of privilege. His frustrations were aimed not only at the hate speech of the white men in the pickup truck but also (and more pointedly) at the orthodox dismissiveness of the white majority. He had experience with his intended audience, and he expressed his frustrations clearly and concisely. His tone was strong but pleading. Head, even as the president of the student body, felt ignored, dismissed, and excluded.

For whatever reason, as Payton Head's post went viral among the students—and even as the campus newspaper was covering the developments—the chancellor at Mizzou, R. Bowen Loftin, did not offer a public response for nearly a week. This delay was viewed by some minority students as a further slight, one that aggravated the injury inflicted by the men in the pickup truck. Others in positions of power at Mizzou responded a bit more quickly than the chancellor. When the story of Head's post was covered in the *Kansas City Star*, five days after appearing on Facebook, Cathy Scroggs, vice chancellor of student affairs at Mizzou, applauded Payton Head publicly and called him a "profile in courage." But there were also early negative reactions. As Susan Svrluga reported, "When the *St. Louis Post-Dispatch* wrote about [Head's Facebook post], some readers were dismissive, pointing out all the resources directed at black students and other minority groups on campus to support them, and saying things like, 'Whiners.'"[7] Even as Head pleaded for those in positions of power and privilege to fully listen to the truth, some failed to hear and consider his message.

Eduardo Bonilla-Silva calls such mental perspectives the "minimization of racism," a posture of dismissiveness that allows white people to accept violence or threats of violence toward Black people while simultaneously accusing Black victims of "being 'hypersensitive,' of using race as an 'excuse,' or of 'playing the infamous race card.'"[8] In Payton Head's Facebook post, we can hear the exasperation caused by previous moments of minimization. Again, he was not merely disturbed and angered at the incident itself—being threatened and harassed by white people in a drive-by rhetorical attack—he was also discouraged by his community's ongoing failure to listen. "For those of you who wonder why I'm always talking about the importance of inclusion and respect," he said, "it's because I've experienced moments like this multiple times at THIS university, making me not feel included here." Head was protesting the overt racism of the men in the truck, but he was also protesting the subtler racism of a campus community that had repeatedly minimized the reality and difficulty of the Black experience.

Head's Facebook post was not an explicit call to action, but it did lead to very dramatic action. His message, which went viral across social media platforms, is widely recognized as the primary catalyst of the campus protests that later made national news. In other words, the post unleashed tremendous energy, in part because Head's Black peers, past and present, had endured years of symbolic and linguistic antagonism. They had been immersed in confederate rhetoric. As 783 Black alumni wrote in a letter of support, "Many of us found ourselves protesting similar incidents on campus, and we find it highly unacceptable that many of these issues are not only continuing, but have become more pervasive."[9] Black alumni and current Black students shared Head's fear, anger, and frustration, and they, too, wanted the white majority to listen to their concerns.

The official response to Head would prove inadequate and, intentionally or not, disrespectful. Of course, most white people at Mizzou would never yell the n-word at a Black person. The young men in the pickup truck represented an extreme minority within the white majority. Many more white people, however, were willing to minimize or isolate Head's report. As one southern sports commentator wrote, "There is actually no tangible evidence of anyone at Missouri doing anything wrong or ignoring anything improper. No crime has occurred on campus, no one has been physically harmed. At the absolute worst a small number of students have been subjected to mean words." Similar sentiments appeared online on Mizzou message boards. Grizzly999, a regular member of tigerboard.com, an online community for fans of Missouri athletics, wrote, "I find it very interesting that the overwhelming support Michael Sam received came from a racist state institution and its students. I'm also trying to figure out how Payton Head was elected MSA president from such a racist student body."[10] The presumption was that Mizzou could not be racist because the Mizzou community had previously supported a gay African American football star (Michael Sam) and had elected Payton Head, an African American man, as president of their student body. This is a common trope used by white southerners to defend themselves or their institutions from accusations of racism. Its illogical and contradictory nature is on full view here, as Grizzly999 is simultaneously using Payton Head as evidence to refute Payton Head. While illogical and contradictory, this tendency to fixate on one instance of racial progress as evidence for a postracial and postracist world is persistent and pervasive, especially among defenders of the status quo.

It is a kind of minimization or oversimplification that requires white people to interpret utterances of confederate rhetoric in isolation. White people can dismiss racist symbols and words by drawing on what Bonilla-Silva terms "argumentative strategies to deny the significance of discrimination." More specifically, such deceptive logic is reminiscent of the phrase "Some of my best friends are black," which has been in recent history a popular and myopic way of dismissing or minimizing the possibility of racism.[11] These rhetorical moves are only possible from a position of safety, from within the protective pale of the white majority. Black students like Payton Head do not have the privilege of ignoring racial inequality on campus or the prevailing legacy of confederate rhetoric. Instead, they feel the oppressive weight of accumulated confederate rhetoric every day of their lives. The results of one election or the exceptional case of Michael Sam's acceptance provide little comfort when compared to the fear and expectancy caused by even one experience of white men yelling the n-word from a passing truck. Black students and alumni were not remembering only one experience of racism. Instead, they had long experienced confederate rhetoric both as an acute condition (slurs, violence, vandalism, etc.) and as a chronic condition (inattention, denial, and dismissal). Again and again over the years, Black students at Mizzou had been confronted by antagonizing confederate rhetoric. And, time and again, the white majority had enjoyed the privilege of dismissing or ignoring such affronts. Not surprisingly, this prevalent form of white minimization—of interpreting instances of confederate rhetoric in isolation—led not to solutions or progress but to the intensification of conflict.

Chancellor Loftin did eventually respond with a statement, seven days after Head's post: "Let me be clear about where I stand as Mizzou's chancellor: one bias incident is too many. . . . The incidents that I have heard about—both blatant and subtle—are totally unacceptable. Our core values of Respect, Responsibility, Discovery, and Excellence leave no room for bias and discrimination."[12] Loftin's tardy statement was, at least, forceful, but it also indulged in the privilege of minimization by relying on careful and vague language and by avoiding the words "race" or "racial," opting instead for broader, more general terms such as "bias" and "discrimination." In so doing, Loftin failed to confront the blatantly racist nature of the episode. Perhaps Loftin was attempting to distance himself and his community from the racists in the pickup truck. Indeed, early coverage of the episode mentioned several times that the white men in the pickup truck may or may not have been Mizzou students. Or perhaps Loftin was simply attempting to cool emotions by using indefinite language. Whatever his motives, Loftin's initial statement stood in stark contrast to Payton Head's passionate and direct appeal on Facebook. While Loftin cited vague ideals like respect and excellence, Head wrote about a close encounter with raw and threatening hatred. The men in the truck had not minced words or invoked lofty ideals. They had used the n-word.

Chancellor Loftin's initial and subsequent statements were consequential rhetorical moments in this unfolding event. Indeed, chancellor statements are always consequential during such crises. When things go wrong, students and others in university communities often pause to hear from the leader at the top of the university hierarchy. There is a natural rhythm to crises like the one at Mizzou, a rhythm that includes this caesura, however brief, during which the community is listening and during which the chancellor or president has the opportunity to speak and to shape reactions and events. Below, I offer a close reading of Chancellor Loftin's responses during this particular crisis because I believe that future leaders can learn from his rhetorical steps and missteps.

The words of chancellors or presidents always do something (in the J. L. Austinian sense). During times of crisis, they may, in fact, do more than usual, marking inflection points in which a crisis can be influenced toward either a positive or negative outcome. As mentioned above, modern universities invest great time, money, and energy into public relations. Yet universities are being challenged, again and again, in their ability to respond adequately to crises caused by eruptions of confederate rhetoric. The reasons for this challenge seem to lie in the disjunction between the playbook of public relations and the less formulaic urgencies caused by moments of public history. Indeed, even for chancellors or presidents who follow the advice and processes recommended by their marketing experts, eruptions of confederate rhetoric can wreak havoc on public relations playbooks, as was the case at Mizzou, where the presumably careful and well-intentioned words of Chancellor Loftin made the crisis worse, not better.

Throughout his first official response, Loftin persistently sidestepped race altogether, choosing words somewhat removed from the reality and urgency of the situation. He remained indirect and vague: "I challenge everyone at Mizzou to stand against acts of bias and discrimination."[13] The "everyone" Loftin addressed is particularly ambiguous. In his challenge to "everyone," was Chancellor Loftin including Black students like Payton Head? Weren't they already standing against racism? Weren't they the targets? This ambiguous challenge was, at best, an awkward rhetorical move. At worst, Loftin's challenge to an undefined "everyone" misplaced some of the responsibility for racism onto Black students. Or if Loftin's "everyone" was not intended to include Black students, why were they being excluded from his official conception of "everyone at Mizzou"? If Black students were not part of Mizzou's "everyone," who were they? The point here is not that Loftin was intentionally further excluding and ignoring Black students. He was, almost certainly, trying to bring the community together and to offer solace to Head and his peers. The point is that Loftin failed to achieve that goal because he deployed vague, color-blind rhetoric in the face of overt and violent confederate rhetoric. He was trying to minimize an already maximized situation.

Indeed, Chancellor Loftin's linguistically circumspect and vague response did not satisfy Black students or alumni at Mizzou. Still stirred by Payton Head's Facebook post, about forty students held a march through the student union on October 1, 2015. They shouted, "White silence is violence, no justice no peace." Here again, like Head, the students were protesting the majority white response, which was chronic inattention, just as much as they were protesting overtly racist language and behavior. As student protester Reuben Faloughi said to the crowd, "I don't like to scream. I don't like to yell. But nobody wants to listen. Nobody listens on the forum, nobody listens on the email." Another student protester, Brittani Savage, put it this way, "We are either told it's not that bad or told that we are just making a big deal out of nothing. And it's ridiculous. It is a big deal, and it does affect everyone's lives." The concluding speaker, Danielle Walker, described the verbal antagonism that she had experienced on campus: "My hair has been called dirty. I've been called ghetto." She pleaded for Chancellor Loftin to make some very specific linguistic interventions: "We want to see a hate crime policy initiated. We want our chancellor to formally make an announcement that we do have a racial problem here on campus and that they are seeking to make sure it gets addressed."[14] Loftin had been slow to respond to Head's Facebook post, and when he did speak, the message was ineffective and ambiguous. His initial statement failed to acknowledge the systemic nature of the "racial problem" at Mizzou. Instead it minimized the harsh reality voiced by Head and recognized by so many Mizzou students and alumni.

Just a few days later, Loftin had another opportunity to respond to an incident of hate speech. On October 5, a white passerby (presumably a student) uttered the n-word at a group of Black students rehearsing a dance for homecoming. While Payton Head had been verbally attacked on the edge of campus, this attack occurred in the heart of campus. It was clearly and undeniably a campus problem. From a conference overseas, Loftin quickly recorded a video message, which was accompanied by a public statement from his office. He was far more direct and clear in this second response. His statement was entitled "Racism at Mizzou" and mentioned the words "race" or "racism" more than fifteen times. It was also far more energetic and passionate. The chancellor's second statement read, "Early this morning, I was furious and disappointed to learn about another person who has harassed Mizzou students and used racist and hateful speech. . . . Racism exists at MU. I want to make it clear that we do not tolerate racism and prejudice on our campus."[15] Loftin's voice was clear, his condemnation strong, and his compassion for the affected students was now front and center.

Yet this second statement also had several instructive weaknesses. First, Loftin addressed it to the "Mizzou family." The use of a familial metaphor to represent an institution is a common tool at modern universities. The label of "family" is meant to evoke a loving community that shares values and space. It accompanies the concept of a campus as a home, and it can be a very effective marketing technique. In the context of a crisis, however, this flimsy conceit is easily exposed as hollow and incomplete. At Mizzou, in this moment of crisis and division, Loftin's invocation of the "Mizzou family" seemed like a romanticized fantasy. Students at Mizzou were not a family living in harmony together on campus. Instead, they were feeling divided and fearful, reeling from two very recent episodes of hate speech. They were not pulling together;

they were pulling apart. In this context, Loftin's aspirational metaphor of the Mizzou family seems mistimed and misplaced.

Another weakness in Loftin's second statement: it is built on an obvious contradiction. Loftin stated, "Racism exists at MU." Here, he was acknowledging directly that racism exists on campus. But in the next sentence, he offered a present-tense declaration that could not possibly be true in light of his opening claim: "We do not tolerate racism and prejudice on our campus." Loftin was acknowledging the presence of racism on campus while simultaneously perpetuating a systemic denial of that racism. Later in the statement, the chancellor specified that the "we" he introduced in the sentence quoted above explicitly included "all on this campus." Yet, in light of the recent racist harassment, the "we" Loftin employed was both inaccurate and misleading. How could the racism on display in previous weeks exist at Mizzou, if "all" at Mizzou rejected racism? Is it credible to claim that "we do not tolerate racism," while also acknowledging that "racism exists" in visible and repeated forms? No, of course not, and Loftin thus became an unreliable narrator.

Such conflicted and illogical rhetoric is commonplace in university statements, especially ones that respond to instances of identity-based harassment or violence. On one hand, such blanket denials and condemnations can be read as strong and comforting. On the other hand, they can be read as deflective and delusional. What Head and his peers were communicating at this time was that Mizzou leaders and others in positions of privilege were failing to fully understand the problem. Students of color wanted listening and understanding. From their minority perspective, episodes of hate speech were not isolated incidents disconnected or removed from the Mizzou experience. Loftin was surely attempting to comfort his campus, but, in the end, his illogical rhetoric was ineffective as an antidote to the hatred and mistrust then circulating so powerfully. The fantasies and contradictions incorporated into his second statement were believable—credible—only from a position of protection and privilege. They were attempts to frame episodes of hate speech as something different and apart from the institution, as isolated incidents. With his second statement, Loftin openly acknowledged racism, but he also included the mistimed metaphor of family and its inherent contradictions so obvious in the current context. He insisted that racism existed on campus but also that "we do not tolerate racism." The tardiness and cursoriness of Loftin's first statement coupled with his second merely perpetuated the inattention that so frustrated Head and the other student protesters in the first place.

Like Loftin, university leaders often seek to dismiss eruptions of confederate rhetoric as singular or exceptional racist incidents. In Bakhtinian terms, campus leaders err precisely because they react to unappealing utterances as isolated incidents, rather than recognizing each as a "link in the chain of speech communication [which] cannot be broken off from the preceding links." In a rush to preserve the institution's reputation and to soothe tensions on campus, university leaders often overlook "echoes" that may be "half-concealed or completely concealed."[16] Perhaps viewing incidents in isolation is a product of formulaic crisis communications, a subfield of public relations that prescribes strategies for managing and moving on quickly from negative headlines. Tracing the evolution of institutional crisis communications is beyond the scope of this book, but it is worth noting that many university leaders seem to follow a common script when faced with a crisis like the one at Mizzou. Similar to Loftin's second statement, university responses are often quick and passionate. These statements emphasize the exceptionality of the incident, present the incident as an isolated occurrence, and propose an idealized community identity as evoked by the image of a campus "nation" or "family." This playbook fails to account, however, for the ever-present and pulsating power of confederate rhetoric on southern university campuses. In the case of Mizzou, the perpetrators of racist verbal harassment were performing these speech acts within a time- and place-specific context and along a continuum of white supremacy. With hateful rhetoric, the white perpetrators in the pickup truck aligned themselves with a long tradition of racism embodied by a campus history of exclusion, discrimination, and violence. Similarly, the Black students who directly and indirectly heard the racist words were pulled into a recognizable history of hate and oppression. White people at Mizzou could view the slurs from the men in the truck as an isolated utterance. Black people at Mizzou could not.

In the wake of racist episodes, southern university leaders often trade immediacy for contextualized understanding, dealing with racial slurs as isolated crises to be managed and then shelved. However, these knee-jerk reactions put administrators, campus communities, and educational institutions in deeper sociolinguistic jeopardy. In the rush to unify and heal campuses, leaders and public relations teams often simplify the story, ignore the layered simultaneity of discourse, and attempt to comfort the campus minority with rhetoric rooted in the dominant perspective of the white majority. At Mizzou, Black student leaders immediately recognized layers of the conversation that their administrators failed to either see or acknowledge. The students' indexes told them that the n-word did not contradict the history and values of Mizzou. Indeed, in the Black student experience, the n-word was consistent with Mizzou's history and values. Perhaps this is why Payton Head's frustration resonated so strongly with other minority students in the first place. Perhaps this explains the virality of his original post. As the protesters chanted on October 1, "White silence is violence."

The stance taken by the Mizzou administration in this instance is a common (and surely inadvertent) form of minimization. It may seem unfair or ungenerous to critique the public statements of well-meaning white leaders who were trying their best to respond to hate and to comfort their campuses. But this study is not about fairness or generosity. It is, instead, about the ongoing power of confederate rhetoric on southern university campuses, rhetoric that governs patterns of racism and often dooms leaders who fail to recognize its longitudinal presence and controlling power. As Jan Blommaert has said, "The different layers of historicity to which people can orient, and from which they can speak, create enormous amounts of tension between continuity and discontinuity in meanings, between coherence and incoherence in discourses."[17] University leaders like Chancellor Loftin at Mizzou will always miss the mark if they react to racist utterances as isolated and discordant incidents.

One student group active during this period was ConcernedStudent1950. The date, 1950, in the group's name refers to the year when the first Black graduate students were admitted to Mizzou. It was ConcernedStudent1950 that organized the protest at the homecoming parade. During that protest, sometime just before or just after being shouted down by the majority white crowd with the M-I-Z-Z-O-U cheer, members of ConcernedStudent1950 were able to block a dignitary's car in the parade. It was a convertible carrying Missouri system president Tim Wolfe. In that moment, he chose not to engage the students. He sat silent in the car. They wanted him to listen to their concerns. Instead, his driver revved the engine and bumped one of the student protesters out of the way. Days later, when students confronted Wolfe after a fundraiser, they asked, "What is your definition of systematic oppression?"[18] Clearly, the minority students at Mizzou were linking recent episodes of hate speech to a continuum of inattention from the white majority. White leaders like Loftin and Wolfe were disoriented and confused. From their place of racial privilege, they did not see the continuum at all.

The disjunction between the white majority perspective and that of the student protesters is evident in the answer that Wolfe gave. He stumblingly responded, "I will give you an answer, and I'm sure it will be the wrong answer. . . . Systematic oppression is because you don't believe that you have the equal opportunity for success."[19] Herein the system president was openly and directly minimizing student concerns and placing responsibility for oppression onto the oppressed. Systematic oppression was "because" Black students did not believe in equal opportunity, rather than because of anything the white majority may have done. The system was not to blame: student perceptions were to blame. Implied in this defensive response was that Wolfe stood on the other side of the issue, that he did not believe in the reality of systematic oppression. Needless to say, this response was not very effective or comforting. These were vulnerable members of his community who were asking for help. They were students who had endured racial slurs and antagonism. They were asking to be heard and helped, but leaders at Mizzou seemed not only inattentive but oblivious. Wolfe's answer at the fundraiser created a secondary firestorm, and he resigned a few days later. Chancellor Loftin followed suit, also resigning shortly thereafter.

What could have been done by Loftin, Wolfe, and other leaders at Mizzou during this intense period to change the discourse and to avoid the subsequent chaos that ultimately resulted in enrollment drops, budget cuts, and a considerable decline in the diversity of the institution? It is a difficult question, perhaps an impossible one, to answer. What is clear is that from the outset of this crisis, Loftin and others in power at Mizzou adopted a white majority interpretive frame and thus failed to hear or understand Payton Head and the other student protesters. Those in power indulged in the temptation to view racist speech acts in isolation. They framed repeated shameful utterances as distinctly different from the imagined (fantasized) culture of tolerance on their campus. Head and his peers, on the other hand, did not have that luxury. They were experiencing instances of racial harassment as recurring symptoms of a broader problem, as common points along a continuum of confederate rhetoric that reified and reinforced a culture of racism. White and Black people may have shared the physical space of campus, but their rhetorical realities held little in common.

Jonathan Butler, a graduate student leader at Mizzou during this period, reflected on the informed and historical perspective adopted by his fellow student protesters when he said, "It's about more than this moment." Butler was part of ConcernedStudent1950. According to reports, he was the very student bumped by President Wolfe's car during the homecoming parade. In the weeks after Head's Facebook post went viral, ConcernedStudent1950 began protesting the inattention and inaction of university and board leaders. These student protests reached a crescendo when, after the homecoming parade, Butler vowed to starve himself to death unless the Missouri Board of Curators fired system president Tim Wolfe, or Wolfe resigned himself. Butler said repeatedly that his hunger strike was necessary because traditional modes of communication (emails, statements, participation in public meetings) and organized protest had not resulted in substantive change. "Every other time we tried to approach you [the administration] in a civilized or respectable manner, you guys didn't listen," said Butler.[20]

After his resignation, President Wolfe seemed to recognize and acknowledge the interpretative gap that so frustrated Head, Butler, and other students:

"So the question really is, is why did we get to this very difficult situation. It is my belief we stopped listening to each other. We didn't respond or react. We got frustrated with each other, and we forced individuals like Jonathan Butler to take immediate action and unusual steps to effect change."[21] With time to reflect, President Wolfe could see the interpretive divide. While in office, however, Wolfe seemed blind to the chasm created from distinct perspectives, differing interpretive frameworks, and an unequal willingness to acknowledge the continuum of racist behavior rooted in confederate rhetoric.

The episodes of hate speech during this period boiled into a crisis at Mizzou, in part, because university leaders were operating from a different index than African American students and their allies. As discussed in chapter 2, Michael Silverstein, Richard Bauman, and Adam Hodges have shown how language can anchor certain messages, thereby limiting interpretative parameters even for future speakers and hearers. At Mizzou, indexical divisions intensified (rather than resolved) conflict. While university leaders isolated and minimized episodes of hate speech in an attempt to preserve the reputation of the university, African American students felt the direct impact of these same episodes. They insightfully viewed these occurrences as indicative of the systemic and cultural racism embedded within the university. Black people within this community understood and felt residual meanings that many white people could not or chose not to understand and feel. Without the privilege granted from whiteness or from administrative power, students like Payton Head interpreted racial slurs as a predictable and routine part of the Mizzou experience. This is another way in which confederate rhetoric can complicate campus crises.

During the latter months of 2015, the student protesters inspired others from the Mizzou community to speak out about their own experiences. Online and through social media came a flood of narratives that contradicted or radically complicated the facile notion of the Mizzou "family." One example came from Mizzou professor Cynthia Frisby. Inspired by her students, Frisby opened up about her own Mizzou reality: "I have lived in Columbia and been at the university for almost 18 years. During this time, I have been called the n-word too many times to count." Such testimonies accumulated quickly, and it was during this period that the 783 "Concerned Black Mizzou Alumni" issued their statement citing a string of racist episodes that over the years left "black students to feel ostracized and unwelcome in their shared living space." This group of Black alumni highlighted "past events to show our own connection to the plight of current students."[22] This flood of counternarratives exposed a stark interpretative variance that had been working for many years beneath the surface. Racism was neither isolated nor unusual at Mizzou;

rather, it was systemic and commonplace, reflecting the confederate rhetoric embedded in the community's history and culture. The white majority may not have seen it or believed it, but the institution was, to a certain extent, defined by reverberating racist rhetoric. Not only were minority students enduring racial slurs and other aggressions, they were enduring dismissiveness and inattention from those in positions of power and privilege.

An Impotency of Strategic Planning

As the crisis was developing at Mizzou from 2010 to 2015, leaders at the university were operating under a new strategic plan finalized in 2010 and based "on more than three years of discussion by faculty, staff, students and administrators." In retrospect, it is ironic that one of the plan's first goals was "to increase the diversity of the campus community."[23] Throughout this document, diversity initiatives are highlighted as important priorities. Yet, despite the intentionality, rhetorical posturing, and polished language of the strategic plan, Mizzou and its public image would soon be overwhelmed by chaos.

Strategic planning as a community composing process, as a genre, has become ritualized in modern universities; thus, the weakness and myopia of Missouri's strategic plan are worth noting. University administrators may view strategic plans as protective documents intended to preserve institutional stability. During the typical strategic planning process, hundreds of stakeholders offer input through surveys and committees. Ideally, the planning process reflects a consensus of these many individual visions for the university. Priorities are agreed on and set. The writers of the plan, usually a small group of people, attempt to codify the top priorities of the broader group, in order to create a sense of community within the final document. If all goes well, the strategic plan thus becomes a credible document, a guide for the coming years to steer decision makers and (presumably) to prevent disorder. Indeed, the writers of the University of Missouri's 2010 plan pointed to this very goal in their executive summary, promising that "the plan safeguards Missourians' 170-year-old, multi-billion dollar investment in their public research and land-grant university."[24] Despite this intentionality and the tremendous effort of Mizzou's strategic planners—an effort to write into reality a predetermined and carefully planned future—events on campus spiraled out of control during the very period of hoped-for protection. Rather than order and progress, the fifth year of the plan was historic for its chaos and dysfunction. Subsequently, the "value" of the University of Missouri dropped dramatically, and the institution took significant steps back from its articulated goals.

Strategic planning is now a cottage industry, and it can sometimes be difficult to tell one university's plan from another, even when the university communities are, in reality, quite different. The genre itself seems to be compromised. Or, perhaps like all genres, strategic plans have a "multifarious nature" that balances (and imbalances) the opposing forces of stability and change.[25] A full rhetorical analysis of the genre of strategic planning is beyond the scope of this book, but the events at Mizzou prove that even highly polished plans can fail miserably. In Mizzou's case, the strategic plan did not safeguard the value of the university at all. Perhaps the incomplete assumptions about the true values of the university underlying the plan can partially account for this failure. The Mizzou plan included generalized statements on diversity and progress, for example, but it did not reckon fully (or even partially) with the confederate rhetoric that was operating so powerfully throughout the history of the school. In other words, the strategic plan merely codified the orthodox inattention that would intensify racial discord. There is an important lesson here for strategic planners. Minimizing unpleasant divisions on campuses may exacerbate problems, may deepen dividing lines. While the goal of strategic planning is consensus building, identity conflicts should never be ignored or downplayed by strategic planners. Nuance and complexity should not be omitted from these documents.

A Catalyst Remembered by Some and Forgotten by the Majority

Indeed, in the same year the strategic plan was published, a major eruption of confederate rhetoric occurred on the Missouri campus. It was an event that Payton Head, Jonathan Butler, and the Concerned Black Mizzou Alumni would reference in 2015, when they formalized their resistance. Late one night in 2010, two white students vandalized the front of the Gaines/Oldham Black Culture Center at the University of Missouri. They spread hundreds of cotton balls across the grass and walkways, turning the front grounds into a cotton field tableau. The perpetrators, both white male students with shaved heads, one a senior and one a freshman, carried out their symbolic and hateful act on one of the final nights of Black History Month. The *Columbia Daily Tribune* called it "a racist act, an overt reminder of slavery."[26]

As a composition of hatred, the cotton ball episode was powerfully persuasive and very effective. It echoed slavery through the material of cotton, the Ku Klux Klan through the shadowy darkness of night, and the white power movement through the shaved heads of its perpetrators. While some apologists on social media saw this as a fairly innocent school prank (what harm could cotton balls do?), many Black students shuddered at what they saw as a carefully constructed incitement of fear and intimidation. Standing outside the Black Culture Center on the morning after, reflecting on the cotton spread across the lawn before her, freshman Ashley Hatcher said, "Racism has never gone anywhere. I don't even have the words to explain how I feel right now. I'm fighting back tears."[27] Mizzou leaders minimized the cotton ball incident as hateful vandalism. They acknowledged the symbolism of the crime, but they also interpreted the episode as an isolated and rogue action. Here again, this interpretation was only available from the safety of the white majority. For Black students like Hatcher, who knew their history, the message sent by the white men in the dark of night was received clearly and chillingly. It was confederate rhetoric, and it was punishing in its evocation of repression.

The official university response was swift and initially strong, as the white student culprits were soon arrested and charged with committing a hate crime. On campus, a town hall gave the community an opportunity to voice their hurt and concern. A few days later, the chancellor at the time, Brady Deaton, alongside the Missouri system president, Gary Forsee, ate lunch with students at the Black Culture Center. They wore "Pick Unity" buttons. On the Friday night following the cotton ball incident, there was a "United We Stand" rally on the steps of Mizzou's main administration building.[28]

Publicly, at least, it seemed that these timely efforts to counteract the hateful tableau were successful. Several news outlets used the word "prank" to describe the event. It seems that many students on campus were convinced by the official university narrative that this was an isolated incident. Lysaundra Campbell, a sophomore, was quoted after the town hall, lunch, and rally: "What these two guys did [with the cotton balls] aren't the views of Mizzou." In responding to this incident, Chancellor Deaton followed the same playbook that Chancellor Loftin called on years later when responding to the racially motivated harassment of Payton Head and other Black students. Deaton quickly acknowledged and condemned the racist behavior, and then in the next sentence declared, "This university is fully committed to tolerance and respect for every one of its members, and this kind of conduct will not be tolerated at MU." Deaton closed his initial public statement by saying, "MU celebrates the diversity of our community and this behavior offends us all."[29]

As I argued earlier, when university leaders like Deaton and Loftin rely on such illogical rhetoric—acknowledging racist acts while simultaneously declaring that "all" in the "family" reject racism—they are trading expediency for actual contextualization, brand protection for historical understanding. Perhaps such tactics are understandable. However, they are also delusional, at least in the long run. Such a statement may serve to momentarily quell a crisis, conquer the news cycle, and help the university move away as quickly as possible from negative headlines. (In the 2010 cotton ball case, this strategy worked well and quite quickly.) But such tangled rhetoric buries (or hides) the recurrent confederate rhetoric that is the real problem at the core of the conflict, allowing the white majority to quickly forget the episode in question and leaving the Black minority to remember in silence. At each turn, eruptions of hatred are isolated and minimized, rather than contextualized and dealt with as an ingrained part of the campus culture.

Why is this a problem? How does isolating and quickly dismissing episodes of hate—eruptions of confederate rhetoric—backfire on universities? First of all, such illogical and scripted responses are often far less powerful than the speech acts to which they respond. This was true for the 2010 cotton ball episode at Mizzou. The symbolic and emotional power of that act was never fully accounted for. The students who created the cotton ball tableau were successful in sending a painful and reverberating message to the Black minority of the present and future. Their targets would remember their rhetoric.

The Black Culture Center at Mizzou was no random choice, of course. The center was named, after all, for students once denied admission to Mizzou because of their race. This included Lloyd Gaines, an African American honors student who challenged his rejection to the University of Missouri School of Law, taking the case all the way to the US Supreme Court in 1939. He won, and his case established part of the foundation for *Brown v. Board of Education*, but Gaines would never benefit from his brave advocacy. He vanished under mysterious circumstances just a few months after winning his mandate against Mizzou.[30] Like many Black people who fought for equality and civil rights, Gaines disappeared into history, and herein lies additional evidence for understanding the divergent responses common to incidents of confederate rhetoric.

Those in positions of power and privilege often view incidents of language and symbols, like the cotton ball episode at Mizzou, which do not cause immediate physical harm or death, as isolated and harmless moments in which otherwise good white kids go too far. Oftentimes, these official narratives highlight the involvement of alcohol, introducing the implication that the motivation is as much inebriation as hatred. African American students and faculty, on the other hand, view the same incidents of language and symbols as episodes along a continuum of violence on which many people have been killed or injured. Within university communities, some have the power and privilege to dismiss or isolate these episodes as pranks. Others read them for their full rhetorical power, as purposeful compositions, as life and death reminders of oppression.

When a set of words or a symbolic action indexes such different meanings for white people than for Black people, university leaders face an intensely emotional and complicated problem. There is, of course, a temptation to isolate and solve the problem of the moment, to push down the violent outcroppings of rhetoric, to counteract the bad news as quickly as possible and to forward a narrative of familial unity. When Chancellor Deaton did this in 2010, however, he merely postponed the university's reckoning. Six years later, Payton Head, Jonathan Butler, and their peers would recognize the pattern and expose Mizzou's convenient illogic. They remembered the cotton ball episode, even though it predated their time at Mizzou. The students of 2016 connected the series of events, refusing to believe the official narrative that incidents of hate speech at Mizzou were isolated or unusual. These students did not accept the metaphors of unity and family because their experiences and knowledge taught them otherwise. Taking a longer view, the students were not convinced by a new chancellor's urgent assurances that such hatred was not coming from within the "family," that "everyone" at Mizzou believed in equality and opportunity. From firsthand experiences, Black students at Mizzou knew better. They remembered. Their indexes of hate speech called forth different meanings than those argued by the official explanations. Black students understood the long running reality—sometimes overt and sometimes covert—of confederate rhetoric at Mizzou.

By 2016 and 2017, "students of all races [had] shunned Missouri, but the drop in freshman enrollment was strikingly higher among blacks, at 42 percent, than among whites, at 21 percent."[31] Missouri had proven to be a place where confederate rhetoric restrained racial progress, overwhelmed any and all strategic planning, derailed access and opportunity, and pulled the institution backward, moving it farther from its own stated and progressive goals for enrollment, finances, and diversity. Confederate rhetoric firmly controlled the campus discourse and destiny during this period. In the end, the anonymous white men who screamed the n-word at Payton Head exerted far more power over the university than did the prominent white men who tried, in vain, to speak officially on its behalf. Administrative limitations were in large part due to ongoing historical failures (or refusals) to acknowledge the presence and potency of confederate rhetoric on campus.

CHAPTER 4

Obfuscation at the University of Mississippi

At Mizzou, the confederate rhetoric that led to protests and resignations was outwardly and obviously racist. When a group of white men yelled the n-word at Payton Head, an African American student leader, no one offered a public defense of the language itself. Although widely accepted as indefensible, the slurs reverberated in dramatically different ways throughout the white and Black communities, which indexed different meanings and implications for the same rhetorical event. Many white people at Mizzou, including the chancellor, indulged in the privilege of interpreting these episodes of hate speech as isolated moments. Black students, like Head and Jonathan Butler, recognized that such interpretative tendencies—to isolate and minimize—were myopic, unrealistic, and unhelpful responses. Black students, unprotected from the punishment of confederate rhetoric, saw a clear pattern of racism inside their institution, a pattern that persisted unrecognized and unacknowledged by those in positions of power and privilege. While everyone could condemn the slurs of white men from pickup trucks, not everyone could agree on the significance and context of those slurs.

What happens on a university campus when the fundamental nature of an utterance of confederate rhetoric is itself contested? What happens when a minority of stakeholders interprets a term as outwardly and obviously racist but the dominant majority interprets the same term as affectionate and inclusive? That is, what happens when confederate rhetoric is hiding in plain sight? This type of rhetoric is what linguistic anthropologist Jane Hill has called "covert racist discourse," and, as she has shown, it "may be just as important in reproducing the culturally shared ideas that underpin racism."[1] This is true, in part, because covert racist discourse often escapes criticism of any kind from the majority. Even when visible and prominent, it is not roundly condemned. Indeed, on the contrary, it is often celebrated and defended by those in positions of power and privilege.

Norman Fairclough has shown that the "opacity of ideologies is a significant part of discourse."[2] Oftentimes, ideologies are strongest when naturalized within discourse communities, turned into common sense, and thereby protected from controversy. This insight applies to confederate rhetoric across the US South, where certain terms and symbols have become deeply embedded in the imaginary of the white majority and continue to influence the power dynamics within southern institutions like universities.[3] To extend another insight from Fairclough, one can say that the confederate rhetoric that has become commonsensical and embedded is the most powerful confederate rhetoric of all, in large part because individuals within systems end up promoting these words and symbols, even if they disagree with their underlying ideologies. People, or "subjects," can be "unaware of the ideological dimensions of the subject positions they occupy." This consequence underlines the reality that ideologies are very different from personal beliefs. In Fairclough's estimation, "it is quite possible for a social subject to occupy institutional subject positions which are ideologically incompatible . . . with his or her overt political or social beliefs and affiliations, without being aware of any contradiction."[4]

These powerful ideas help us understand the dynamism and longevity of confederate rhetoric within southern universities. In this chapter, I undertake a detailed analysis of a period of discourse at the University of Mississippi, one that was intense, heated, and also prolonged. I find that confederate rhetoric, sometimes disguised as tradition or commonsense, enforced real limitations on university leaders, who were in good faith attempting to move their institution forward and to understand and reconcile multiple eruptions of confederate rhetoric. This struggle, which was publicly documented through committee reports, official statements, press interviews, court documents, tweets, and local and national news stories, reveals much about the perniciousness of opaque language and symbols. The struggle also demonstrates how confederate rhetoric can survive (and grow stronger) across time. Finally, it shows how inherited confederate rhetoric can handcuff university leaders, forcing them, often unknowingly, to obscure and thus strengthen words and symbols that reify ideas or ideologies that the leaders themselves despise. In short, the following case study from UM reveals how confederate rhetoric strengthens systemic racism.

Burning Obama Signs and Yelling Racial Slurs

At the University of Mississippi, the most "successful" example of covert confederate rhetoric is the abbreviated name "Ole Miss" itself. As I demonstrated in chapter 1, the term has deep ideological roots and has performed disturbing cultural work across its history. Even so, the majority of the university's community members view the name as "affectionate" instead of problematic,[5] although sometimes brave members of the Black minority and others call it into question. For example, as mentioned in chapter 1, Jackie Certion cannot forget the term's legacy within the system of slavery after reading the transcript of a WPA interview of her enslaved ancestor who used the term to refer to the wife of the man who enslaved her; Certion now regularly edits her conversations and emails to avoid using "Ole Miss" in favor of the more formal "University of Mississippi." Such linguistic resistance, though, is quite rare within the overall university community. Or, perhaps more exactly, it is not orthodox or mainstream. Most people, white and Black, at UM ignore or dismiss criticism of the term. They may have heard vague references to its affiliation with the antebellum South, but those references are ambiguous, contested, or not given much weight. Most of the time, the term is accepted as simply a nickname that has become commonsensical, traditional, and beloved. In other words, the use of "Ole Miss" usually passes without notice.

It is not surprising that linguistic resistance to "Ole Miss" is rare, at least in the sphere of public discourse, a sphere that continues to be controlled by the traditions and preferences of the white majority. This privileged majority can and does routinely ignore or deny the problematic nature of confederate rhetoric. As a white lawyer and UM alumnus said to me at a party in Oxford, "I've heard that the name Ole Miss might be related to slavery, but I don't think that story's right."[6] Such dismissiveness is not hateful, but it does blindly privilege white comfort over historical reality. Indeed, questioning the term's legitimacy or beneficence is simply something that most people do not want to talk about, a possibility to be minimized or unacknowledged. With this context in mind, I explore in this chapter a moment when the term "Ole Miss" *was* publicly (though subtly) challenged. The intensity of the backlash reveals much about how confederate rhetoric—and the ideology it strengthens and embodies—is protected and preserved across time.

In the early morning hours of November 7, 2012, just after Barack Obama was elected to a second term as president of the United States, African American and white students at UM clashed in what they themselves described on social media as a "riot." By most news accounts, the event was less a full-scale riot than an intense social confrontation. Some four hundred students were participants and/or witnesses. Racial epithets, including the n-word, were shouted. Student journalists at the scene described hateful interactions, the smell of alcohol and marijuana, and widespread chaos and fear. As I noted in chapter 2, the Hotty Toddy football cheer was used on this night as a rhetorical weapon by white students to taunt and exclude Black students. There was little, if any, physical violence, but the University Police Department made several arrests for disorderly conduct. At some point in the night, a group of white male students gathered together near a dormitory and burned Obama-Biden campaign signs. Other white students gathered around these young men, watching and cheering the ceremonial conflagration.[7] Pictures of the hateful rally went viral on social media, and the episode made national news almost immediately.

Once again, the university had a serious public relations challenge on its hands. Jarring confederate rhetoric had emerged without warning, and campus leaders reacted quickly to counteract the negative headlines and reset the public narrative. In the days following the incident, Chancellor Dan Jones and other university leaders worked alongside students and faculty to formulate and communicate a public response. Their message was strong in its repudiation of hatred and bigotry. A group of student leaders, which included both the president of the College Democrats and the chairperson of the College Republicans, issued a public letter with a crystal clear summation: "To students who believe what happened on our campus is somehow acceptable, and to those who partook in hateful speech: you are not welcome at the University of Mississippi. We do not want you here. Our campus is not a safe haven for hate." Chancellor Jones reinforced this rejection of hatred with his own statement, which was released on November 7: "As we have acknowledged throughout this year of recognizing fifty years of racial integration at our university, despite evidence of progress, we still live in an imperfect world. All of us in the university community must recommit ourselves to condemn hate and to continue our work to assure our university is a safe and welcoming place for every individual every day."[8] In the following days and weeks, other official voices from the University of Mississippi were coordinated and strong in their communal rejection of racism and hatred. From a public relations standpoint, these efforts were successful. Soon the negative national attention had faded from front-page headlines and Twitter feeds. Yet something on campus, something within the community, was unsettled and unsettling. The conflict on election night had been real. It had been ugly. It had been racial.

Unfortunately, the university's internal reckoning was slowed by a tangential linguistic debate. Before members of the UM community could decide what the election night incident meant about their past, present, and future, considerable time and energy was spent attacking a single word—the noun "riot"—which had been used in some of the earliest coverage of the event. One of the first people to use "riot" to describe the election night conflict was a student reporter who witnessed the events firsthand in the middle of the night. Following her characterization, the *Daily Mail* and other outlets began using the word in their coverage.[9] Right away, the label struck a nerve for Chancellor Jones and others in the white majority at UM. It evoked the events of 1962, a full-scale riot that had been deadly and that had been aimed at blocking James Meredith from becoming the first African American student at the university. The 1962 riot made the history books and is never far removed from the community's collective memory.

In the fall of 2012, the 1962 riot was especially fresh on the minds of those on campus. A few weeks before election night, on September 30, Chancellor Jones, a progressive voice on matters of race, led the university in publicly marking the fiftieth anniversary of the 1962 events.[10] Also, just a week before the election night conflict, ESPN aired an hour-long documentary focusing on the 1962 UM football team. Based on an insightful article written by local author Wright Thompson, this documentary both critiqued and gently romanticized the period of the Meredith riot and its aftermath. If schools like the University of Mississippi are constantly trying to overcome their traumatic legacies—or at least to control the public narrative around those legacies—the ESPN documentary and, much more so, the racialized election night conflict that was being called a "riot" by newspapers and television networks were both rhetorical setbacks, moments when old wounds were opened and exposed. Rather than receiving positive attention for the campus commemoration of the fiftieth anniversary of racial integration, the university was, once again, presented as a site of turmoil and racial conflict.

When the *New York Times* ran its story on November 7, reporter Robbie Brown used the word "riot" twice and highlighted the recent event's connection to the deadly riot of 1962. The term had now spread beyond the social media posts of student reporters to the country and world. To some extent, the word "riot" set the tone of the coverage, so that by the evening of November 8 university officials were doing whatever they could to actively dispute a singularity, the word "riot." A Reuters story published that afternoon stated that "campus police Chief Calvin Sellers dismissed reports describing the incident after Tuesday's election as a riot. He said a few individuals caused a small disturbance."[11] This type of minimization became a major theme of the orthodox response at UM. Even while Jones and others were admonishing the bad behavior of students and acknowledging the racist overtones of the conflict, they actively attempted to counteract any and all associations with the events of 1962, specifically by vigorously attacking the use of the word "riot."

Jones and other UM officials went on the defensive, blaming the media for overreacting. The most prominent person on campus at this time was head football coach Hugh Freeze who led the way in blaming the media: "In the thirty or so kids that gathered to do whatever they were going to call that, which by the way happened at a lot of places across the nation and not just at Ole Miss. I'm very disappointed in our local media who took it upon themselves to run with it and make it into something it wasn't. We are our own worst enemy when we do those kinds of things. It's not, in my opinion, proper journalism, and that's frustrating."[12] Freeze minimized the event as much as possible, implausibly reducing the number of "kids" to "thirty or so." He was careful to avoid using the word "riot" at all, even while attacking the usage of that very word. Freeze offered the excuse that it "happened at a lot of places across the nation." He then directly attacked reporters (including UM student reporters) for making too much of the events.

Blaming the media became a common refrain during the community's response, so much so that news stories were written about the attacks on news stories. Reflecting on the media coverage and on insider reactions, Steven Godfrey, a sports reporter who covered UM extensively, wrote in *SB Nation* on November 15 that "frustrated fans, alumni and students targeted the precarious use of the word 'riot' to describe the event. Whereas any other university might not be as sensitive to that specific label, Ole Miss's history combined with present day southern zeitgeist has created a powerful mistrust of the national media." This sensitivity to the label "riot" had become a key part of the official university reaction, and it appealed to many UM stakeholders. Writing in the *National Review*, conservative columnist and talk radio producer Lee Habeeb, a resident of Oxford with some influence in the UM community, offered the most aggressive and cogent attack on the media, calling CBS, ABC, and other news organizations that covered the election night conflict "media bloodhounds." His long piece from November 12, 2012, titled "Mississippi Yearning: Ole Miss 'Race Riots,'" gives tremendous insight into the frustrations of many Mississippians, folks who were tired of negative news stories about their state and who often felt attacked for their conservative views. From Habeeb's perspective, the election night conflict was not only *not* a "riot," it was "a non-event that turned into a national one." Habeeb dismissed the incident as just "a few students not happy with the election results" who "went outside and blew off some steam. One burned a paper Obama-Biden sign. Some said racial slurs were shouted. Others denied it. They surely acted poorly. It didn't matter." From this kind of perspective, the problem was less the extant racism and more the eagerness of the national media to perpetuate stereotypes of white southerners as racists. Like other vocal UM allies, Habeeb focused his attack on the word "riot."

One central assumption of this book is that words and symbols are contested whenever they are important. In this case, the mainstream UM community's focus on the word "riot" reflected white sensitivities around the word's connotations to a shameful historical moment of racist violence. From a public relations perspective, the university leadership's sensitivities were logical and warranted. The chancellor wanted prospective and current students to feel safe on campus. It was a time of growing enrollment and burgeoning budgets. Bad press coverage could have certainly threatened such progress. The football coach, Hugh Freeze, wanted his recruits, many of whom were African American, to feel good about coming into the program and onto campus. His aim was to build a strong football team, win games, and win fans. Obviously, these marketing or image concerns, directly linked to campus finances, animated some of the official displeasure with the word "riot." The university's prudent concerns about the impact on campus funding help explain, perhaps, the intent behind the united minimization effort. Officials like Freeze and Jones did not defend the racist words or actions on election night, but they did seek to downplay the entire episode, to protect the university's image. Just like at Mizzou, this response proved problematic because it minimized very recent, raw, and real experiences of minority students who had been attacked by confederate rhetoric and who were now feeling hurt, unsupported, and oppressed. Leaders in these kinds of situations do not intend such negative outcomes, but intent is far less important than effect.

This coordinated detour from the substance of the debate may have delayed progress toward an antiracist UM campus. The prevalent preoccupation with the word "riot" distracted from a potential communal reckoning with the bald racism expressed on election night, when white students yelled the n-word at Black students, screamed the Hotty Toddy at them as a means of exclusion, and burned Obama-Biden campaign signs in a zealous, rally-like atmosphere. The events of that November night may not have been a riot, but they were highly racialized and deeply disturbing. To argue over the label not only missed the main point, but it also distracted the community from prosperous reflection and reconciliation.

Many in the white majority promulgated the defensive notion that the real problem during the election night episode was the mislabeling of the event as a "riot." Although this was a distraction fallacy, one somewhat glaring in hindsight, it did give ample cover to insiders who wished to minimize or ignore the harsh reality of the actual event. Read through a rhetorical lens, the critiques of the media and of the term "riot"—like all claims of "fake news"—served as barriers to what could have been a kairotic moment for progressive forces within the UM community. Such distractions perform cultural work by slowing or delaying debates over real racial divisions.

Traditional rhetoricians might protest against the weakness of distraction fallacies. Students are often taught to identify and avoid logical fallacies of all kinds. Indeed, composition textbooks, like one in use at UM during this very period, advise students that logical fallacies "are misguided or dishonest uses of legitimate argumentative strategies." Yet, as Walter Minot suggested long ago, we should not kid ourselves. Logical fallacies might be misguided or dishonest, but they are often quite effective argumentative strategies, despite their fallaciousness.[13] Such was the case here. Blaming the national media and protesting against the word "riot" may have been a distraction fallacy, but it was also quite unifying and effective, at least within the UM majority.

When the Media Moves On: Internal Reverberations of Confederate Rhetoric

In the days immediately following the election night conflict, Chancellor Jones issued statements, held meetings, and organized a candlelight vigil. Within a week or so, this rapid and coordinated response had succeeded in deflecting national attention away from the university. His next step was to attend to internal campus perceptions. By November 15, a group of more than one hundred faculty had signed a letter of concern drafted by political science professor Marvin King.[14] The letter urged the chancellor to launch a full investigation and to take concrete steps to prevent this kind of racialized conflict from occurring on campus again. The letter was sent privately to the chancellor, and shortly thereafter, he appointed a special group, the Incident Review Committee (IRC), co-chaired by a faculty member of higher education and an associate vice chancellor of student affairs. This committee of twelve faculty and staff worked expeditiously across the Thanksgiving and December breaks to produce its report on January 25, 2013.

Within the report, the sensitivity to the word "riot" and the commonplace suspicion of the media were on full and official display. It is here that these ideas grew into orthodoxies and were inscribed into institutional history. An early section stated, "Although not a 'riot,' as erroneously suggested by social media and news media outlets, the events carry with them the duty of reflection on racial concerns." A subsequent footnote included this critical rationalization: "Members of the student media picked up the term 'riot' from students' tweets and used 'riot' in their coverage (including tweets) to describe the events. Student media tweets were retweeted by students and then recirculated by the regional and national media." The report went further to discredit the word "riot" by blaming a Memphis television reporter, Kym Clark, who "relied on erroneous early morning information provided by producers" and who later ceased using the word. The implication was that Clark and other reporters regretted their word choice. Later in the report, a UM student journalist received direct criticism:

> Local media and social media were among the first to publish the word "riot" to reference the event, which was then re-circulated by regional and national media. One student journalist defended the decision to do so by saying that she was quoting the term as it was being used by other students. Unfortunately, this did not resonate through her messages and later the broader news media also picked up the term. This same student journalist asked others what had been occurring and then tweeted out their reports. Unfortunately, most of these tweets proved to be inaccurate. She noted that, if she had it to do over again, she would only tweet what she had personally witnessed.

Again and again in this short report of the "incident," the writers returned their focus to the word "riot" and to perceived mistakes made by the media. Another footnote summarizes this preoccupation: "While no student interviewed used the term 'riot' to describe the event (and most adamantly argued that it was NOT a 'riot,' rather an incident 'blown out of proportion' by the media), its effect on our students and community was profound."[15] This sentence encapsulates some of the competing—and ultimately irreconcilable—tensions within the report.

On one hand, the university—as represented by the IRC—was working very hard to minimize the incident, to deflect from the obvious reality that white students had launched late-night protests over the reelection of a Black president, yelled racial slurs at their Black peers, burned Obama-Biden campaign signs in a ritualistic performance that echoed darker southern traditions, and used the Hotty Toddy fight song (a supposedly unifying tradition) to punish and exclude their Black classmates. On the other hand, it was also documenting and acknowledging these racialized realities of the evening. As a result of this tension, the report itself reads as strained and conflicted. It is more defensive than objective, and it attempts (rather skillfully) to make a difficult argument: the "riot" was no big deal and certainly not a riot, but, by the way, it was profound. The students on the scene acted badly, but the media was also to blame for its exaggerations and inaccurate coverage.

As an institutional document, the IRC report seems to undermine itself at various points. The writers attempted to balance forthright contrition with minimization, to document the racism of the evening while also isolating the event from other episodes of racism in UM history, most notably the riot of 1962. Nearly as strongly as it criticized the students who yelled racial insults and burned Obama-Biden campaign signs, the report excoriated "irresponsible" student journalism and "inflammatory" social media posts, chastening student journalists for using the word "riot" to describe their experiences and criticizing the regional and national media for repeating the term. The report acknowledged that the word "riot" was used on the night in question, but it attempted to discredit that usage by emphasizing that "no student interviewed [for the report] used the term 'riot' to describe the event (and most adamantly argued that it was NOT a 'riot,' rather an incident 'blown out of proportion' by the media)." In all caps, the report screamed, this was NOT a "riot"! Although the co-chairs of the committee wrote later that the IRC was "only a fact finding entity" and was charged to "not posit an opinion," the document they produced is clearly argumentative in nature.[16]

The report's "fake news" line of reasoning may have satisfied those in the community who felt that the University of Mississippi was too often a victim of biased media coverage, but it did little to further an understanding of the underlying problems of hatred and bigotry that fueled the behavior of the white student offenders. The argument was an unfortunate distraction, one that shifted the UM majority into the role of victim and thus displaced the true victims of the evening: Black students who had endured frightening hate speech and threats of racist violence for publicly supporting an African American president. In other words, the entire debate over the word "riot" served to minimize and isolate the real problems and to defend the institution from charges of broader contamination. If the university could cast the coverage as overblown, the problems themselves might not seem so severe. Perhaps not surprisingly, the Incident Review Committee's report satisfied some at UM and angered others.

Faculty, staff, alumni, and students of southern universities often grow tired of the seemingly endless cycle of racist incidents and intense media coverage. As the editors of the UM student newspaper, the *Daily Mississippian*, wrote in a 2014 editorial, "These [racist] events continue to happen semester after semester, and year after year. All of our actions seem fruitless and impotent, leaving us broken, scared, humiliated and with burning, difficult questions: What do we do about it? How do we stop these events from transpiring? How do we fight an idea?"[17] Such frustrations are certainly understandable. People associated with schools like UM want to love their institutions and want them to be celebrated. They want to be proud of their universities. They have a natural impulse to defend their schools in the face of external threat or criticism. This desire to fully associate with their educational institution, to fully engage as members of the community without reservations or misgivings, is a salubrious sign of loyalty and gratitude to institutions that provide them with educational, social, economic, and cultural growth. Quality institutions like UM and Mizzou provide profound and formative experiences. They are places that create meaning in people's lives. They are sites of transformational and positive change.

However, in the US South, the longitudinal presence of confederate rhetoric often undermines and corrupts these positive feelings, weakening regional institutions through racial divisiveness that persists from previous eras. Confederate rhetoric as an operative force often converts pride into shame. When sullied language and symbols are intertwined so closely with an institutional identity—when they have created that identity in many ways over many years—they can seem to work mysteriously. To insiders who either fail to recognize or deny the fundamental flaws of their linguistic investments, the repeated pattern of conflict, healing, conflict, healing can create feelings of impotence and frustration. For the editors of the *Daily Mississippian*, racist episodes seemed to continually come from nowhere and be fueled by nothing. They were and are chaotic and disruptive incidents that leave most community insiders feeling perplexed or scared or embarrassed or angry. Whatever the emotion after such episodes, it is always negative.

The other terrible reality is that covert confederate rhetoric can compromise even those moments of actual progress and change that should be celebrated and savored. At schools like the University of Mississippi, many community members feel exasperated and discouraged by the recursive, Sisyphean process of race relations. When members of the white majority protest that their institution has come a long way but receives national media recognition only for negative episodes, they are (partially) correct. It's a well-founded complaint. Many (perhaps most) white people on modern southern campuses are striving for an identity that is unified, communal, and harmonious, but something unseen by them (covert) is always getting in the way, disrupting or slowing progress and sullying external perceptions. A major problem, often hidden or denied by the white majority, is confederate rhetoric: a semiotic legacy that is always performing its cultural work, creating divisions, catalyzing incidents like the cotton ball episode at Mizzou and the election night "riot" at UM. Blaming the media or minimizing such deeply disturbing and meaningful moments by isolating them, by decontextualizing them from the rest of university history, is a misguided and ineffective strategy, one that only perpetuates underlying problems.

After the negative regional, national, and international attention for the election night "riot," leaders at UM followed a typical plan for crisis communications. They were largely successful in the short term. Their first attempts to reconcile these events internally, however, were less successful. Internal unity was not easily achieved, in part because the loudest and most official voices on campus concentrated first and foremost on attacking the media and on contesting the characterization of the events. When the members of the Incident Review Committee formalized these defenses in their January report, they inscribed the distraction into institutional history. Their report was a defensive document that protected the traditional institution as much as it addressed the traumatized reality of present-day African American students.

I have already discussed why and how ingrained confederate rhetoric can lead to such defenses. When racialized terms and symbols are present, but unrecognized, they set limiting parameters and motivate defenses that are tangential and additionally divisive. By attacking the media and debating the word "riot," many in the UM community, including the Incident Review Committee, sought to isolate the election night episode, to disassociate it from the traumatic events of 1962 and from other racist moments in UM history. This impulse was understandable, but it was ultimately counterproductive to the goals of the committee itself. The election night incident was not isolated, no matter how much officials wished it to be so. History is continuous and interdependent. Rhetoric is ongoing and interrelated.

Proof of the reverberating power and longitudinal effectiveness of such eruptions of confederate rhetoric continued to be evident throughout the two-year period that followed the election night episode. The initial university response may have satisfied the external media, but many students and faculty on campus, those within the community, remained shaken and disturbed. In a letter to the campus newspaper, the *Daily Mississippian*, on February 1, 2013, sociology professor Ross Haenfler offered insightful criticisms of the IRC's report: "The dominant story, if left unchallenged, suggests a few bad apples started a non-riot . . . and that the big bad international media picked up on some misreporting, casting our otherwise racially harmonious campus as backward and racist. But anyone who has been here a while knows our ongoing history of racist events. Election night was simply the latest." Such dissenting calls for confronting and contextualizing the racism displayed on election night were neither frequent nor predominant, but they were influential enough to keep the conversation alive.

Even before the IRC had completed its report, Chancellor Jones asked the standing Sensitivity and Respect Committee to expand its membership. Upon receiving the IRC report, Jones charged the Extended Sensitivity and Respect Committee (ESRC) "to study race relations and make recommendations with the aim of improving the racial climate on campus"—all "in light of the Election Night incident."[18] This much larger committee, composed of twenty-two faculty and staff members and thirteen student members, worked during the spring and summer of 2013, issuing its report to the chancellor just before the beginning of the 2013/14 academic year.

In some ways, the ESRC's report relied on the IRC's report. In fact, the ESRC's first task was to review the IRC's report, and there are clear alignments of messaging between the two documents. Both reports condemned in direct and strong language the racism displayed by white students on election night. In other ways, however, the two documents are quite different. While the IRC's report pursued the distracting tangent of media criticism, the ESRC's report remained focused on the generative problem of the election night disturbance: namely, the strained racial climate on campus. The second report struck a deliberate tone and took a broader view of the racism underlying the incident. It acknowledged the event's connections to the university's history and did not attempt to offer an institutional defense of any kind. What's most important for the purposes of the present analysis, however, is the fact that this second report concluded with recommendations for action and introduced criticism of Old South symbols on campus, including a specific reference to the revered and orthodox term "Ole Miss." Granted, the report's reference to the term is brief and gentle: appearing under the fourth recommendation—"Enhance our communications and marketing strategies to ensure that race and inclusiveness are a central part of our messages"—the report listed "promote 'The University of Mississippi' along with 'Ole Miss'" as one of six possible actions.[19]

When local news outlets wrote about the ESRC's report, few focused on this specific idea—to use "The University of Mississippi" alongside "Ole Miss"—probably because this was already a practice that had been followed within the community for decades. The names "Ole Miss" and "University of Mississippi" were currently being used interchangeably by the majority of students and alumni, and the ESRC's report did not directly challenge this practice. The recommendation that seemed to equate the two terms was vague. Perhaps it signaled some possibility of progress to the progressive minority on campus, those who felt uncomfortable using "Ole Miss," but it did not stir the majority, those who loved the term and who were devoted to defending it. Even if the critique was gentle and not confrontational, the introduction of the critique would soon prove consequential. The ESRC's report served as an official acknowledgment, however indirect, that some in the community had doubts about the term. The report also suggested the hiring of outside consultants to review all symbols.[20] The recommendations seemed destined to lead to semiotic progress.

In October 2013, just a few days after receiving the ESRC's report, Chancellor Jones issued a response that was positive, general, and quite brief. It signaled a methodical, deliberate approach to undertaking the recommendations of the ESRC. It also exposed disagreements within the committee and sought to relocate many of the institution's problems on race, distancing them from the institution by labeling them as age-old problems that plagued all of humanity: "Implementation of some of your recommendations will be easy and others will be much more difficult. It is not surprising that on some of the more difficult issues your committee had difficulty gaining consensus or unanimity. These issues of conflict, hate language and being disrespectful of those who are different from us have existed for the entire span of humanity. Exemplary leaders like Gandhi and King have literally given their lives to dealing with these issues and yet there's still work for us to do." If Jones was attempting to minimize the problems on the UM campus by framing them as typical and universal, he also offered some localized and concrete promises. Jones detailed an action plan to respond to each of the ESRC's recommendations, and soon after his statement, he initiated this work. He asked various university administrators to "develop implementation plans," "prepare implementation," and "plan implementation." In what would become, perhaps, the most consequential move, Jones decided to follow the ESRC's recommendation of hiring outside consultants to "conduct a review of all of our divisive symbols."[21]

Chancellor Jones was moving deliberately and methodically, perhaps in an effort to calm passions and to make sustainable progress. But this approach would soon be tested by another highly publicized and hateful enactment of confederate rhetoric. Just as the external consultants were beginning their work at UM, three white fraternity brothers asserted their opinion about diversity on campus. They did so not during a public meeting or through committee service or in response to an official survey. Instead, late one night in February (Black History Month), they tied a noose around the neck of a life-sized statue of James Meredith standing in the heart of campus. Next, they draped a version of the Georgia state flag that incorporated the Confederate battle flag around the statue's shoulders. Two of the men returned the next morning to admire their handiwork, holding fists in the air and screaming "White Power" and "Fuck Niggers," all within sight and earshot of a maintenance worker. He called the university police, and the two student offenders were later identified by video surveillance footage. They were soon arrested. As sociologists from the UM Critical Race Studies Group noted, this "symbolic lynching" of "James Meredith, the first African American to attend the university . . . became the university's latest incident of racism to spark international headlines." Indeed, the *New York Times* reported that the incident ignited "a new round of soul-searching in a place where past and present still restlessly coexist."[22]

Like the men at Mizzou who spread cotton balls across the grounds of the

Black Cultural Center, the white students at UM chose their target carefully for this volley of confederate rhetoric. The Meredith statue commemorated the university's first African American student, James Meredith, and was the most public marker of racial progress on campus. In fact, it was, at the time, one of the only public markers of racial progress. By choosing to desecrate the statue, Austin Edenfield and Graeme Harris, along with their anonymous comrade, were sending a message of racial intolerance and hatred. How can we know their intent? Court documents, informed by an FBI investigation, make it clear that these students were acting with racist purpose. In their own words, this was an act of "white power." Before creating their tableau, they considered their context, their audience, and their methods. Theirs was an act of public composition and hateful creativity: "During the course of the evening, HARRIS decided that he wanted to create a sensation on campus using a Confederate flag. Harris frequently used racist language, and often voiced his belief that African-Americans are inferior to whites. . . . HARRIS [and his fellow students] decided that they would place an old Georgia state flag (which prominently features the Confederate battle flag) and rope around the neck of the James Meredith statue. Edenfield recalled HARRIS saying: 'It's James Meredith. People will go crazy.'" The federal filing goes on to say that these three students knew their institutional history. They realized that James Meredith was the first African American student at UM. They knew that people had died during the riot that preceded his registration. They knew that African American students and faculty would "reasonably perceive the Confederate flag and rope as a form of intimidation and as a potential threat of violence."[23] In other words, this was no lighthearted prank or drunken mistake. It was, instead, a premeditated and hostile rhetorical action.

Almost immediately, even before the students were arrested and the FBI established the facts, this expression of confederate rhetoric disrupted the ongoing discourse about race on campus, a discourse that had been catalyzed more than a year before by the election night episode. The University of Mississippi had yet another public relations nightmare on its hands, even before it had dealt fully with the previous nightmare. It seemed that the institution's most recent attempts to ameliorate the racial discord on campus had failed. White students had just performed a symbolic lynching of the community's most famous civil rights hero during a period of heightened awareness, dialogue, and progressive action. How could such an act be explained?

From within the community, there were widespread declarations of condemnation. Whereas many had minimized and isolated the election night episode, very few attempted to do so in the present case. As the editors at the *Daily Mississippian* wrote on February 19, 2014, in their "Experience Informs

Our Consciousness" editorial, "We are aware that a series of similar, intolerant events makes it seem as though they are no longer isolated but instead institutionalized." Throughout this passionate editorial, there is palpable shame and confusion. There is frustration that "still nothing has changed," that "these events continue to happen semester after semester, and year after year. All of our actions seem fruitless and impotent, leaving us broken, scared, humiliated and with burning, difficult questions: What do we do about it? How do we stop these events from transpiring? How do we fight an idea?" This raw and unflinching reflection—published in the campus newspaper and spread on social media—marks a rhetorical milestone for the UM community. The student editors were frustrated, hurt, and confused. They were grappling with existential questions on behalf of their community. They were performing journalistic soul-searching at its most honest and open.

Indeed, at this moment, the UM community seemed united in its interpretation of the noose around the neck of the Meredith statue. Chancellor Jones issued his strongest and most unequivocal statement to date. The alumni association offered a $25,000 reward for information leading to arrests. Fraternity leaders offered public condemnation. At first, there seemed to be no room this time to blame the media or to disassociate the event from the riot of 1962. The facts were clear and undeniable: white students had performed a symbolic lynching of the university's first African American student. They had carefully composed and sent a clear and unambiguous message of hatred and exclusion.

Of course, the national media arrived quickly to cover the story. When Alan Blinder wrote a long piece in the *New York Times* on February 20, 2014, he placed the noose episode in historical context, citing the 1962 riot. He also interviewed Charles Eagles, an outspoken history professor at UM and the author of the definitive history of James Meredith's integration of the school. Eagles openly criticized the administration's "careful pace" and called into question the most beloved of UM symbols: the name "Ole Miss" itself. "If I could do one thing, the place would never be called Ole Miss again," said Eagles. Many white people in positions of power or privilege recoiled at this suggestion. They saw Eagles's jump to the beloved name as overreach. As Blinder noted, within the university community, Eagles's words "come close to heresy." In response to Eagles, Frank Hurdle, an Oxford lawyer and UM alumnus, was quoted in the same article countering with a familiar and orthodox defense. He urged caution and deliberation: "It's a mistake to base any decision on this [incident], whether it was done by white racists or whether it was a hoax. Now, if you can show me that several hundred students got together in a meeting and did this, then I will be the first one to say that we need to have some systemic changes made. But we all know that's not what happened." Hurdle failed to note the election night episode from the previous year, in which hundreds of students had indeed gathered and performed racist speech acts. He also attempted to minimize the noose episode by introducing the word "hoax." Once again, in the face of a vile and racist episode, some in the white majority could enjoy the privilege of a dispassionate perspective. They could recommend slow, cautious deliberation. For some white insiders, the noose episode did not represent a "systemic" problem at all.

But white insiders were no longer fully in control of the discourse. The national media was present, but there was now another external audience, one who had been invited into the campus community by Chancellor Jones, and thus one who was more difficult to demonize. Following the recommendation of the Extended Sensitivity and Respect Committee's election night report, Jones had secured two consultants to review campus symbols. Ironically, those consultants had been conducting their reviews when the noose episode occurred. They had come with the election night "riot" in mind, but they now had a fresh incident to consider. Edward L. Ayers, the former president of the University of Richmond, was one of the consultants, and his trip to Oxford happened to coincide with the symbolic lynching of James Meredith. A few days following the noose episode, Ayers was on campus interviewing students, holding focus groups with faculty and staff, and discussing the campus climate with several key committees. He spent the next few months compiling his report. At the same time, the FBI took the lead in officially investigating the noose incident.

The rest of the spring semester was relatively quiet on campus as far as issues of race and racism were concerned and while this important work churned beneath the surface. In April 2014, Chancellor Jones spoke to the campus newspaper about his hopes for racial progress, but he avoided specifics: "Because we don't have both [consultant] reports in, I want to wait so the university leadership can digest those and draft a specific response."[24] Another school year came to a close. The freshmen students who had participated in and witnessed the election night "riot" would be juniors by the coming fall. Everyone was waiting on the reports from the consultants and more importantly on the chancellor's response. What, if anything, would change at the University of Mississippi?

Some of the answers came late in the summer, during the quiet period of early August, several weeks before most students and faculty returned to campus for the fall semester. In a six-page memo addressed to "All Who Love The University of Mississippi," Chancellor Jones detailed an action plan in response to the consultants' reports and the work of the Extended Sensitivity and Respect Committee. In his long introduction, Jones struck a moderate and open tone:

> People with different views will likely find parts of this action plan they like and other parts they do not. Some will agree or disagree with individual comments reported by our consultants. As our consultants noted and as readers should remember, the comments reported here did not result from scientific research or a random sample. They are thoughts from people who felt strongly about the issues we have faced as a university, people who were encouraged to be candid. To whatever degree they do or do not reflect majority opinion, they are important views to air. It was important that we hear from everyone who loves this university. Too often when viewpoints are wide-ranging and emotional, the easy answer for leaders is a non-decision, freezing people at a point in time and putting progress off to another day. To me, that is not leadership. And our mission as a university is to lead.

Within this setup, Jones demonstrated his awareness of his complicated and divided audience. He knew that insiders from various perspectives would "agree or disagree" with "our consultants." He gently undercut the approach of the consultants by emphasizing the qualitative nature of their research methods. Or perhaps he anticipated and attempted to weaken criticisms of their methods. Either way, Jones elaborated on the methodological limitations of the consultants by pointing out that some of the gathered comments may or may not reflect the majority opinion. He stated that all opinions are important. He wanted to "hear from everyone who loves this university," and he reflected that he—and the university—must now lead toward progress. He next issued a challenge to his internal audience: "Whatever the views may be on different aspects of this report, I am hopeful that people who read it and find places to agree or disagree will honor a process that encouraged open and honest dialogue and valued every idea. I am also hopeful that with decisions made, we have found common ground to move this university forward."[25] In other words, Chancellor Jones was asking everyone to respect his recommendations and to move forward in a spirit of unity, or at least in a spirit of peace.

It was not to be. Soon after, the chancellor found himself at the center of a community firestorm, one caused by the "majority" reacting to his action plan and to the reports of the consultants, which had been released as appendices to his action plan. For anyone interested in preserving oppression and exclusion at UM, there were some real provocations in the action plan. Through his responses to the consultants, Jones initiated a new vice chancellorship of diversity, endorsed the work of a faculty committee studying slavery at UM, renewed his support of the William Winter Institute for Racial Reconciliation, committed to creating new and visible campus symbols to honor Black Mississippians and racial progress, and pledged to contextualize existing buildings and spaces on campus that honored the Confederacy or persons who had been antagonistic to civil rights. These were aggressive responses: a litany of real actions that were certain to infuriate racists like the men who hung the noose on the Meredith statue. Ironically, these proposed changes were not the most controversial or publicized portions of the action plan. Instead, it was the sixth and final action item that created tremendous conflict in the weeks ahead.

In a typically strange twist, Chancellor Jones angered the conservative university base not by *attacking* the name "Ole Miss" but by *defending* it. How so? The consultants recommended that "the University consider the implications of calling itself 'Ole Miss' in various contexts." In his only rebuttal of a recommendation, Jones disagreed and openly sided with the status quo:

> Our longstanding nickname is beloved by the vast majority of our students and alumni. A few, especially among our faculty, are uncomfortable using the term "Ole Miss"—some at all, and some within the academic context. Some object simply because it is a nickname and prefer the more formal name, and some express concern about its origin, believing that the term is racist.
>
> Some of what we learned about the "Ole Miss" name over the last year or so, in a purposeful evaluation, includes:
>
> - The vast majority of current students of all races embraces the name and does not attach any meaning to it other than an affectionate name for the university.
> - National research revealed that there is no greater association with negative racial history for either "University of Mississippi" or "Ole Miss." In fact, a significant margin likes and prefers the "Ole Miss" name. And a very small percentage of respondents associates the university with negative race issues, whatever the name.
> - Regardless of its origin, the vast majority of those associated with our university has a strong affection for "Ole Miss" and do not associate its use with race in any way. And the vast majority of those who view us from a distance associate the term "Ole Miss" with a strong, vibrant, modern university—and the Manning family, *The Blind Side*, the 2008 Presidential Debate, and great sports teams.

> We are fortunate to have a highly favorable national reputation for our university, especially our fine academic programs. Applications and enrollment continue to soar. The quality of our applicants improves every year. And the affectionate term "Ole Miss" is and will continue to be an important part of our national identity.[26]

The rebuttal of the consultants (on only this single recommendation) was striking for its defiance. Chancellor Jones stated directly and clearly that "'Ole Miss' is and will continue to be an important part" of the school's identity.

Jones built his defense of the name on several fallacies already popular within "Ole Miss" circles. One, he avoided taking a specific position on the racialized legacy of the term. Indeed, he reiterated the ridiculous but orthodox position that the term may or may not be related to slavery, saying only that "some [mostly faculty] express concern about its origin, believing that the term is racist" and, later in the rebuttal, that "regardless of its origin, the vast majority . . . has a strong affection" for the term and does "not associate it with race in any way." As noted in chapter 1, such ambivalence may be popular, but it is not credible. The only way to conclude that "Ole Miss" may or may not be related to slavery would be to leave the matter unexamined.

Yet to deny or question the term's origin—its relationship to slavery—has been the definitive rhetorical strategy of the white majority for decades. This elision has proven to be an effective defense of the term. White traditionalists can avoid confrontation and controversy through a determined and prolonged erasure of the origin story. In this instance, Jones fell back on this very strategy. His rebuttal of the consultants was a plea of ambiguity and ambivalence that gave him the room to equivocate and to marginalize those minority voices who expressed their concerns during what was, supposedly, an open dialogical process. Going a step further, Jones also forwarded the fallacy that the "majority" does not find "Ole Miss" objectionable, thus it is not objectionable.

It was (and is) true, of course, that most in the UM community do not question the term. Indeed, it has almost never been questioned by more than a handful of people, at least not in a prominent or sustained way. Instead, the term has become what Fairclough would call commonsensical or naturalized.[27] When voices like that of Charles Eagles or Charles Ross have questioned the use of "Ole Miss"—and when others spoke about their concerns to the consultants—they were knowingly expressing dissent in moments of rhetorical and (presumably) risky transgression. Chancellor Jones was right when he said that the vast majority of people in the UM community do not voice objections to the term. He was wrong, though, in his conclusion that its use was thus not objectionable or harmful. Visible in this obfuscation is how confederate rhetoric can be perpetuated and protected over time. The appeal, which is in part a democratic fallacy, is often successful, as it was in this case. Jones instituted many changes based on the consultants' report. He did not, however, threaten the revered "Ole Miss."

When confederate rhetoric hides in plain sight, it becomes a semiotic repository of problems, a protective vessel for the remnants of racism. When modern leaders in the South fail to confront such words and symbols, and instead reify their commonsensical and accepted status, these leaders are (usually inadvertently) forestalling progress and priming ongoing conflict. Civil rights victories in the South during the 1960s often required a forced confrontation of inequalities that had long gone unnoticed or unacknowledged by the white majority. Jones's logic that "most" do not see a problem with using "Ole Miss," and therefore there is no problem, provides a clear dramatization of institutionalized racism. Such faulty logic could have been used to defeat any recommendation posed by the consultants—or to undermine any single point of racial progress in the school's history, or in the history of the US South for that matter. The idea of majority rule may appeal to patriotic citizens of a democracy, but majority rule can sometimes produce horribly unjust outcomes. If a deciding vote had been held in Mississippi in 1962, for example, James Meredith would never have been admitted to the flagship state university in the first place. Here in 2014, a University of Mississippi chancellor was invoking the concept of majority rule as an oversimplification to rebut the consultants' recommendation to reconsider the name "Ole Miss." Jones was using the concept of majority rule to muffle dissent.

When institutional leaders hide or fail to examine shameful aspects of their institution's histories, they often cite economic justifications. In his single rebuttal of the consultants, Chancellor Jones cited a mysterious and rather vague market study that had already been completed; this study was never published, but it does exist and was referenced by Jones within the context of his rebuttal. Jones said that "over the last year or so" there has been "a purposeful evaluation" of the term "Ole Miss." He pointed to conclusions of this evaluation without elaborating and without providing many details. Instead, he (presumably) quoted from that internal document, citing evidence that "we are fortunate to have a highly favorable national reputation." In the course of my research for this book, I was told by a UM librarian that university communications officers were the last to look at many of the files I was using and the last to ask questions about the origins of the name "Ole Miss." Apparently, they did this research quietly and without sharing their conclusions with the broader campus. If their internal report still exists, that document could be rich source material for scholars of rhetoric. Certainly I would love to read it.

Thus far, however, it has not been made available. We must infer its existence and findings from Jones's subsequent and very clear conclusion: that weakening "Ole Miss"—a national brand name—would weaken the school itself.

Again, Jones rebutted the report of the consultants and defended, rather ardently, the use of "Ole Miss." His reassurances in print, however, were not enough to calm one very vocal segment of the UM community: those insiders deeply committed to the name and to other examples of confederate rhetoric. Their reaction dramatizes the depth of their ideational and emotional investments in Old South words and symbols. On August 8, 2014, UM student Bart Wilbanks launched an online petition "calling for [the] resignation of Dan Jones." In his introduction to the petition, Wilbanks wrote, "Chancellor Dan Jones has done more to divide the fans, alumni, students, and supporters than anyone in my lifetime. . . . The final straw was August 1, 2014, when Chancellor Jones announced an action plan including discouraging use of the nickname 'Ole Miss' when talking about the University of Mississippi." Wilbanks was confronting the action plan, and he went on to list other grievances, including Jones's banning of the song "Dixie" from football games and the previous removal of the Colonel Rebel mascot. His concise summary made clear the agenda of the petition itself, which read:

> By signing this petition, I certify that I am an Alumni, Fan, Student, or supporter of The University of Mississippi aka "Ole Miss", and that I support the unrestricted use of the nickname "Ole Miss" as an interchangeable alternative to "The University of Mississippi."
>
> Further, we demand the resignation or if necessary termination of Chancellor Dan Jones for abusing his power to push an agenda that is not supported by the majority of the Alumni, Fans, Students, and other supporters. And that he be replaced by an alumnus who has enough sense to listen to the voice of the majority of the Alumni, Fans, Students, and supporters!
>
> We are "Ole Miss"!

On Twitter, the petition was accompanied by the hashtag #FireDanJones. In short order, the petition received tremendous attention. By March 2015, the petition had garnered 3,364 signatures and more than 30,000 views.[28] Clearly, some significant portion of the UM community did not trust Dan Jones and felt that the name "Ole Miss" was, for the first time in the school's history, under serious threat.

Suddenly, Chancellor Jones was facing a crisis that directly threatened his chancellorship. He had defended the use of "Ole Miss," guarding the name against the interrogations of the consultants, yet many of his conservative constituents had interpreted his defense of tradition as an attack on tradition. The moment illustrates the pressure and difficulty of the modern chancellorship or presidency. If Jones had been trying to satisfy the white majority through this strong rebuttal of the consultants, he was now being portrayed by many within that majority as the enemy of "Ole Miss." How did he respond? Jones and his public relations team, in concert with UM athletic director Ross Bjork, produced (very quickly) a highly polished video that was posted on Vimeo and widely distributed through social media.[29] The four-minute video was shot with close-ups in the style of *60 Minutes* (fig. 16). Remarkably, the video message worked very well and promptly extinguished the conservative firestorm. In this regard, it was a rhetorical masterstroke, effective by any measure and worthy of study by scholars of public relations. In just four short minutes, Jones made his own position on the term "Ole Miss" perfectly clear. It was an instructive affirmation of the majority view, a strong polemic that repudiated—with a feeling of finality and solemnity—any lingering doubt about his position on the name.

Wearing a prominent "Ole Miss" lapel pin and sitting within the historic Grove on campus, Chancellor Jones was introduced by the university's popular athletic director, Ross Bjork. At the time, Bjork was among the most admired of UM celebrities. Young and enthusiastic, he often talked publicly

Figure 16. Chancellor Jones in his video defense of the term "Ole Miss." Note his "Ole Miss" lapel pin and the nostalgic setting of the Grove, regarded by many Mississippians as sacred space. (Ole Miss Sports Productions, "We Are Ole Miss: A Conversation between Athletics Director, Ross Bjork, and Chancellor, Dan Jones," online video, Vimeo, 2014, last accessed 2018. Screenshot by the author.)

about leadership and was regarded by many university stakeholders as a tremendous asset. Bjork opened the video by pitching a question to Jones about the term "Ole Miss." Jones responded, underscoring that when it comes to "Ole Miss," you are either with us or against us.

> Before I became chancellor, I heard the rumors that "Ole Miss" was going away, and many people have had conversations with me about it over the whole time I've been chancellor. In 2009, in my first year, I said publicly several times, "I love Ole Miss. I love the words Ole Miss." . . . First and foremost, the vast majority of people in the Ole Miss family love the affectionate term Ole Miss and see it as a symbol of a great American university. . . . There's never been any confusion internally about who we are. Those of us who have loved this university for a long time use those terms Ole Miss and University of Mississippi interchangeably, so one is our formal name and one is a nickname. . . . Those of us who've been around this university a long time don't have to stop and think consciously am I going to use Ole Miss or am I going to use University of Mississippi. Just like I don't have to stop and think am I going to use Dan or Daniel. We've affirmed, we are Ole Miss.

The video is rich with visual and textual messages. Chancellor Jones created and emphasized an oppositional discourse with a clear "we" standing against a less defined but clearly present other. The "we" is for "Ole Miss"; the other is not.

It is a jarring line to draw when considering dissenters like Jackie Certion and Charles Eagles. Jones, a chancellor, used strong words to push certain faculty and staff members beyond the pale. He fell back on confederate rhetoric in a time of crisis, thereby reiterating the oppressive power dynamics that his own action plan was designed to confront. In this context, the video is difficult to watch, as it grinds away at the very idea of an inclusive community. In his denials of internal debate and confusion about the term "Ole Miss," Jones was conveniently but tragically widening gaps between the white majority and the mostly Black minority. He was using synchronization ("there's never been any confusion") to sweep the minority view under the rug and enforce a false chronological continuity. As one signer of Wilbanks's "Fire Jones" petition wrote a few days before the video's release, "Staff, faculty and students who are ashamed of the school's history are free to go somewhere else." Or, as another signer of the petition commented, "Maybe the few who don't care for the way things are done at Ole Miss should just pack up and leave. There are lots of other places they could go to if they are ashamed of who we are . . . True Ole

Miss Rebels."[30] Jones echoed such sentiments in his video, formalizing (and making official) a heretofore folkloric and commonsensical loyalty test, one built on confederate rhetoric.

Indeed, Chancellor Jones steadily prosecuted this binary of "for versus against" throughout the four-minute video. Early in his remarks, using active voice and direct language, he drew his rhetorical line in the sand. He was emphatic: "I love Ole Miss. I love the words Ole Miss." Next, he strung together three metaphors that established the term as a presupposition, a name with permanency. The metaphors also enforced the regional dimension of "Ole Miss," which became here not simply a generic presupposition but a presupposition with southern appeal. First, Jones introduced an often-used metaphor, presenting the University of Mississippi as not just a university but a family: "The vast majority of people in the Ole Miss family love the affectionate term Ole Miss." Without naming or giving voice to the dissenters, this trope clearly located the dissenters as familial outcasts. In the American South, where family is often valued above all else, such familial exile is undesirable, to say the least. Who would want to oppose the "vast majority" of their family, to reject "love," to reject an "affectionate term"? This was regionalized and masterful rhetoric on the part of Jones.

The chancellor's second metaphor was one of nativism: "Those of us who have loved this university for a long time use those terms Ole Miss and University of Mississippi interchangeably." Here again, Jones left the dissenters unnamed, alluding to them vaguely as shadowy newcomers. If "those of us who have loved this university for a long time" use "Ole Miss," presumably those who don't love the university and/or those who have not loved the university a long time are the only people who do not use the term. This trope exploits a long-standing white southern tradition of disdain for outsiders, one dating back to the carpetbaggers of Reconstruction and reappearing with the Freedom Riders of the civil rights era. Concomitantly, there is a southern tradition of appreciating birthrights. Being native—being born in Mississippi, for example—remains a marker of credibility even in the twenty-first-century South. Jones had earlier referenced his own Mississippi hometown. His metaphor here may seem gentle, but it is also deeply rooted and resonant. What self-respecting southerner would want to identify with newcomers over "those of us who have loved this university for a long time"?

The chancellor's third metaphor combined nativist and familial sentiments into a culminating trope of inheritance: "Those of us who've been around this university a long time don't have to stop and think consciously am I going to use Ole Miss or am I going to use University of Mississippi. Just like I don't have to stop and think am I going to use Dan or Daniel."

Here, Jones reinforced his appeals to familial and nativist preferences and, once again, suggested a false unity by keeping the dissenters in the shadows. There is a southern dimension to this metaphor as well. "Ole Miss" was foregrounded as the primary and familiar label for the University of Mississippi, no different than Dan is to Daniel. By personalizing this metaphor with a simile of his own first name, Jones invoked a deeply emotional component of his own familial inheritance: the name given to him at birth by his mother and father. What honorable and respectful southerner would dare question or complain about his or her own name? Who would dare dishonor his or her own parents in such a way?

Jones deployed these three metaphors to conceal his actual argument. His video did not engage the opposing view that generated the controversy in the first place. Instead, it dismissed those voices through elision and minimized them through a robust presentation of the majority view. "Ole Miss" the term became a familial and southern treasure, something inextricable from the collective identity, an official birthright. At the video's conclusion, Jones returned to concrete language and active voice, this time speaking not just for himself but for the entire university "family." His tone was strong, reassuring, and fatherly. His culminating assertion was conclusive: "We've affirmed, we are Ole Miss."

At the moment it was released, the video was a rhetorical masterstroke. In a few short minutes, Chancellor Jones established and reified the presupposition that the term "Ole Miss" was beloved and beyond question. He used a tripartite and extended metaphor—one with regional appeal—to dismiss contention and foreground unity. The message had its intended effect, quelling a brewing controversy and reestablishing the chancellor's credibility among the majority of university stakeholders. One UM sports fan expressed his satisfaction this way: "[Jones] values Ole Miss as both a term and an institution, and has no designs to get rid of or significantly alter it."[31] The #FireDanJones movement petered out. In many ways, the video is a lesson in leadership. Chancellor Jones delivered a strategic message using familiar and reassuring metaphors, averted a crisis, deflated a social media campaign calling for his removal, and reassured the vocal "Ole Miss" majority with rhetoric of force and conviction.

In many other ways, however, the video is disturbing evidence for the power of confederate rhetoric to limit progress and protect problematic ideologies within supposedly progressive institutions. At the time of the video, Chancellor Jones was leading a modern, public research university, a place where dissent and questioning not only are allowed but are essential ingredients for achieving its stated mission "to create, evaluate, share, and apply knowledge in a free, open, and inclusive environment of intellectual inquiry."[32] By castigating critiques of language and excluding dissenters, Jones worked in direct opposition to UM's stated mission. He silenced people who questioned a label, who arrived at different interpretations than the one embraced by the majority, who engaged in intellectual inquiry and critical thinking. Marginalizing dissent is in no way compatible with the modern concept of research, teaching, and learning. University leaders must protect the rights of students and faculty to write and speak freely. Language in all its variables must be accessible and available for use. It may have been expedient for Jones to dismiss debate about the words "Ole Miss," but it was also detrimental.

University leaders should protect and encourage linguistic explorations. After all, reconsidering orthodoxies is an essential mindset within any healthy university community. When terms like "Ole Miss" are interrogated, those interrogations should be supported, not shunned. In the ideal, such linguistic interrogations would stand at the very center of any university enterprise. As Norman Fairclough has said, "Educational institutions are to a greater or lesser extent involved in educating people about the sociolinguistic order they live in." Universities, in particular, aim to equip their students with "an essential prerequisite for effective democratic citizenship, the capacity for critique of language."[33] In his video, Chancellor Jones encouraged the opposite. He successfully closed debate. He silenced and excluded minority voices.

It was an unfortunate position for a university leader. It was also flawed rhetoric for another, very important reason: his message, no matter how forcefully delivered, no matter how temporarily effective, was simply not true. As it turns out, there were by this point many people who had loved the University of Mississippi for a long time but who did, indeed, have to stop and think consciously about using the term "Ole Miss." There were influential voices on campus calling for its elimination entirely. Charles Eagles, Charles Ross, Joe Ward, and Jackie Certion were just a few of the insiders who voiced critiques. These were people who loved the university, who contributed to it every day, who did not want to leave just because they dared question the history and meaning of a label or brand name. This important minority not only questioned the term "Ole Miss"; they viewed it as language of suspicion, exclusion, and even hatred. It was confederate rhetoric that had yet to be contextualized or confronted.

Lessons from the UM Community

In this chapter, I analyzed an episode during which covert confederate rhetoric was momentarily exposed and threatened. In response, influential people within the UM majority quickly defended it as a culturally shared and highly valued semiotic tradition. And so the name "Ole Miss" itself was ultimately strengthened by those in positions of power and privilege. To paraphrase Jane Hill, the effect was the reproduction and reification of a shared symbol that underpinned long-standing racist practices within this particular institution. This episode demonstrates just how rhetoric can become and remain naturalized. The majority at UM viewed the term "Ole Miss" as commonsensical and unquestionable, and they rallied to protect it and to keep its full capacity hidden from view, an enactment of denial, of protection.[34] This example shows just how deeply confederate rhetoric can become embedded at a university and how individuals can often end up promoting Old South words and symbols—and their accompanying ideologies—even when they disagree with those accompanying ideologies. My claim here is not that Chancellor Jones, Coach Freeze, and many others in the UM community are racists. I do not believe that to be true. My claim is that they and many other people in the UM community rallied together in this case to protect racist discourse. Confederate rhetoric is thus one mechanism for the transmission and survival of systemic racism, of marginalization, of white discoursal control.

A terrible racial schism still exists in America, particularly in the US South. As many historians and public commentators have observed, the optimism of the Obama era—optimism for a postracial America—is now regarded as a premature hope. In 2019, the racial divide remains and has only deepened in the time since the incidents discussed in this chapter. Indeed, in the 2016 election season, Donald Trump used racial divisions to fortify his voter base and catapult himself into presidential office. He defied expectations, in part, by tapping into messages and sentiments thought to be taboo by mainstream pundits. Since being elected, Trump has used the bully pulpit of his presidency to further emphasize divisions and to stoke racial tension. Journalists at Democracy in Color, a political organization dedicated to racial justice, have documented more than two hundred examples of the Trump administration's racist messaging from January 2017 to August 2018. From segregationist language used by the attorney general to the president's own habit of blaming people of color for crime and other problems, the online report establishes a Trumpian pattern of hateful rhetoric. One effect of this messaging has been the emboldening of white nationalists, who have stepped from the shadows and moved closer to the mainstream. As the Anti-Defamation League concluded in a 2018 report, this "white supremacist resurgence is driven in large part by the rise of the alt right," and "it was Donald Trump's entry in 2015 into the 2016 presidential race that really energized the alt right and caused it to become highly active." As the president has used hateful rhetoric from the White House, hate crimes have increased and hate groups have been emboldened.[35]

But it is important to always remember that Trump did not invent the rhetoric of exclusion and division. He is not a semiotic innovator. Instead, he simply identified and tapped into a long-standing American tradition of hateful rhetoric. If former presidents like George H. W. Bush, Bill Clinton, George W. Bush, and Barack Obama favored the rhetoric of compassion and reconciliation, Donald Trump has favored the rhetoric of vitriol and division. Rather than trying to counter our worst rhetorical traditions, Trump has capitalized on them. Disturbingly, it has been a highly effective political strategy.

This reversal of rhetorical progress is having immediate consequences within the many small communities that form the larger community of our country. University communities have proven frequent battlegrounds for national symbolic conflict. The white supremacist violence at Charlottesville was a battle over symbols. It marked a very public reemergence for white supremacists. The University of Virginia campus and the surrounding town became the battleground between those who cherish confederate rhetoric and those who reject it. Trump encouraged the white supremacists involved in the Charlottesville violence, both before and after the events, now famously elevating them to a morally equivalent and respectable position. He condemned Charlottesville as an "egregious display of hatred, bigotry, and violence on many sides." A few days later, he rationalized and defended the white supremacists even more clearly: "You had people in that group who were protesting the taking down of what to them is a very, very important statue. . . . You're changing history; you're changing culture." He once again blamed the counterprotesters: "I think there's blame on both sides. And I have no doubt about it. You had a group on one side that was bad and you had a group on the other side that was also very violent."[36]

Again, though, such equivocation and denial are not new strategies. These tactics have long been white strategies for the defense of racist symbols and words. Trump may be giving unprecedented modern prominence to this kind of racist discourse, but he is not inventing it. As the rhetorics of the extreme converge on the rhetorics of the mainstream, these contradictory stances are increasingly converging on university campuses. A few years after Charlottesville, several neo-Confederate groups, who had participated in that conflict, set their sights on Oxford and the University of Mississippi campus.

Confederate 901 and the Hiwaymen of Arkansas, two regional hate groups, decided in 2019 to organize an "Ole Miss Stands" march in defense of the Confederate monument on campus. In a series of Facebook Live posts, leaders of these groups spent time reading Trump tweets, spewing typically repugnant racist tropes, and heckling UM student activists petitioning the administration to remove the monument. As one of the Confederate 901 organizers explained on February 20, 2019, they were "tired of these little punk ass bitches trying to tear everything out of Ole Miss. If they tear all that stuff out of Ole Miss then what separates it from any other university out there? Nothing! It's the history and heritage that makes Ole Miss University Ole Miss University. And if you don't want to go to Ole Miss University because you don't like the flag or you don't like seeing Confederate monuments—nothing makes you do it! You have that freedom—to pick what college you want to!"[37] This statement marks a clear convergence between the rhetoric of a neo-Confederate, white supremacist hate group and the president of the United States. Both are defending Confederate monuments. Also apparent is a disturbing rhetorical convergence between these hate groups and Chancellor Jones from a few years before, when he defended the term "Ole Miss" using a similar binary (accept or leave), the same faulty logic (the majority is not bothered), and the same defiant posture. Of course, his tone was more respectable and his vocabulary more polished. His message, though, analyzed at length earlier in this chapter, was eerily similar in some ways. Confederate rhetoric and the identity of the University of Mississippi were presented as inseparable and timeless. They were defended with zeal.

Uncovering and contemplating such discoursal convergences is important, if sometimes painful or unsavory, work. We make meaning of our world through symbols and words, and our communities are the most immediate context for this creative and ongoing formative process. As James Paul Gee and Michael Handford have said, "We shape, produce, and reproduce the world through language in use. In turn the world we shape and help to create works in certain ways to shape us as humans. This mutual shaping process can have profound consequences for people's lives."[38] What are the consequences for our lives when the rhetoric of our communal leaders parallels the rhetoric of our most extreme and hateful fringe groups? What problems are such convergences perpetuating? What problems are being protected or hidden? Only through close analysis can we expose and understand language and symbols in their full and interrelated power. Only through close analysis can we look beyond the intent of rhetors and to the consequentiality of rhetoric.

Racism in the US South is a multidimensional problem. In this chapter—and in this book—I have argued that to understand racism and its stubborn foothold in the US South, scholars must attend to the semiotic dynamics at work within individual southern communities like universities. The case study of "Ole Miss" illustrates just how confederate rhetoric destabilizes notions of interracial unity and disrupts, quite profoundly, racial progress. The next chapter shows how confederate rhetoric has worked within and against even one of the South's most revered (and supposedly unifying) traditions: college athletics.

CHAPTER 5

Football, Flags, and Rhetorical Fury

> Rhetorical success depends upon the rhetorical situation. Just as a blurted-out statement or an alleged misstatement can reveal us positively or negatively, so can our silence, whether controlled, instinctive, or imposed. Just as we use words to obfuscate meaning or to buy time, we use silence, sometimes productively, sometimes not—just the way we use speech.
> CHERYL GLENN, *UNSPOKEN*

> What we cannot speak about we must pass over in silence.
> WITTGENSTEIN, *TRACTATUS LOGICO-PHILOSOPHICUS*

WITHIN MANY SOUTHERN INSTITUTIONS—AND CERTAINLY within southern universities—there is a reverence for tradition. In and of itself, tradition may sometimes be an underlying structure that limits or slows racial progress. How so? Tradition is concerned with time and, more specifically, with the ways in which people present time. Specifically, any given tradition represents some human arrangement of individual historical moments into a perceptible continuum that can be understood and agreed on by members of a particular community. Traditions tend to compress history and create uniformity. Oftentimes, the process of constructing and maintaining a tradition is salubrious: a way of creating order, of making meaning, of emerging and reemerging some shared notion of togetherness across years and even across generations. Think of family traditions such as Sunday dinners or July Fourth barbecues. Each week or year, the family replicates a similar experience, thereby creating a string of memories for individuals within the family and a continuum of touchstone moments shared communally. Thus tradition can organize collective or familial memory and be an effective tool for unifying individuals and for cultivating a sense of togetherness and belonging.

Tradition is not always experiential, though. Some of the South's most powerful traditions are semiotic. Think of colloquial usage of the word "y'all," which may have once been purely natural but which is now oftentimes purposeful, self-aware, or intentional. "Y'all" is distinctively regional. Its usage is a way of signaling membership, of making identity, of emerging and reemerging some shared and comforting notion of togetherness—of southernness. With every use of "y'all," individual southerners are connecting to the past, consciously or not, and, in a sense, compressing history. They are deploying and participating in a semiotic tradition.

But not all semiotic traditions are charming or benign. When considered as the rhetorical rearrangement of time, some semiotic traditions can be quite unhealthy for communities. At the University of Mississippi, for example, leaders have sometimes invoked tradition in order to defend Old South words and symbols from previous eras. In the previous chapter, I described how Chancellor Dan Jones engaged in this strategy while defending the term "Ole Miss." By framing pieces of confederate rhetoric as part of a wholesome tradition, members of a discoursal majority can protect those words and symbols from criticism or change. This defensive strategy often relies on synchronization, a rhetorical tactic for incompletely connecting the past to the present. Within a community that reveres tradition, one way to shelter a problematic word or symbol is to place it beneath the protective notion of tradition. As Jan Blommaert has shown, historical or temporal synchronization necessarily erases divisions and debates, creates silences, and imposes the (false) notion that particular words or symbols are timeless, constant, and unquestionable in their meaning. Traditions can create feelings of unity within communities, but those same traditions can also marginalize or overpower alternative perspectives and minority voices.

In this chapter, I explore two more traditions at the University of Mississippi—Blind Jim Ivy and the Confederate battle flag—analyzing them as rhetorical traditions that have performed a particular kind of cultural work. These examples dramatize the difference between public history and public relations, demonstrating the dangers of tradition as an unreliable synchronizer of the past and present. They also explain much about the way power has worked in the US South. Specifically, they illustrate how those in the majority have exerted discoursal control over their communities and the region. Lastly, they reveal much about the rhetorical nature of tradition and show how traditions can sometimes create oppressive silences.

The Tradition of Blind Jim

James Ivy was born in Alabama sometime around 1870 to Matilda Ivy, a formerly enslaved woman who moved to the Oxford area and helped found the First Colored Baptist Church in Lafayette County. As a young man, he worked construction jobs until he was blinded in an accident on a bridge project over the Tallahatchie River. No longer able to work in construction and with his job options now limited by both his race and his disability, James Ivy forged ahead. He opened a business selling peanuts and candy on the University of Mississippi campus. His best opportunity for visibility and sales came at athletic events, where his booming voice could be heard, above all others, cheering on the home team. One day, when the baseball team was losing badly to the University of Texas, Ivy's persistent encouragement catalyzed an unlikely rally that resulted in a comeback victory for UM. The ecstatic students credited Ivy for the win, and thus began his legend. James Ivy would soon become a university tradition, "the most persistent presence on campus during the first half of the twentieth century."[1]

Students called James Ivy "Blind Jim," a moniker that remains well known on the campus even today, more than sixty years after his death in 1955. During his lifetime, Blind Jim grew in popularity, becoming more than a vendor of snacks. To the all-white student body, he became a sort of celebrity and mascot. As Curtis Wilkie has written, Blind Jim "hung around campus for sixty years, selling peanuts, dispensing folk stories, and cheering its athletic teams. He liked to boast that he had never seen Ole Miss lose a game."[2]

Previous scholars have contextualized Blind Jim and his relationship to the all-white student body. UM historian David Sansing wrote, "The relationship between Ole Miss students and Blind Jim was genteel racism in its purest form and it broke none of the codices of white supremacy." Joshua Newman argued that Ivy's celebrity was "constructed out of his nonthreatening, accommodating 'Otherness.'" It was an otherness that the student body read as twofold: Jim's race and his disability. Charles Eagles agreed, detailing how Ivy's status was built, at least in part, on both his blindness and his self-deprecating and race-deprecating sense of humor. Blind Jim was known for his jokes and his humorous "convocation" speeches delivered every fall to the freshman class. Ivy's comedy was in line with *Amos 'n' Andy* and other popular radio programs and cartoons in which Black characters were portrayed as dumb, humorous, and inept.[3] It was also comedy consistent with many of the racialized jokes and cartoons found in the *Ole Miss* annuals contemporaneous to Blind Jim's more than fifty-year period of prominence.

Blind Jim was beloved by the all-white student body not despite his Blackness but because of his particular performance of Blackness. As Anthony James has written, Ivy's rise to iconic status within the UM community "represented a remarkable relationship over time and a high level of racial tolerance by white students, administrators, and staff. Paternalism, however, soured this acceptance."[4] Consistent with many of these scholars, my own view is that Ivy capitalized (intentionally) on white southerners' predilection for paternalism. He played his part, realizing that white people in positions of power and privilege would support him as long as he displayed compliance and loyalty. He navigated a racist system with tremendous skill and rhetorical prowess, finding ways to monetize his status and become a beloved university tradition, in and of himself.

Kurt Edward Kemper has found that many southern universities "sheltered" Black men like Ivy, who were almost always connected to athletic programs as water boys, helpers, or "general hangers-on." According to Kemper, "these black retainers were always men; intensely loyal [and] the most legendary of their number provided long-standing service." At the University of Georgia, there was Clegg Stark, "described by one white Georgia partisan as 'a flap-mouthed Negro water boy . . . who doesn't know his own age or how long he has been there.'" At the University of Alabama, there was Merrill Collins, who lived in the basement of the athletic complex and who relied on the charity of players and coaches; they saw Collins as a lucky mascot and would rub his head before the Auburn game. And at Auburn University, during the same era, when Auburn was known as Alabama Polytechnic, Coach John Heisman employed an African American man named Bob Sponsor, who was portrayed by Heisman in *Collier's* magazine as undyingly loyal and unfailingly stupid.[5] In the first half of the twentieth century, many university communities imagined, tended, and paternalistically cherished Black male figures who reified orthodox conceptions of Blackness and who provided a strangely cheerful and comedic counterpoint to the more violent enforcements of Jim Crow happening around the South.

It is worth noting that all of these examples were connected formally or informally to the athletic programs at their respective universities. Later in this chapter, I discuss the role of athletic programs in preserving and sometimes eroding confederate rhetoric. For now, I argue more broadly that men like Blind Jim at the University of Mississippi were, for those in the white majority, embodied examples of confederate rhetoric. As flattened, dehumanized, and appropriated figures, these popular (even legendary) African American men became symbols in service to the white imaginary. Future researchers might prosper from detailed historical excavations of these figures, in order to complicate and chart the fullness of their humanity and relationships. Some such work has already occurred. For example, it is known that Jim Ivy was twice married, preached sermons at his church, and traveled beyond the South to Chicago to visit family, but such complicating details are not part of the Blind Jim mythology or tradition that was created and preserved by generations of white students and faculty at UM. From the white perspective, Blind Jim was always one-dimensional, compliant, and beloved for his ignorance, dependence, and goodwill, and, above all, for how his presence made the white majority feel superior and benevolent.

In many photographs of Blind Jim from across the decades, a sign hangs around his neck. It appears that he would change the text regularly, and in most of these old photographs, the text is impossible to decipher. In one image, however, taken by local photographer J. R. Cofield in 1944 or thereabouts, the sign is legible. The image shows Jim Ivy seated inside the Old Chemistry building at UM.[6] As was often the case in photographs of Blind Jim, he is surrounded by smiling white faces. The sign around his neck reads:

> Read Blind Jim's Message
>
> For 48 years I have been on the campus and I would like to continue being here, but since the war has started I cannot get candy to sell. Other arrangements will have to be made. My only hope is a cup with this sign asking for help.
>
> Yours for Ole Miss,
>
> Blind Jim

Like a statue with an inscription, Blind Jim, sitting in one of his usual spots on campus, was accompanied by a textual reminder of his status, his benefactors, and his purpose. His dependence and history were inscribed almost directly on his body. As symbol and tradition, Blind Jim was passed down year after year by the white students at "Ole Miss." Like many traditions, he became beloved and consistent. Viewed another way, his audience gave him little room for growth or change. Every fall, the freshman class purchased Jim Ivy a new suit of clothes, thereby continually creating his dandified caricature. His renewal became ritualized each year as his clothes were refreshed, as he delivered a speech to the freshmen, as he appeared at football games to lead the Hotty Toddy and other cheers.[7] The all-white community at UM cemented their conception of Blind Jim, and they left little interest or room for James Ivy the man. They continually synchronized his image, oversimplifying a human being and creating a racist tradition that was timeless and constant in its meaning.

As such, Blind Jim served ideological purposes and performed cultural work, in the same way that other types of confederate rhetoric like statues or flags did. He sat in just a few specific spots on the UM campus, for example, becoming a kind of landmark in the memories of generations of white students. As confederate rhetoric, he offered the all-white campus much more than peanuts or candy: he offered racial reassurance. Even today, given his folkloric status, Blind Jim, although long-dead, continues to serve those ideological purposes and perform that cultural work. Despite his tremendous influence and historical presence within the life of the institution, Jim Ivy has not been widely contextualized or reinterpreted at UM. After decades of synchronized oversimplification, Blind Jim remains (for many) a flattened symbol, carrying a particular type of racist residue forward into time. Relevant here is Jan Blommaert's observation that "perhaps synchronization explains a lot about the way power works in societies." He continues, "[Synchronization] may be a tactic that suggests clarity, coherence, and transparency . . . by eliminating attention to the nature of differences and contradictions. It is powerful, for it connects to everyday rationality: we do not observe the deeper layers of our system, we see and experience its surface. Thus, someone who can make us feel that our own experiential reality is the only relevant one and our historical position the only 'normal' one, stands a good chance of convincing us that we are right after all."[8] Blind Jim, as synchronized image, suggested for decades a particular type of Old South clarity and coherence. As confederate rhetoric, he made white people at "Ole Miss" feel that their worldview was correct and normal. As a superficial reassurance, he served as evidence for a white southern argument in favor of patronizing racism, one that devalued and flattened African American bodies.

This observation might not be of much contemporary importance, if the modern UM community had worked through its problematic reverence for Blind Jim as a symbol of Black inferiority and white paternalistic domination. Instead, because the community has never come to terms with the fullness of this important figure, because the dominant narrative about Blind Jim has been prevalent and promoted for more than fifty years in the life of the institution, the symbol of Blind Jim has lived into the present as a tradition of covert and uncontested confederate rhetoric. It is a tradition that continues to create problems.

Three modern examples in which Blind Jim continues to be known and discussed in his flatness, not in his fullness, within the UM community prove my point. Although the Blind Jim tradition is mostly folkloric, it does sometimes find its way into print, even today. For example, in a 2017 news release about a major gift from an alumnus, there is this quote from the donor alongside "context" from the UM writer: "'Nobody but Blind Jim ever had more fun at Ole Miss than I did,' [the donor] recalls, referring to James 'Blind Jim' Ivy, a peanut vendor on campus known for his 60-plus years of enthusiastic loyalty to Ole Miss athletics."[9] In this pairing, Blind Jim serves as a symbol of fun and humor, a symbol used for white self-deprecation. The donor employed Blind

Jim as a reference that he believed those in his audience (the UM community) would understand. The UM employee who wrote the story not only chose to use this quote in the first place, but also chose not to complicate the reference, not to offer an updated description of Jim Ivy, but to simply repeat the conventional (and incredibly flat and patronizing) view that Blind Jim was "a peanut vendor on campus known for his 60-plus years of enthusiastic loyalty to Ole Miss athletics." This example demonstrates the durability and effectiveness of both tradition and confederate rhetoric. Blind Jim, as symbol of the Old South, has been preserved into the twenty-first century.

Historian Charles Eagles documented an unsuccessful movement to create a campus memorial to Blind Jim just after his death in 1955: "Immediately after Ivy's death, an ad hoc committee, including Athletic Director Tad Smith, Provost Alton Bryant, and Financial Secretary W. C. 'Chuck' Trotter, continued to raise money. Organized to solicit contributions to provide for Ivy's final needs, [the committee] announced after his death that it would continue to seek donations to pay Jim Ivy's remaining bills but also to erect a memorial to him on campus."[10] No memorial was ever erected. What form might the proposed memorial have taken? Would it have stood as a monument to Jim Ivy, the man, or Blind Jim, the character? How would that memorial be perceived today? These are interesting questions to ponder. It would have been the first public memorial on the UM campus dedicated to an African American, predating the James Meredith statue by some fifty years. It also, in all likelihood, would have presented Blind Jim as the flat and loyal servant, not James Ivy as a full and complex human being.

Even though the white majority at UM did not create a statue, portrait, or plaque to honor their conception of Blind Jim, they had, by some accounts, already found a way to perpetuate his image, even before his death. According to popular legend and some historians, Blind Jim Ivy was the visual inspiration for Colonel Rebel, the official UM mascot for more than sixty years. At the time that Colonel Rebel was created, during the 1936/37 academic year, Blind Jim was an established fixture at the University of Mississippi; he continued his prominent role at football games, for example, serving as both a mascot, of sorts, and a cheerleader. In his official history of the university, David Sansing speculated that "Blind Jim may have been the model for Colonel Rebel who first appeared on the cover of the yearbook in 1937." In his notes, Sansing traced this idea of a connection between Blind Jim Ivy and Colonel Rebel to Frank Everett, the same UM legend discussed in detail in chapter 1. Other scholars have followed Sansing and have explored the complications of this idea: the strange but credible possibility that a Black man, perceived as a loyal servant, was the inspiration for the image of a white mascot, one framed as an aristocratic plantation owner, presumably someone who enslaved people of African descent. Joshua Newman noted that "over time, the Colonel came to be known by other names, including 'Johnny Reb' and 'General Nat'—with the latter a reference to General Nathan Bedford Forrest, Confederate war hero and founder of the Ku Klux Klan." Newman argued that Blind Jim and Colonel Reb offered similar reassurances to white southerners: they both signified and celebrated the "'harmonious times' of the Old South; whereby an all-White student body exercised its dominance over subservient Blacks."[11] They were both, in other words, examples of confederate rhetoric.

Certainly the campus environment during the 1936/37 academic year was dripping with nostalgia for the Old South, and that nostalgia remained alive and active through pervasive instances of confederate rhetoric. The 1937 *Ole Miss* annual contains not only the debut of Colonel Rebel on the cover but also within its pages a photo of Blind Jim, a photo of a student homecoming float that featured the Confederate flag, prose in praise of ancestral honor and southern glory, cartoon depictions of industrious and loyal enslaved people alongside their white enslavers, and, most joltingly, a half-page image of a Ku Klux Klansman riding his horse with a burning cross in hand (fig. 17).

Figure 17. Detail from the opening page of the "Fraternities" section of the 1937 University of Mississippi yearbook. The annuals were replete with confederate rhetoric, and this image of a Ku Klux Klansman riding at night with a burning cross in hand is overtly racist and jarring. It appears, without comment or context, alongside pages of happy college students engaged in activities that would look typical and commonplace on today's campus. (University of Mississippi, *Ole Miss, 1937*, 138. Special Collections, University of Mississippi Libraries.)

It was out of this milieu that Colonel Rebel was born and in this context that Blind Jim was patronizingly cherished. Whether there is a causal connection between the two figures—Blind Jim and Colonel Reb—is a fascinating topic, one that still needs to be explored by historians. What's most important for the purposes of this discussion, however, is that there is a clear rhetorical connection between these two figures. The white majority at "Ole Miss" invested much in its conception of Blind Jim. Even more, it actively crafted this conception, buying his clothes (or costume) every year, ritualizing his humorous and self-deprecating speeches, celebrating in various ways his subservient manner, and providing financial support by patronizing his peanut stand. This ongoing process of white composition of Blind Jim elided James Ivy in his more complex and real form. The all-white student body repeatedly erased James Ivy and repeatedly created Blind Jim. The creation and valuing of confederate rhetoric is always centered selfishly within the white majority, and in the case of Blind Jim, an Old South image was created and traditionalized. It was a durable image that thrived well into the twentieth century. Blind Jim—well-dressed, polite, deferential, seemingly ignorant, disabled—was a reassuring servant to "Ole Miss" ideals.

In this way, Blind Jim as an image relates directly to Colonel Rebel, the subsequent mascot who recalled, in white form, the same racial order and uncomplicated hierarchy of the plantation-era South. From this perspective, the race of both figures—their whiteness and Blackness—recedes in importance as other visual elements become salient. Blind Jim and Colonel Rebel, aesthetically, share mustaches, hats, and light summer suits. They both serve as mascots and cheerleaders, champions of the institution in its most orthodox form. They both evoke the mythic gentility and racial stability associated with the ideology of the Old South. One might think of this implied and underlying commonality as a figure in and of itself, something one could label "plantation man."

Such a momentary experiment in imaginary forensics allows for fitting both Blind Jim and Colonel Rebel into a continuum of such images from across time that were valued by the "Ole Miss" community. For example, Blind Jim was preceded on campus by "Uncle Bob," another African American man who had long been valued by white students for his "loyalty and faithfulness." When Bob died in 1912 or 1913, he was eulogized in the 1913 edition of the *Ole Miss* annual: "God make the final wrenching . . . gentle and without pain, and find the good old darky a place of rest after long, long toil." It was within this era that Blind Jim was first installed—by the students—as the most prominent and faithful Black figure on campus.[12] Later, after Blind Jim's death in 1955, another "plantation man" image is present within this discoursal community. Figure 18 is an image of unknown origin that can be dated generally to the time of James Meredith's integration. One copy of the image remains in the University of Mississippi's Race Relations Collection. On a small flier, which may have been distributed on campus, is the cartoon of a Black man dressed in the white suit and hat of a wealthy plantation owner. The caricature is drinking a mint julep, smoking a cigar, and lounging in a rocking chair on what seems to be either the front porch of the Lyceum, UM's

"Now THIS is what me and Martin Luther had in mind!"

Figure 18. Racist ephemera from the University of Mississippi. This cartoon was probably created and distributed around the time the school integrated in 1962. It is a complicated rhetorical image blending visual racial elements traditional to white representations of the plantation-era South. Far from an isolated image, this is but one example in a long continuum of confederate rhetoric. (Racist ephemera from the University of Mississippi, n.d., box 1, folder 26, control #00-420, Race Relations Collection, Special Collections, University of Mississippi Libraries.)

main administrative building, or the front porch of an Old South plantation. The caption reads, "Now THIS is what me and Martin Luther had in mind!" The image presents an intersection between Blackness and whiteness that occurs at some imaginary point in the future, one in which a Black man occupies the dominant position of an Old South landowner, a person with time and money enough for leisure. The Black man in the cartoon is presented with all the exaggerated features of a typical racist caricature. As the caption makes clear, the point of view of the anonymous cartoonist is the point of view of the white majority, poking fun at the agenda of the civil rights movement. The image echoes Blind Jim, Colonel Rebel, and all the racist cartoons published over the years in the *Ole Miss* annuals. Like those images, this one evokes the Old South in a way that is clearly argumentative and racist.

My main point in discussing these examples is to show that within the white UM community there has been a long-standing impulse to create and promote images related to what one might call the "plantation man." Through this lens, Blind Jim is a key, but not solitary, image. He can be understood as part of what Laurie Gries has called a single multiple image that has lived a complicated and ongoing rhetorical life. Blind Jim, and other resemblances, including Colonel Rebel, have gone viral and have been consequential—they have become traditions—because as confederate rhetoric they have furthered ideological goals. Such an insight is possible on account of Gries, whose materialist approach to visual rhetoric allows one to trace circulating images as they transform in a variety of ways and as they become "actants" in collective life.[13]

One of my arguments is that Blind Jim—as a single multiple image—does, indeed, remain active and consequential within the UM community, even into the second decade of the twenty-first century. As evidence for this claim, I offer the unsettling truth that many people within today's UM community argue for and value the idea of a direct linkage between Blind Jim and Colonel Reb. Notably, the Colonel Reb Foundation is the most organized proponent of this connection. Following its motto, "Tradition Matters at Ole Miss," the Colonel Reb Foundation was created in the summer of 2003, just after the Colonel Rebel mascot was officially retired by the university administration, as part of Chancellor Khayat's effort to step gently away from some of the school's most glaring Old South symbols. According to the foundation's website, the group has organized a "Grove lapel sticker campaign" in which "over 500,000 Rebel fans have worn the 'Colonel Reb Is My Mascot' stickers on gamedays." Also according to the website, the Colonel Rebel Foundation initiated a student chapter on campus, which became by 2012 the "largest student organization . . . as evidenced by the signatures on last year's [2011] petition for the Colonel's restoration. A total of 4,160." The foundation "believes that Colonel Reb is the only mascot for Ole Miss, despite a fraudulent 'student-led' poll in 2010 that introduced 'Rebel the Black Bear' as the administration's new on-field mascot. The Colonel," argues the foundation, "is a lovable, unique, recognizable and historic tradition of Ole Miss. The Colonel loves nothing more than to bring smiles to kids' faces, shake hands with alumni and cheer the Rebels to victory. Hotty Toddy, Go Rebs!"[14]

Not only does the Colonel Rebel Foundation demonstrate the contemporary function of Blind Jim as a flattened and possibly adapted and defended image, but it also demonstrates the broader, present-day investments in confederate rhetoric, as well as that rhetoric's continuing power to motivate southerners to action. On the foundation's website and social media feeds, this "conservation" group has emphasized David Sansing's speculation that Blind Jim's mustache, face, hat, and suit served as the visual inspiration for Colonel Rebel, the cartoon and costumed mascot. The foundation seems to value the notion of a connection between Blind Jim and Colonel Reb because it provides a defense to the criticism that its beloved mascot is racist for his appearance as a wealthy Old South plantation owner and enslaver. If Colonel Reb's image was partially based on a Black man, how could Colonel Reb invoke racism? While this is obviously a weak argument by any objective measure, it has been a powerful and effective argument within the UM community nonetheless.

As an organization, the Colonel Rebel Foundation has been quite successful in arguing its case, furthering its cause, and garnering support. In fact, as a coalition designed around the defense of words and symbols, the foundation merits further study. It remains active more than fifteen years since its founding and has outlived the chancellor it was formed to persuade and the replacement mascot (a black bear) it argued so vehemently against. At present, its focus has shifted to attacking the new mascot, Tony the Landshark, a substitution that members of the foundation seem to hate as much (or more) than the black bear. In August 2018 the official Colonel Rebel Foundation Twitter account retweeted sports journalist Clay Travis, who wrote, above an unmanipulated photo of the new landshark mascot, "What the fuck, Ole Miss? Landshark Tony?! You killed Colonel Rebel for this? Shameful." The tweet received 3,800 likes and 541 retweets within less than a month.[15]

There are potential lessons for the modern UM community in the story of James Ivy, lessons about the ways in which an all-white majority regards and confines African Americans, about the terms of white approval and acceptance, about the myopia of turning human beings into mascots. Unfortunately, these lessons are not yet readily available to most within the modern UM community. Returning to Blommaert's idea of synchronization, the image of Blind Jim has been taken up only by those insiders—like the Colonel Rebel

Foundation—who wish to synchronize the present with the past, who wish to promote continuity and stasis. Thus, Blind Jim as confederate rhetoric lives on within the popular imagination only in his reduced form, while James Ivy as human being remains mostly overlooked and neglected. And so Blind Jim is being used not to stir reflection or debate about race at UM but as promotional evidence that the Colonel Rebel mascot is neither racist nor problematic. In other words, Blind Jim is still being used by a white majority to promote Old South ideologies and racial inequalities.

The Tradition of the Confederate Battle Flag

Within southern institutions like the University of Mississippi, confederate rhetoric still maintains the power to motivate and unite a significant segment of white stakeholders, to garner tweets and retweets, Instagram likes, and Facebook comments, and to create and coalesce emotional and rhetorical energy. This dynamic is likely true at every southern university. And, perhaps for these same reasons, confederate rhetoric has been—and continues to be—attractive to athletic programs seeking to energize and unite fans to buy tickets and T-shirts and make donations. Indeed, for most of the twentieth century, the football program at UM has embraced and amplified Old South words and symbols. Beginning around 1948, the Confederate flag was central to school spirit at football games. Thousands of small Confederate flags were purchased using UM funds and then distributed by cheerleaders before every kickoff. In addition to these small, individual flags, the "Pride of the South" marching band would unfurl the world's largest Confederate flag during its halftime shows. School beauties posed with Confederate flags and presented them to campus guests as mementos. Throughout the 1950s, 1960s, 1970s, and 1980s, the Confederate battle flag was the most prominent symbol of UM athletics. And, in turn, UM athletics was one of the most prominent national promotors of the flag. Just before the Meredith riot in 1962, for example, *Sports Illustrated* featured UM cheerleaders both wearing Confederate flag uniforms and flying Confederate flags on the cover of its "College Football" issue.[16]

Not surprisingly, as the school made steady progress on issues of race, the ubiquity of the rebel flag became a growing concern for progressives. The story of that symbol's slow retirement at UM has been told from various angles by previous scholars, including Charles Eagles and John Coski. After a decades-long and recursive debate, the Confederate flag was finally banned from the football stadium by Chancellor Robert Khayat in the late 1990s. In his own book, *The Education of a Lifetime*, Khayat detailed the firestorm created by his 1997 decision to review the university's relationship to the Confederate flag and other symbols associated with the Old South. As Khayat said to the campus newspaper at the time, "For way too long, the public perception, and sometimes our internal perception, has been inaccurate and too heavily influenced by negative events of our past. We need to get rid of negative perceptions. They impede our mission and our destiny." When the news story from the campus paper was picked up and spread by the Associated Press, Chancellor Khayat and his staff were inundated with angry letters and calls. Khayat remembered that the UM campus became "a flashpoint for radicals on the far right, liberals on the far left, and every point in between."[17] He realized that the Confederate flag and the University of Mississippi remained nearly synonymous in the minds of most insiders and outsiders.

Khayat proved to be a brave and progressive leader, a man who combined vision and charm, and the story of his struggle to manage symbolic progress at UM is fascinating. As he said in his memoir, he soon realized that "blind devotion to Confederate symbols ran deeper" than he had ever imagined. His decision to review the image of the university—and to include Confederate symbols in that review—triggered a deluge of protest letters from around the country and from within Mississippi. "Letters from friends, classmates, former teachers, and coaches pleaded with me to stop erasing symbols that held deep meaning for them and the school they loved," remembered Khayat. He faced the criticism not with anger or offense, but with understanding and civility. As a native Mississippian who loved the University of Mississippi, Khayat undertook this struggle as an insider, a member of the old guard with academic credibility, as a law professor, and athletic credibility, as a former UM football standout. Khayat's personal network of friends and allies was broad. He knew many of the letter writers personally, and he knew that most of them were not violent racists. Instead, they were people whose identities had been formed and contained by a system they themselves did not fully understand. As Khayat later reflected, "Those of us who grew up in the white South, and particularly Mississippi, were so accustomed to Old South songs and sights and symbols during sporting events that the origins of the emblems weren't carefully considered. Nor was the pain they caused others."[18]

Khayat himself was white and the product of a segregated Mississippi and of the University of Mississippi of the 1950s and 1960s. As chancellor, Khayat decided to focus his reform efforts on one Confederate symbol in one particular context: the rebel flag at the football stadium. Khayat's well-known strategy of banning sticks rather than flags from the stadium worked brilliantly. His thinly veiled prevarication was to invoke safety concerns over sticks and poles, rather than to outwardly declare a ban on the flags themselves, which Khayat knew could be reasonably challenged as unconstitutional. Fans got the point, and the football stadium seemed to transform nearly overnight. The sea of rebel flags disappeared. This episode is detailed in Khayat's memoir and adeptly summarized in John Coski's seminal study of the Confederate flag. Two details about this struggle to end an entrenched tradition of confederate rhetoric are most important for the purposes of the present discussion.

Khayat was successful in achieving this major step forward not because UM football fans were unable to find a way around the stick ban. They could have bypassed the ban by bringing in flags without sticks or by wearing rebel flag hats, scarves, and so on. Some of this type of symbolic resistance did occur, but not on a large scale. UM fans were not outsmarted by Khayat. They were not tricked. Instead, they were persuaded. Khayat made an argument to the UM faithful, and they conceded that argument. The argument was for reform in one particular context, the football stadium. The articulated motivation behind the ban leveraged two key desires shared by nearly every UM stakeholder: the desire to overcome a nagging, negative national reputation and the desire to win football games. Khayat's success with the stick ban should also be understood as a culmination of several previous and unsuccessful university-sanctioned attempts to eliminate the rebel flag from the stadium.

The University of Mississippi of the 1990s had a problematic reputation, having received negative coverage for its handling of issues related to race from numerous national outlets. As Khayat has detailed in his book, the football coaches were having trouble convincing Black athletes to attend UM. Meanwhile, other SEC football programs successfully portrayed UM as a hotbed for racism and as a dangerous place for Black recruits. As Tommy Tuberville, the head football coach, said to Chancellor Khayat after a disappointing season in 1996, "We can't recruit against the Confederate flag." It was a stark and desperate conclusion that Tuberville had already been declaring to the UM fan base. A few months before, in fact, Tuberville had released a statement aimed directly at students and published in the campus newspaper. It was relayed by the Associated Press and thereafter published in many newspapers around Mississippi and the South under the lede "Ole Miss head football coach Tommy Tuberville has a message for the school's football fans: Rebel flags are not welcome." Citing an increase in the number of flags on display in the Grove and in the stadium, Tuberville pointedly asked fans to leave the flags at home for the upcoming game against Vanderbilt, which was scheduled to be televised nationally. "I was hired to win football games," said Tuberville in an interview, "and other schools are using the Rebel flag against us in recruiting black athletes." Students and alumni responded defiantly to Tuberville's open challenge of their tradition. They appeared at the Vanderbilt game with more flags than ever before. After that game, when the UM team traveled to Knoxville to play the University of Tennessee, the Knoxville chapter of the Sons of Confederate Veterans passed out eight hundred Confederate flags to UT and UM fans alike; it was a show of white solidarity and intercampus support between two rivals.[19]

If Tuberville's pleas backfired in the short term, Tuberville had at the very least opened the argument about the Confederate flag as a hindrance to recruiting. As he built some credibility through victories on the football field, ending the 1997 season at 8–4, winning a minor bowl game, and being named the SEC Coach of the Year, Tuberville also began to win over more of the fans, many of whom were ready to reconsider his logic in relation to the flag. Chancellor Khayat, a skilled rhetorician and a trained lawyer, proposed the stick ban at this very moment. He did so with a straight face, giving the university a legally sound avenue for banning the flag and giving the UM faithful an avenue toward respectable surrender of their beloved tradition. As Coski noted, "Few flags have appeared at Ole Miss football games in the years since."[20]

The second detail often overlooked about this struggle—but a highly important detail for the present study—is that Khayat was successful in removing the Confederate flag from the UM football stadium, in part, because he did not actually remove the flag, at least not entirely. Years earlier, the university had introduced an official alternative, known as the "Battle M" flag, what Coski has called "essentially the Confederate battle flag but with a star-studded blue M replacing the St. Andrew's cross."[21] The "Battle M" flag was not widely adopted and did not, at the time of its introduction, win over many white students or fans, but it did garner support from the Black Student Union and the faculty senate. Although Confederate flags consistently outnumbered the "Battle M" flag during the 1990s, it was present as an odd marker of both continuity and progress. After the "Battle M" flag, another version appeared on the scene of UM football games. This one, too, shared a visual lineage with the Confederate flag. In the newest version, the "Battle M" became the words "Ole Miss" in nostalgic cursive script. The color scheme of red and blue was preserved. Even as the Confederate flag diminished in visibility at football games, its close relatives remained prominent, and the words "Ole Miss" surged in importance, replacing the stars and bars and the "Battle M" on the flags flown in the stands and on the field. This evolution happened visibly and materially on the flags themselves.

These flags, taken together, are another example of what Laurie Gries has termed a "single multiple image." As Gries has shown through her analysis of the Obama Hope image and its many iterations, an iconic visual image can break apart and reassemble, leaving some parts of its design behind while carrying other parts forward. When this happens, a single multiple image is formed, which "actualizes" in new ways, gaining rhetorical power for its new associations and complexities. If Gries's insights are applied to the present case, the single multiple image of the Confederate/"Battle M"/"Ole Miss" flag becomes "an active and lively mediator that not only experiences but also produces rhetorical transformation."[22] The continuum of flags at UM football games allowed Khayat to ban the Confederate flag while simultaneously preserving the tradition and memory of that flag. The original image was transformed, but it remained alive and accessible to the white campus community (fig. 19).

The single multiple image of the flags at UM and the surrounding, fierce public debate, which framed the transformation as an elimination, reveals much about the extant conflicts and divergences within the UM community and about the oftentimes superficial goals of external audiences. When Khayat and his leadership team buried (or evolved) the Confederate flag in the context of football, transforming it into the "Ole Miss" flag that still flies today, they certainly improved the university's external image. To outsiders, this shift appeared to be a straightforward and unqualified victory. The stadium had been awash with Confederate flags, and then suddenly it was not. On the other hand, from the perspective of insiders at UM who were Confederate flag supporters, this moment had been preceded by many preparatory signals. The "Battle M" flag had been introduced alongside the Confederate flag. The

FIGURE 19. Top results from a Google Image search of the words "Ole Miss football flag" on March 5, 2020. Although no official linkage between the Confederate battle flag and the "Ole Miss" flag has been acknowledged, the succession of flags, including the "Battle M" flag, and the visual consistency and practices of usage make the connection clear. (Screenshot by the author.)

coaches had asked fans publicly to adapt their traditions in order to benefit recruiting. The chancellor had given them a way to save face. Most importantly of all, the Confederate flag on the field, presented with music and fanfare for decades, was transformed (synchronized) into the "Ole Miss" flag of the present. It was still presented in the same way and in the same context and in the same colors. In fact, from the stands, if one squinted, one could imagine quite easily that the new flag was the old.

This analysis is not to downplay the progress or to de-emphasize the furor, divisiveness, and potential violence that Khayat and his administration navigated so skillfully. That fury was real and would emerge again, in stronger and more organized forms, when the next chancellor, Dan Jones, attacked the song "Dixie," also a game day tradition, one that had long complemented the presentation of the Confederate flag. It is the same fury that forced Jones to defend the term "Ole Miss" in the video analyzed in chapter 4. And it is the same fury that will surely emerge again at the University of Mississippi, when some future chancellor dares to challenge the name "Rebels," the colors red and blue, the modified version of "Dixie" still played on game day by the band, the rebel flags still flying unofficially in the Grove, or (apocalyptically perhaps for this community) the name "Ole Miss" itself. Within communities like the one at UM, southerners who have invested so much in confederate rhetoric—whose very identities have emerged, in part, through these Old South words and symbols—will no doubt be ready to engage in rhetorical conflict again, whenever their remaining rhetorical traditions are threatened.

Confederate Rhetoric in High Schools

While the focus of this book is the presence and power of confederate rhetoric in southern universities, it should be noted that confederate rhetoric has also been active in other educational institutions, including many high schools across the South (and beyond). In Mississippi, for example, Carroll Academy has long used the Colonel Rebel mascot, the nickname "Rebels," and the Confederate flag emblem as their official symbols of school spirit. Like other segregation academies in Mississippi, Carroll Academy received support and assistance from the White Citizens' Council, a now infamous group formed by "respectable" southern white supremacists to resist racial integration. In some ways, schools like Carroll Academy became outlets for the council's propaganda and publicity. Even after the demise of the White Citizens' Council, its successor organization, the Council of Conservative Citizens, championed all-white schools like Carroll Academy. For example, a photo spread of Carroll Academy students is featured in the pages of the council's regional publication, the *Citizens Informer*, from July 1975. Student award winners are pictured, some in front of a large Colonel Rebel drapery. The accompanying story applauds the local chapter of the council, which "recently presented [the] white private Carroll Academy . . . with a check for $2,500 to be applied to the gymnasium fund. . . . The money was raised at a barbeque and political rally at the academy in May sponsored by the Council. Over a thousand persons attended. Music was provided by the Christian Crusaders." In this example, elementary, middle, and high school students were being celebrated and affirmed within a sea of confederate rhetoric. Words and symbols associated with the Old South became naturalizing elements completely intertwined with more common educational milestones like athletic recognition, citizenship awards, and communal fundraising events. And this intertwining did not end in the 1970s. Even in 2018, Carroll Academy continued to embrace the old Colonel Rebel mascot and the nickname "Rebels."[23]

Beyond Mississippi, many other high schools around the South have used confederate rhetoric to define themselves, unify their white student populations, and strengthen their school spirit. In Chattanooga, Tennessee, the Brainerd High School "Rebels" also adopted the Confederate flag emblem, the song "Dixie," and other Old South words and symbols. By the late 1960s, these prominent displays were creating tensions between Brainerd High School and neighboring schools like Alton Park, which predominately served Black students. As Brainerd High itself integrated, the Old South words and symbols that had once unified an all-white student body began to create serious internal tensions. By 1969, Black students at Brainerd High were walking out of pep rallies "to protest the use of the Confederate flag and the song 'Dixie' as school symbols." At a football game that same year, Black students raised their fists to protest the symbols and then marched together from the stands to the field to ceremoniously burn a Confederate flag. School officials and police intervened. Over the coming months, the conflict between students escalated and spilled out into the broader community. On one school day in October, 400 white students staged a walkout in defense of the Confederate flag and the song "Dixie." Later, white students, parents, and community members formed a long caravan of some 100 to 150 cars, "a cavalcade of cars with individuals waving and otherwise displaying Confederate flags" on a long and loud drive through the city. Such protests and counterprotests continued throughout early October. In one incident, "a group of white Brainerd students and others held an impromptu pep rally at the Eastgate Shopping Center during the night . . . where they repeatedly sang the song 'Dixie' and hanged Dr. Lawrie [an administrator] in effigy. A small motorcade of flag waving students and others passed McCallie Avenue during this night shortly before 11 p.m. Several negro youths in the Burger Chef ran out and began throwing rocks and bottles at passing cars." In a detailed account of this period, historian John Coski noted that the entire city of Chattanooga seemed entangled and transfixed by the conflict begun at Brainerd. At one point in the fall, Chattanooga officials imposed a citywide curfew that lasted five nights.[24]

In and around Brainerd High School, there were periodic clashes and eruptions of violence over the next months. By April 1970, Brainerd was ordered to be closed. Students were promptly dismissed in the middle of an afternoon. They spilled out of the school doors and formed two large groups, dividing themselves along racial lines and jeering at each other. The white students joined together to chant a form of the "Hey-Hey, Ho-Ho" athletic cheer, changing the final words to "blacks gotta go, hey, blacks gotta go."[25] This story of conflict, one ignited and fueled by confederate rhetoric, is long, winding, interesting, and deserving of further study. For now, the example proves that confederate rhetoric has been destructively active within high schools beyond Mississippi.

There are many other examples from around the US South. In Virginia, there is Robert E. Lee High School in Fairfax County, one of many high schools named in honor of the famous Confederate general. Not surprisingly these "Lee" schools often embrace Confederate imagery. Lee High School in Baytown, Texas, for example, may be known as the home of the "Ganders," but the Confederate battle flag was long featured at football games and made regular appearances in the pages of the school yearbook. A cursory review of the 1973 annual revealed more than fifteen images of the Confederate flag, including a photo from the band's halftime show, when the marching students would form a human Confederate flag some eighty yards wide. In Park Hills, Missouri, there is Central High School, home of the "Rebels" located on Rebel Drive and featuring in 2019 a Colonel Rebel mascot on the header of the homepage. In Georgia, Effingham County High School declares itself to be "Rebel Country" where "the tradition lives on." As late as 2008, students displayed Confederate flags at Effingham football games and "lynched" models of opposing mascots. In Alabama, there is Vestavia Hills High School, home of the "Rebels," whose motto in 2019 was "Once a Rebel. Always a Rebel."[26]

These and many other examples have dotted the landscape of the US South, influencing communal identities, reifying racial divisions, and inflicting steady reminders of Old South hierarchies on African American people. Oftentimes, this localized confederate rhetoric has lived for decades without being challenged, thriving within nearly all-white spaces or institutions. Along the way, such words and symbols have sometimes been retired or de-emphasized by white leaders. Coski cited some of these stories in his book-length study of the Confederate flag, noting that "statistical evidence substantiates the decline of Rebel team names and symbols" at southern high schools beginning around the time of forced integration.[27] But, as a rhetorician, I suspect that most retirements and revisions of confederate rhetoric do not come naturally or easily. I suspect that most have been prompted by some kind of localized conflict or argument, even if most of those conflicts have not been nearly as public as the long and violent episodes at Brainerd High School or as the well-documented debates and brouhahas at the University of Mississippi.

Sometimes, a national tragedy has triggered a wave of changes. Negative press around Confederate symbols surged in 2015, after Dylan Roof committed mass murder in Charleston in the name of white supremacy. The sheer horror of the crime and Roof's undeniable motives seemed to shock some high school communities into partially reappraising their long-standing Old South symbols. Vestavia Hills, for example, was publicly castigated by comedian John Oliver one month after Roof's crime. On his national broadcast, Oliver highlighted Vestavia Hills' use of the Confederate battle flag and the "Rebel Man" mascot. "Your logo is a plantation owner," mocked Oliver. This negative attention reinforced nascent local opposition, especially from the more diverse communities of nearby Birmingham. Administrators from Vestavia Hills responded by undertaking a "rebranding" campaign. The old Confederate colonel mascot was retired, but other confederate rhetoric was reemphasized, including the motto "Once a Rebel. Always a Rebel."[28]

It is not surprising that confederate rhetoric is deeply rooted in high schools across the South, but Old South words and symbols have also taken hold in high schools in other parts of North America. At least five high schools in Iowa were using the nickname "Rebels" in 2015. In Kirkland, Washington, Juanita High School continues to embrace the "Rebels" nickname, although administrators there did discontinue using a version of the Confederate battle flag for the school crest in 1990. In Anaheim, California, the "Rebels" of Savanna High School used the Confederate flag to cheer on their football players well into the 1990s. A tall "Johnny Reb" statue stood prominently on Savanna's urban campus until 2009. And, in Canada, the Georgetown High School "Rebels" used Confederate flags on merchandise and equipment until at least 1989. Even later, student athletes and award winners routinely posed with Confederate flags for yearbook photographs.[29]

That confederate rhetoric can be found outside the US South demonstrates the fallacy of considering the South wholly different from the rest of America. James C. Cobb, W. J. Cash, and others have long since complicated any facile binary that places the South on one side and the North on the other. As Cobb has documented, history is full of moments when the South proved it was no better than the North and when the North proved it was no better than the South.[30] Perhaps the emergence and persistence of confederate rhetoric across North America is simply more evidence for the commonality of racism within all our communities. But, as I have shown throughout this book, confederate rhetoric is not merely a symptom. It is not merely an inert and harmless relic of the past. It performs cultural work and prosecutes harm as long as it is present. Perhaps confederate rhetoric has been a southern export, and has found markets beyond the South, precisely because it can unite white communities and communicate enmity to others, serve as a very effective tool in the promotion and preservation of racial dominance, keep people divided along racial lines, and promote and preserve systems of inequality and dominance. Finding confederate rhetoric in many local communities—in the US South and beyond—is a reminder that the problem of confederate rhetoric is widespread and enduring.

Conclusion

For any community, there are often vast differences between public history and public relations. Historical progress requires a full accounting of the truth, transparency, and reflection. Marketing victories, on the other hand, can often be achieved through partial honesty, as some marketing techniques frequently rely on prevarication and dismissiveness. In this chapter, I explored two rhetorical traditions at the University of Mississippi. Neither the legacy of Blind Jim nor the legacy of the Confederate flag has yet been fully considered by the university community. Instead, both traditions have been altered without being eliminated or reconciled. Both have been swept under the rug, preserved as active memories and as accessible ideological symbols. This type of synchronization is a way to preserve problematic traditions, and it has occurred at many southern universities. Traditions of confederate rhetoric, like the displaying of the Confederate flag in athletic contexts, have not been problems confined to the University of Mississippi.

At other southern schools, from the majority (white) perspective, there are now—and always have been—frequent calls to let bygones be bygones, to forget about racial divisions, to move on. For example, consider the comments section of Saturday Down South, a website devoted to SEC football. In 2015, ESPN published a story about the ongoing presence of Confederate flags at SEC football tailgates and games. The article included the perspectives of white and Black SEC coaches and players who openly criticized the flag. In response, many of the reader comments reflected the sentiments "move on" or "get over it." One self-identified Auburn fan under the username cdh72469 put it this way: "For over 30 years my family has given to Auburn University, purchased season tickets, invested money, time, emotion and energy into following Auburn on Saturdays to watch mostly young African-American men represent our Alma mater on the football field and the color of their skin never enters our minds. They're all wearing the AU on the helmet and the navy and orange. They are Auburn football players . . . period. I am sure most supporters of other schools here feel the same way." The commenter was arguing in defense of the rebel flag, suggesting more broadly that any discussions or stories about race are fictions manufactured by what he earlier labeled "the progressive media." Notably, cdh72469 did not directly engage the comments of the players and coaches, which highlighted experiences and feelings that contradicted his own (seemingly white) narrative of unity and color blindness. This type of deflection or avoidance was a common trend in this comment section. SCBAMA, a self-identified Alabama fan, was more pointed and direct: "You can ask any black and most of [them] will bring up racism, the flag has nothing to do with race, get over it and let it go!"[31] Accepting such calls today would mean accepting extant confederate rhetoric as a harmless and quaint tradition. That is, it would mean abandoning uncomfortable analysis of the kind undertaken by this book and blindly promoting university traditions without attempting to shape or question them. Is that the right approach? Has enough progress been made on issues of race to stop pursuing racial progress? Has some postracial utopia been achieved? Of course not. White people in the South (and in America) do have the power, oftentimes, to enforce a false synchronization, to avoid confrontations with words and symbols that divide people along racial lines. But they should not use that power. To do so would be to overlook the reality of Black life in the modern US South and to actively ignore minority voices.

For leaders of southern universities, confederate rhetoric presents both a tool for synchronization and a barrier to genuine reconciliation and progress. Because fundamental aspects of school pride have been built on confederate rhetoric—because communal identities at places like the University of Mississippi have emerged from and been strengthened by Old South words and symbols—it remains tempting to use confederate rhetoric to unite and unify a majority of stakeholders. This strategy would be effective in many cases, as it was in the case of the Jones video analyzed in the previous chapter. Confederate rhetoric can inspire and unite some significant part of these southern communities. The problem, of course, is that synchronization, however tempting for leaders, stands in direct opposition to some of the most fundamental aspects of a university's mission and responsibility: open inquiry, critical thinking, and a willingness (even zeal) to interrogate orthodox histories and viewpoints. The other problem, of course, is that synchronization reifies inequities and historical injustices that modern universities publicly oppose and purposefully seek to rectify. Rather than providing voice and agency to minorities, "synchronization elides all kinds of possible voices"; it creates undemocratic absences.[32] It silences. Allowing confederate rhetoric to live on in peace allows it to prosecute its cultural work in the present and to survive into the future.

Any honest process of reconciliation requires pain and persistence. It requires not defensiveness or elision but honest and open reflection on difficult realities of the past, especially when those realities have heretofore gone unacknowledged or unexamined. Leaders and others in positions of power within southern universities should consider embracing this process when faced with public relations crises—and even and perhaps especially when no crisis is present. Rather than promulgate a falsely synchronized past and present, those in positions of power should fully engage with the complicated, unsynchronized versions of their institutions' histories. They should view moments of alumni outrage over threatened confederate rhetoric not as disturbances to be quieted but as opportunities for fresh identity formation and learning. If words and symbols can emerge and reify divisive identities related to the Old South, they can also emerge and reify unifying identities related to the future South.

What might such proactive rhetorical strategies look like? I explore this question in more detail later in this book. For now, let me highlight an ongoing process of contextualization at the University of Mississippi. In 2018, new plaques were collaboratively written and installed in front of buildings and spaces with problematic names or histories. This was a communal project of public history, one that sought not to quell an unexpected controversy or acute crisis but to calmly and deliberately confront and learn from a painful past.[33] Such efforts seem constructive and encouraging, and they could, if multiplied many times over, form the foundation for a new southern rhetoric, one that substitutes forthrightness for nostalgia. It might take time, of course, but the contextualization plaques of today are the communal memories of tomorrow, and they will undoubtedly give future UM stakeholders new options for forming and reforming identities better and more inclusive than those of the present. Indeed, at the University of Mississippi and at other southern universities, there are many opportunities for this kind of healthy redress because there are many instances of confederate rhetoric that have been hidden away or de-emphasized but that remain active parts of the communal consciousness. These historical elisions are waiting on a new kind of audience, waiting as deeper opportunities for reconciliation and learning.

CHAPTER 6

Origins and Repercussions

The Continuum of Confederate Rhetoric

> Rather than treat contested memory as an element of history that becomes salient only at moments of crisis or dislocation, we instead should acknowledge it as a central and enduring feature of the history that shapes daily lived experience.
>
> W. FITZHUGH BRUNDAGE, *THE SOUTHERN PAST*

AT PREDOMINANTLY WHITE UNIVERSITIES ACROSS the US South, yearbooks have long been vehicles for the promotion and reification of Old South values. As communal exercises in public memory, yearbooks compile and display the edited testimonies of young, educated people. These publications are more granular than generational, providing yearly windows into the progress or stasis of cultural attitudes and trends of all kinds. If one were interested in the history of fashion in the US South, for example, the yearbooks of the region would provide mountains of sartorial data. Likewise, for my current interest—the influence of Old South words and symbols—the same yearbooks provide mountains of rhetorical data. Although they have sometimes been viewed as lighthearted publications not worthy of serious study, school yearbooks are, in fact, rhetorical rituals of self-identification and memorialization. They are communal self-portraits painted year after year and archived faithfully by local librarians. In other words, yearbooks merit serious attention from scholars of rhetoric. They are rich and accessible primary sources.

Taken together in chronological order, the yearbooks of any particular school unfold like an instructive continuum, revealing insights into that school's ideational and emotional identity. In chapter 1, I used the yearbook *Ole Miss* to trace the birth and growth of a particularly consequential piece of confederate rhetoric: the term "Ole Miss" itself. While yearbooks may have something to say about individuals (usually immature individuals), they deliver much more reliable information about institutions, communities, states, and regions. They are showcases of culture: vehicles for the preservation and transmission of tradition, contemporary snapshots of a particular and fleeting present, and purposeful projections into the future.

Having spent several years looking at yearbooks from universities across the US South, I was not at all surprised by the images that surfaced from Virginia yearbooks in 2019. In his medical school yearbook from 1984, Governor Ralph Northam was one of two men pictured in blackface or Ku Klux Klan regalia. (Northam admitted being in the photo but did not remember or disclose which racist costume he had worn.) The resulting firestorm and complicated reckoning nearly cost Governor Northam his job and brought turmoil to Virginia politics.[1] None of this was surprising to me, because people who acquire power in the US South usually do so after attending universities and graduate schools in the region, and confederate rhetoric has long been a staple of yearbooks from those schools. Thus, some powerful people like Northam inevitably will be found in disturbing images or will be found to have written or edited yearbook content with racist overtones. Confederate rhetoric in southern yearbooks is not the surprising exception; it is the predictable rule.

In the wake of the Northam scandal, journalists across the region began scouring university yearbooks for offensive images. They found many. Other powerful people were caught up in similar scandals. At Wake Forest University, Martha Allman, the dean of admissions, was one of those people. Before she was a staff member at Wake Forest, she was a student, and in the 1982 Wake Forest yearbook, she was one of many students pictured in front of a large Confederate flag. When this photo resurfaced in 2019, Allman faced her own firestorm and nearly lost her job.[2] Such scandals will likely proliferate, and public outrage will probably continue to focus on prominent individuals featured in offensive photographs or otherwise connected to examples of confederate rhetoric.

Focusing on individuals, however tempting and understandable, is also a misleading enterprise, an oversimplification that plays well on social media but that does not necessarily further public discourse around issues of race. Photographs such as the ones that captured Northam and Allman are not unusual. My argument here is not that such individuals should not face consequences for their actions but that such individuals should not be scapegoated.[3] Scapegoating these individuals overlooks a deep cultural and societal flaw within the US South and mistakes examples of confederate rhetoric in yearbooks as youthful indiscretions, as individual or isolated errors in judgement. Instead, confederate rhetoric is an ingrained part of the yearbook genre in this region; representations of blackface, Klansmen, or Confederate flags are as expected and predictable as photos of students lounging on the grass or photos of the football team in action. Throughout my research for this book, I have found university yearbooks to be rich and disturbing sources of confederate rhetoric. Take, for example, the front and back cover of the 1953 *Ole Miss* annual depicted in figure 20.

To be alarmed or surprised that individual members of such communities posed with Confederate flags or dressed in blackface is to ignore (or in some cases deny) the depth and breadth of the problem. Most predominantly white colleges and universities within the South have long been communities of confederate rhetoric. As institutions, they have shaped and influenced generations of white students. What their yearbooks reveal is just how deeply and longitudinally antagonistic these environments have been toward minorities and just how commonsensical and common racist symbols and words have

FIGURE 20. Front and back covers of the 1953 University of Mississippi yearbook. Everything contained within this yearbook could be considered confederate rhetoric given the boldness of this encompassing image. Throughout the South, the Confederate flag and other Old South words and symbols have long been ubiquitous elements of school yearbooks. Such confederate rhetoric is not exceptional but instead commonplace. (University of Mississippi, *Ole Miss, 1953*. Special Collections, University of Mississippi Libraries.)

been over the decades. Northam and Allman were not intruders but insiders in their yearbooks. They were not sources of discordant messages of hate and exclusion but were, instead, conveyors of conformist messages. Their messages were accredited and published by larger groups. When the photographs were taken, Northam and Allman were not caught in a subversive or unconventional act. They were, instead, creating memories of conventional, mainstream college experiences. They were displaying their whiteness in encouraged and orthodox forms. Southern society may still have an individual problem, but southern society has, more urgently, many institutional problems. And the problems have existed—confederate rhetoric has flourished—during every decade since Reconstruction. Looking back from the 1980s to the 1950s to the 1920s to the 1890s, one can see that confederate rhetoric in southern yearbooks has been normal and ubiquitous.

When the Defeated Remain in Power and When They Witness

In *Commonplace Witnessing*, Bradford Vivian calls on scholars to "dramatically expand and diversify our normative assumptions about the particular types of historical subjects who bear witness." For Vivian, the act of witnessing "encompasses a public rhetoric composed of doxastic expressions, available means of persuasion, and customary symbolic displays with which communities seek to understand, draw meaning from, and render judgment on the most pervasively remembered injustices and tragedies in Western modernity."[4] While Vivian is most interested in the expressions, arguments, and displays made by actual victims of historical injustice, particularly those victims who have not traditionally had audience or voice, his concept of witnessing also proves useful in understanding acts of witnessing by rhetors who perceive themselves as victims. In other words, even if and when witnesses have experienced only partial or incomplete victimhood or defeat, Vivian's concept of witnessing provides a tool for understanding their rhetorical impulses. I am thinking here of every white southerner of every generation who has identified at all with the sense of loss and defeat collected beneath the umbrella concept of the Lost Cause. They have retained power and privilege within their region, but they have still regarded themselves as victims of injustice and tragedy. This perception shades their rhetoric and their memories.

I am also thinking here of the white people in the nineteenth-century South who created the Lost Cause concept in the first place. Those few generations of white southerners had lost the Civil War (and their preferred social order) but then managed to quickly reassert agency and voice. After losing the Civil War and enduring the humiliation (for a time) of Reconstruction, white southerners embarked on a multidimensional effort to maintain power within the region, to reassert the preexisting social order, and to reaffirm their self-imagined racial dominance. As part of this effort, white southerners used the rhetorical process of witnessing (as described by Vivian). They did so through yearbooks and countless other avenues, deploying symbols, language, expressions, and means of persuasion of all kinds. While the white South failed to win the war, afterward it succeeded in dominating public rhetoric within the region. Historical conditions, such as the North's abandonment of the project of Reconstruction, created openings for white southerners to prosecute this rhetorical project, to witness on their own terms without much risk of being challenged or contradicted. The North occupied the South with troops for a short period after the war; it occupied the South with words and symbols for no time at all. In other words, the construction of confederate rhetoric—both during and after the historical era of Reconstruction—can be understood as the witnessing of white southerners who grappled with their own perceptions of victimhood and defeat for many generations.

Applying Vivian's concept of witnessing to white people in the US South illuminates the purposefulness and strategy involved in the sowing and propagation of confederate rhetoric by white southerners in positions of power. When Jubal Early, a leading southern voice, called in 1873 for his rebel compatriots to bear witness to "the grandeur of the sacrifices endured and of the deeds performed by a people who were fighting for their sacred rights, against such odds and difficulties as had never been encountered in any previous struggle," he was concerned explicitly with claiming autonomy over the historical narrative. "Are we willing that our enemies shall be the historians of our cause and our struggle?" asked Early. "No! a thousand times No!" Instead, Early urged his fellow (white) southerners to use language and symbols "to vindicate the honor and glory of our cause."[5] Early's was an influential and early call for a strategic, southern rhetoric.

Jubal Early had achieved fame during the war as a Confederate general, but he secured his place in history during the postbellum years as an outspoken advocate for the Lost Cause. As the first president of the Southern Historical Society, Early organized efforts to record the witnessing of Civil War battle accounts from a southern perspective and memorialize through the discipline of history the valor and supposed righteousness of the Confederacy. In fulfilling its mission, the Southern Historical Society "rekindled flames of Confederate patriotism by exhorting good southerners to contribute" documents and memories that could cement favorable views of the Confederacy within the historical record. Interested first and foremost in battlefield accounts and wartime documents, Early and his contemporaries were also suggesting a larger project of linguistic and symbolic memorialization. As Richard Starnes has written, the Southern Historical Society "dedicated itself to the creation of a Confederate historical memory" that was idealized in a variety of ways.[6] The organization sought to author and collect public memories of military battles and to canonize southern soldiers as valorous, but it was also interested in looking further back in time, in order to revise the terms and rationale of the original Confederate cause. The group was making an argument about its communal past.

Many historians consider Jubal Early the leading voice—the coordinating voice—of this Confederate rhetorical project. As Gary Gallagher has written, "Early understood almost immediately after Appomattox that there would be a struggle to control the public memory of the war, worked hard to help shape that memory, and ultimately enjoyed more success than he probably imagined possible." Early rallied southerners to take control of the historical narrative, to write and speak into the public record a blend of documentation and idealization. In this vision, there were many distortions and simplifications that became precedents. For example, Robert E. Lee became an admirable strategist to be revered, while Ulysses S. Grant became a dullard, a person victorious but uninspiring.[7]

At the same time that they were establishing imaginative parameters around the history of the Civil War, Early and other creators of the Lost Cause myth were also looking ahead, urging a new southern generation to wage broader rhetorical battles that could salvage many of the Confederacy's essential values and beliefs. Thus, their witnessing of the past revealed their aspirations for the future. As Stephen D. Lee wrote to the Sons of Confederate Veterans in 1899, "We will commit the vindication of the cause for which we fought. To your strength will be given the defense of the Confederate soldier's good name, the guardianship of his history, the emulation of his virtues, the perpetuation of those principles which he loved."[8] Perpetuation of principles was a clearly stated goal of such unrepentant Confederates.

Stephen D. Lee was one of many writers and orators within this communal project of witnessing on behalf of the Confederacy. If Early was the national leader of the movement, Lee was a regional advocate. He was the first president of Mississippi State University (then called Mississippi Agricultural and Mechanical College), serving from 1880 to 1899.[9] A heralded lieutenant general during the Civil War, he found solace and refuge in the academy after the war. While promoting a modern concern—agricultural science—Lee also promoted the backward and slanted pursuit of history by writing and supporting southern revisionist and apologist views as president of the Mississippi Historical Society.

Some of Lee's writings remain in print today, including his most influential essay entitled "The South since the War," which is, as scholars James W. Loewen and Edward H. Sebesta have pointed out, overwhelmingly preoccupied with glorifying and preserving the old racial order. In detailing "the negro problem," Stephen Lee attempted to counteract some of the supposed wrongs of "Yankee" Reconstruction, such as the enfranchisement of Black people in the South. Writing "to justify taking black citizenship away, [Lee] concocts a fantastic history of Reconstruction that blames African Americans for the inequalities they suffered." Lee wrote that "the great Negro problem . . . has been a running sore in this country . . . [a] vexed problem [that] has caused division, irritation, bitter political discussions, sectional animosities, and conflicting interests. . . . The negro since the war was still the irritating cause which kept the sections wide apart, and was responsible for the harsh reconstruction epoch." Later in the essay, Lee lamented that during Reconstruction "the negro . . . was made to face the white man in the great problem of competition, while his aspirations and instincts were entirely different from the stronger ruling race." Lee expanded on this paternalistic and racist theme: "I do not believe that any one can forecast the future of the negro. One thing is certain, when left to himself without the strong will and example of the white man in the black belts, he tends to retrograde." And Lee later asserted that "it was a wise provision also that the races are kept separate in the schools, in churches and in railroad cars. . . . It will be a long time, if ever, before the children of the two races will attend schools in common."[10]

Stephen D. Lee's essay, published in a popular 1899 collection, serves today as a concrete example of the strategic and purposeful witnessing undertaken by Confederate apologists during the years immediately following the Civil War and then Reconstruction. Their project was about more than simply documenting the heroics of Confederate soldiers. It was about justification, glorification, and race. After being defeated on the battlefield, Lee and others organized and led rhetorical battles, hoping to breathe new life into some of the Confederacy's most disturbing ideals. To a large extent, they were successful.

Such men often led the rhetorical fight from within southern universities and colleges, places where their legacies remain most active today. For example, Stephen D. Lee remains a heralded figure in Mississippi, best remembered as the long-serving first president of Mississippi State University. Indeed, at the center of that campus, without context or explanation, today stands a bronze bust of Lee, complete with a small Confederate flag lapel pin (fig. 21). As of 2019, this memorial has seemingly attracted very little controversy within the Mississippi State community. The bust, raised high on a pedestal, stands prominently in front of Lee Hall, named for Stephen D. Lee and used today as the university's main administration building. The statue's gaze is constant. Its only adornment is the aforementioned Confederate flag pin. Although there is no modern context provided for the statue, the original inscription remains: "Stephen Dill Lee, Lieutenant General CSA, First President, Agricultural and Mechanical College of Mississippi."

Figure 21. The bust of Stephen D. Lee positioned at the center of the Mississippi State University campus. The small pin on the left lapel shows a Confederate flag. (Photograph taken by the author in May 2019.)

This very public commemoration of a leading local voice of Lost Cause ideology is fairly typical around the South. Through such public displays, Confederate rhetoricians became confederate rhetoric themselves, memorialized in statuary, building names, town names, and so forth. Stephen D. Lee's statue stands guard more than a century after he and other elder "witnesses" organized their calls for the younger generations to learn, witness, and carry on the rhetorical fight for the Confederate cause. Students at the modern Mississippi State University may not read Lee's racist writings, but they are continually interacting with his visual representation: a glorifying marker of Old South words and symbols.

Stephen D. Lee was not the only unreconstructed Confederate issuing calls to witness from the perch of a university position. Many other members of the Southern Historical Society, for example, also held faculty or administrative positions at southern institutions. Daniel H. Hill, former Confederate general and publisher of *Land We Love*, a periodical instrumental in establishing the myth of the Lost Cause, served from 1877 to 1884 as the president of the University of Arkansas. John William Jones, editor of the *Southern Historical Society Papers*, held positions at Washington and Lee, the University of Virginia, and the University of North Carolina.[11] These intersections between southern higher education and purveyors of the myth of the Lost Cause should be scrutinized by scholars in a variety of fields. For the purposes of this study, it is enough to point out the connection and acknowledge that many of the men and women who were creating and catalyzing confederate rhetoric during the postbellum years—the white people who were organizing southern witnessing[12]—were doing so from within the gates of universities and colleges. In this regard, they were purposefully training, mentoring, and encouraging the next generation of white southerners.

My point here is not novel, but it is central to the arguments forwarded in this book. The broader project of deploying words and symbols to defend (to argue for) the righteousness and valor of the southern cause took strong root in southern universities during the decades following the Civil War. Men like Lee, Hill, and Jones found fertile rhetorical retreats in these institutions. Campuses across the South became greenhouses for the remnant seedlings of Old South values. Defeated "heroes" cultivated the southern cause at colleges and universities, embedding and archiving their ideals. In the decades following the Civil War, this process was purposeful, rhetorical, and highly effective. Chapter 1 detailed an extended example: the invention and flourishing of the term "Ole Miss" at the University of Mississippi. It was not until 1897 that this particular piece of confederate rhetoric was adopted and embedded within the campus culture, and it proved to be a highly influential and effective way to rebrand the university, to bind its identity to a historical but highly idealized and myopic notion of the Old South. At the same moment that the University of Mississippi was entering the twentieth century and attempting—in other ways—to grow beyond its provincial roots, it was anchoring itself to the traumas and defeats of its past: it was becoming "Ole Miss." This purposeful intertwining of a university identity with Old South imagery and values had profound and limiting cultural consequences—and those consequences continue to unfold into the present day.

Historians have shown us (through their careful and accumulated scholarship) that for men like Lee, Hill, and Jones this rhetorical cultivation was no accident. It was, instead, as strategic and coordinated as any military offensive. Many southern leaders in their generation wanted to use words, symbols, and monuments—rhetoric—to perpetuate Old South values. Some of their most enduring successes can be found at southern universities, where younger southerners responded enthusiastically to their elders' rhetorical calls to arms. These students and future southern leaders created enduring and stubbornly intractable confederate rhetoric. As every example in this book demonstrates, confederate rhetoric became a dynamic force within these institutions and beyond; it was not merely reflective of past culture but was, instead, generative of the region's present and future culture.

Long after every Confederate general had died, confederate rhetoric was active and formative within southern universities and colleges. By the 1950s, when universities in other regions of the country were opening their doors to African American students, institutions like the University of Alabama and the University of Mississippi continued to be defined by rebel flags, magnolias, and simplistic notions of race. These identity markers, which created boundaries of racial resistance, were not the silently held opinions or psychological postures of an intellectually passive generation. Instead, the white people who controlled these communities, generation after generation, actively reinscribed and often extended Old South words and symbols within their institutions. The result was an argumentative continuum formed and strengthened by ongoing investments in Old South words and symbols.

At the University of Mississippi, the primary case study in this book, that argumentative continuum is long and clear: Elma Meek's invention of the moniker "Ole Miss," the yearbook editors' repeated inclusion of Klan references over the decades, the cheerleaders' overwhelming deployment of Confederate battle flags, the football team's embrace of the mascot Colonel Reb, the fraternity and sorority system's various Old South parties, the students in the 1950s who produced blackface minstrel shows in the university's main performance hall, the burning of a Black fraternity house in the 1980s, the threatening late-night protest of white students after the reelection of Barack Obama, the overnight lynching of the James Meredith statue. These rhetorical episodes are not isolated moments along the timeline of this institution's history. They are, instead, typical moments along a continuum of confederate rhetoric. For more than a century now at UM, white students have used words and symbols to create and re-create an ethos that would have seemed familiar and comforting to Confederate heroes like Stephen D. Lee and Jubal Early. The confederate rhetoric circulating at UM during the twentieth and twenty-first centuries—the continuous witnessing of white southerners—would have likely made the unreconstructed rebels of the nineteenth century quite proud.

Here may lie one of the primary, daily mechanisms for the perpetuation of racism within the educated classes of the modernizing South. White learning or indoctrination often has not been something happening outside of the formal education process. Instead, it has been embedded within educational institutions. It has been rhetorical and experiential, and it has been unifying within individual generations and also across multiple generations. Think again of those white UM students who performed minstrel shows in 1950 and of the hundreds who laughed and applauded at those shows in Fulton Chapel, the campus's largest performance hall (see fig. 10). Those students were performing and enjoying nineteenth-century stereotypes. They were coming together and celebrating through laughter and applause racist tropes, fictions on which some portion of antebellum southern culture was built. At the same time, in other ways, the UM students of the 1950s were also modern, progressive Americans. Yearbooks from the era show modern scientific laboratories at the university, contemporary musical performances, and many other signals of broader cultural participation. These students were never completely isolated, naïve, or provincial. As historian Charles Eagles noted throughout his seminal study of the university, "Without causing any controversy, fraternities often hired African American musical groups for their parties and dances. In the 1950s the university also featured concerts by jazz musicians Lionel Hampton, Louis Armstrong, and Duke Ellington."[13] The wider world has always been available to students within the UM community, but narrower worldviews—narrower arguments about the nature of race—have consistently won the day. Confederate witnessing may have been merely one project among many others, but it was one of the most consistent and stabilizing projects across time. Confederate rhetoric held the majority of the UM community together even during eras of disruption and jarring cultural development. It was present at the university during the roaring twenties, the hippie sixties, the preppy eighties, and the hip-hop aughts.

A consistent thread of confederate rhetoric has survived within many universities—and within other types of institutions or nested communities—of the US South. Whereas the unabashed racism of the kind promoted by Stephen D. Lee has fallen out of favor and is no longer tolerated at Mississippi State, for example, Lee himself, as a traditional icon, remains an embedded and revered symbol at the school, where his statue still stands, where the main administration building is still named in his honor, and where Stephen D. Lee Scholars are recognized for having perfect GPAs upon graduation.[14] In Vivian's terms, the witness remains prominent and revered, even though the unseemly details of the witnessing may now be overlooked or de-emphasized. Stephen D. Lee, who promulgated confederate rhetoric while alive, continues to thrive long after death, serving now as confederate rhetoric himself.

As I mentioned in the introduction to this book and in various chapters, such confederate rhetoric often hides in plain sight, which is an important dimension of its power. At Mississippi State, Stephen D. Lee has not yet been rehabilitated, reconciled, or transformed. Instead, the darker aspects of his legacy have merely been de-emphasized or elided. When asked about the Lee statue in 2017, following the events of Charlottesville, Mark Keenum, president of Mississippi State, wrote, "With respect to Stephen D. Lee, I will say that his bust on the Drill Field is a reminder of the work that Mississippi State's first president did to build a new institution that looks to the future and not to the past. It's important to remember that President Lee was a leader of reconciliation efforts after the Civil War."[15] While Mark Keenum is a talented leader and administrator, his presentation of history here is incomplete and misleading. It is myopic at best and whitewashing at worst. Only from the comfort of the white majority could someone imply that Lee was an advocate for reconciliation, at least in the modern sense of that word. Like the term "Ole Miss" at the University of Mississippi, Lee the icon contains problematic complexities worthy of analysis and attention. But the leaders at Mississippi State have not yet begun to undertake that difficult work. In 2019, Lee remains as an Old South witness, carrying forward latent ideologies and bigotries forged in the fires of Reconstruction. Lee's racist and argumentative essays may no longer be on reading lists, but his views (his witnessing) remain accessible through his prominent image and name. He is central, orthodox, and largely unquestioned. Transformed into confederate rhetoric, Lee the revered icon continues to communicate a legacy of white supremacy and a nostalgia for the Lost Cause.

THE PERSONAL INTERACTION AS POTENTIALLY REDEMPTIVE

White men like Jubal Early and Stephen D. Lee—and white women like Elma Meek at UM—enjoyed success within the confines of southern universities, where their project of persuasion and memorialization has been carried on by generations of educated white people. By design, confederate rhetoric has been one tool of this success. It is confederate rhetoric that has carried the seeds of racialized conflict across time, propagating old and pernicious orthodoxies in generation after generation of white southerners. This process has had negative consequences on a regional scale, but the process itself has occurred on the personal, individual scale, within small communities like those gathered around universities.

When Ralph Eubanks decided to attend the University of Mississippi in 1974—twelve years after James Meredith integrated the school—he did so because he was a passionate student "smitten," in his words, by the town of Oxford, which had lived in his imagination since his first encounters with the fiction of William Faulkner. Eubanks was a talented student from rural Mississippi, seemingly a perfect recruit for the state's most academically elite university. But he was also African American, and the UM of the 1970s remained overwhelmingly white. As Eubanks recalled in his memoir, he had faced racial divides and barriers before in his hometown of Mount Olive, but nothing had prepared him for "Ole Miss": "The Confederate era still held sway there and was brandished in your face at every turn. . . . On the one hand, Ole Miss was a welcoming and encouraging place, even giving some degree of personal attention to the black students in the freshman class to encourage us to stay the whole four years. On the other hand, however, Ole Miss existed as a world unto itself, like one big memorial to the lost cause of the Confederacy."[16]

Eubanks's memory serves as a counternarrative to the (still) popular defense from some white people that Confederate symbols have nothing to do with race, that they harm or bother no one. As one Alabama fan wrote in a 2015 online debate, "The [Confederate] flag has nothing to do with race, get over it and let it go!" Or, as *Dukes of Hazzard* star John Schneider said in defense of the frequent Confederate flags on his 1980s show, "If the flag was a symbol of racism, then Bo and Luke and Daisy and Uncle Jesse were a pack of wild racists, and that could not be further from the truth." Such denials and misleading arguments persist. Whether confederate rhetors actually believe in this ideational separation or not, Ralph Eubanks and other Black people who have been on the receiving end of confederate rhetoric provide the most trustworthy insights into the full power of the flag and other symbols. For most Black students at UM, Confederate symbols are now—and always have been—hurtful and punitive. In another recollection, Eubanks remembered the sting of the "rebel flags carried by young men in Confederate dress at sporting events." He also joined the small number of isolated individuals to criticize the name "Ole Miss," pointing to it directly as a "reference to plantation aristocracy, when blacks were slaves and whites were masters." Contrary to the majority white view of his day, Eubanks recalled that even in the 1970s, antebellum language and symbols "made many black students uncomfortable." Indeed, Eubanks remembered stories from his Black classmates "of their being booed in church when the preacher announced they were going to Ole Miss. Special prayers were sometimes requested."[17]

Ralph Eubanks moved into his dormitory at UM as a freshman in 1974. It was his first day on campus, and his father accompanied him from their small Mississippi hometown of Mount Olive. As they carried clothes into the campus dormitory and found Ralph's room, they encountered something both predictable and alarming. The story of this moment is powerful and worth quoting at length:

> I was assigned a white roommate. By 1974, Ole Miss did not make dormitory assignments based on race. When I moved into my dorm room at Twin Towers, my roommate, Mark Crain, had already settled in and decorated the room in typical Ole Miss fashion: a Confederate flag was placed right above his bed. After I opened the door with an armload of clothes, we shook hands and I introduced him to my father, who had come to help me move in. Both my father and I ignored the flag, but I was having a difficult time not noticing it. It was so big it almost filled the entire wall. "Just don't pay any attention to that Rebel flag," my father said to me soothingly after Mark left for the afternoon. My father sensed that its prominence made me uncomfortable. "If you're going to survive here, you're just going to have to get used to seeing them everywhere," he added. Although I knew he was right, being in the same room with the flag was not the same as seeing it off in the distance on a football field. I continued to unpack and then we went out to lunch before my father left to go home.
>
> When I came back, the flag had been taken down. "I didn't want to offend you with the flag," Mark told me later that evening, when he came back from a fraternity rush party.[18]

On prominent display within this episode are complex truths about the ways in which confederate rhetoric operates within and between individuals—and thus how it influences the very idea of community at the University of Mississippi.

First, this episode shows how the Confederate flag (like any Confederate symbol or association) can contribute to the construction and strengthening of simplified notions of communal membership. For Eubanks, the jolting appearance of the flag was an initiatory moment that reified doubt and worry about the university community he had chosen to join. For Crain, who is white, the same flag was reassuring décor that signified affiliation and belonging within the community he had chosen to join. Both students carried certain racial expectations with them to campus. Eubanks carried understandable fear and misgiving. Crain carried an understandable expectation of comfort and sameness. We know that Eubanks and Crain brought such different feelings and expectations to campus that day in 1974 because the University of Mississippi was still then almost entirely white. Only fifty or so African American students matriculated among a class of more than eight hundred incoming students. Also, we can deduce from Crain's subsequent reaction—his taking down the flag after meeting Eubanks—that he was not a virulent racist in any personal or ideological sense and also that he was not at all expecting a Black roommate to appear in his dorm room.

A symbol of fear for Eubanks and a symbol of collegiate belonging for Crain, the flag played the critical role in this moment of discomfort and division. Both men were relating to their new college—and to each other—through the Confederate flag, which mediated and controlled this key moment of their campus orientation. Dorothy Holland and others have explored the predetermining power of "figured worlds," the concept that we all carry around and rely on simplified notions about what is normal or typical in the world. As explained by James Paul Gee, "What is taken to be typical or normal . . . varies by context and by people's social and cultural group."[19] In the episode above, Crain, a white freshman, was operating in a different figured world than Eubanks, a Black freshman. Had Crain's expectations been met (that is, had his roommate been white, as happened for the vast majority of white students on move-in days during this era), the normalcy and supposed positivity of the Confederate flag in his room would have been reaffirming, for the flag was a ubiquitous and official symbol of school spirit at this time. When difference appeared, however, the normal script of reification was interrupted. Confronted by the unexpected arrival of a Black roommate, Crain was forced to think beyond his figured world and to admit other meanings for the flag. The episode is a wonderful example of personal hospitality and manners overriding, if only momentarily and incompletely, institutionalized racism. It is also a clear rebuttal of the facile but popular notion that Confederate symbols, like the flag, have nothing to do with race. If Confederate symbols had nothing to do with race, Crain would not have felt compelled to take down the flag upon realizing that Eubanks was Black.

Stories from the UM Black minority are rarely prominent compared to the nostalgic perceptions of the white majority. In his memoir quoted above, Eubanks is remembering the University of Mississippi of the same era memorialized by Frank Everett in his nostalgic speech about all things "Ole Miss." As I noted in chapter 1, Everett's romanticized and racially purified vision of "Ole Miss" (a "citadel where beauty dwells . . . an ocean of waving crimson flags with white stars on blue bars . . . an unbreakable unity, a lasting living bond between those past and those present") became revered scripture within this community. It became an orthodox frame for understanding the school. Even today, it is a revered communal memory, one that has been printed in newspapers across the state, sold by the alumni association as framed art, and even emblazoned in bas-relief lettering on the walls of the Ole Miss Student Union.[20] Everett's verse continues to be regarded as doctrine within the mainstream (white) UM community. Meanwhile, Eubanks's witnessing—his memories of the same era—have been elided and eschewed. While Everett and other white people in the majority used confederate rhetoric to romanticize UM as a glorious bastion of the old, "better" ways, African Americans connected to the school felt understandably uncomfortable and marginalized by that same rhetoric. The "Ole Miss" that Everett personified as a caring and loving mother was viewed by many Black students as a dangerous and threatening place, one to be avoided or that required special prayers of protection before entering. While Everett's speech, given to an all-white audience at a private club in Vicksburg, became an orthodox and revered frame for understanding the UM community of the 1970s, the reality experienced by Black "members" of the university would have been lost to history if not for a few writers like Eubanks who were bold enough to record memories that are disjunctive to the continuum of confederate rhetoric that still dominates the school.

This privileging of one narrative over another demonstrates the white community's need and ability to control the discourse around a particular southern institution. More specifically, it shows just how investments in Old South words and symbols have been safeguarded and have grown over time. Eubanks left Mississippi after his time as a student at the university. Even now, after his stories of student life have been published, after he has made UM proud by achieving great success as a writer, after he has, in fact, returned to campus to teach in the Honors College, his minority perspective on confederate rhetoric is often either downplayed or ignored, especially when compared to Everett's revered vision. At student orientation sessions during the summer of 2018, for example, the Associated Student Body president welcomed new students into the UM community by quoting Frank Everett's speech, by citing the romantic ideals of "Ole Miss" as higher and more lasting than those of the University of Mississippi.[21] The division encountered by Eubanks in 1974—the confederate rhetoric that divided him from his roommate—still existed in less glaring forms in 2018. The Confederate flags are no longer on public display, perhaps, but other subtler examples of confederate rhetoric continue to greet UM students of all races.

Again, confederate rhetoric dominates and punishes in very personal ways. It silences minority views. As the semiosis of power and whiteness in the US South, it tends to assert—and then embed—itself within institutions like universities. Thus, confederate rhetoric becomes a repository for ideational and ideological traditions. It becomes indispensable for new generations trying to initiate themselves and others into the community. More often than not, these new generations would never consciously promote division along racial lines. They would never welcome their classmates with harsh and obvious racialized language. Because confederate rhetoric cloaks itself, however, it becomes a pernicious mechanism by which racism can be reified and reinscribed across generations.

The Personal Intervention as a Mechanism of Hope

Stephen D. Lee remains an unexamined but prominent symbol at Mississippi State. Frank Everett remains in control of the majority narrative of identity at the University of Mississippi. But their power lies in the very fact that their legacies have been obfuscated, as they have been incompletely presented and edited. The personal dynamics of confederate rhetoric often explain how it has caused tremendous pain and suffering. Those same personal dynamics, however, offer pathways for reconciliation and healing.

When Mark Crain met Ralph Eubanks in that dorm room in 1974, Crain realized almost immediately that the Confederate flag was delivering painful messages to his new roommate. In that moment, Crain had all the power and was in the majority. Eubanks, on the other hand, was a silenced member of the minority. Just moments before their meeting, Crain had hung the flag as a marker of belonging, as an official symbol that he was truly an "Ole Miss Rebel." He was behaving normally and in alignment with his figured world by simply defaulting to an acceptable and standard semiotic practice. Just as Martha Allman, who was discussed at the start of this chapter, operated within the majority frame at Wake Forest, so too did Mark Crain in signaling to his imagined peers that he belonged. He was hanging the flag that in his time and context was an apt symbol of membership and belonging.

Like all young and nervous people arriving at college, Crain probably wanted to belong. He wanted to fit in, to succeed, to become a member of his new community. Within the system of this southern institution, the Confederate flag would have facilitated that process, at least under normal circumstances. Like many white people in the US South, Mark Crain was not an outwardly racist person. He was not hateful when confronted with an interpersonal situation. Instead, he was seemingly embarrassed and regretful in this moment. Once he realized that Ralph Eubanks was Black—and once he understood, either through nonverbal signals from Eubanks or through simple reflection and intuition, that the flag was offending Eubanks—he removed the flag. Before Eubanks's arrival, Crain as a member of the white majority had been able to deploy the flag without much thought regarding race. When Eubanks arrived, Crain was forced to broaden his thinking, to confront a realization. His decision at that moment to remove the flag and to explain hospitably to Eubanks why he removed it demonstrates the potential power of personal interactions in counteracting even long continua or traditions of confederate rhetoric.

Such stories of white people revising their traditions, of resisting hateful defaults, should be celebrated and encouraged. If the white majority controls discourse at the University of Mississippi, the white majority maintains the power to improve it. In a more recent example, Roun McNeal was serving as the Associated Student Body president at UM during a heated debate over the song "From Dixie with Love." In 2009, this song was played regularly at football games, and the (majority white) student body would conclude the song by adding a loud chant to the end: "The South Will Rise Again!"—certainly an example of overt confederate rhetoric. McNeal led the student government in voting to ban the chant, recommending an alternative: "To Hell with LSU!" The resolution passed after a lengthy and public debate. What's most interesting for the purposes of this discussion is McNeal's explanation for how he was converted to this cause. McNeal, a white student leader who was part of a traditional fraternity, had previously yelled "The South Will Rise Again!" at football games for many years. He decided to stop forever at one particular football game. "I said the chant one day and there was a black family sitting in front of me and they turned around and gave me this look like I hurt them," explained McNeal.[22] It was this interpersonal moment—a moment when confederate rhetoric was deployed at close range and when the pain of that deployment proved undeniable to a young member of the white majority—that changed McNeal forever and that contributed to the campus-wide retirement of a clearly racist tradition.

Moments of white realization and conversion must be multiplied within southern communities if the region's long traditions of confederate rhetoric are to be substantially weakened or eliminated. Change will accelerate only if members of the current dialogical majority become members of the current dialogical minority. Conversions must occur. Lines must be crossed. Otherwise, embedded traditions of confederate rhetoric will continue to perform their work, often unrecognized or denied by those in control of the words and symbols. Confederate rhetoric is extraordinarily resilient.

Too often, though, members of the white majority in southern institutions are unwilling to surrender their beloved sociolinguistic traditions. Moments of realization and change, like those experienced by Crain in 1974 and McNeal in 2009, are less common than moments of obliviousness and stasis. Sometime around 2015, an African American student at UM experienced this more typical episode before a football game:

> I avoided The Grove my entire freshman year, but when sophomore year rolled around I vowed to go and have a nice time. Some friends and I pre-gamed a bit before we went Groving so we were all in good spirits, laughing, joking, and just enjoying ourselves as we walked to The Grove. As I walked around, I began to feel very uncomfortable. There were Confederate flags hung up everywhere, old white people eyed me curiously as I passed, Colonel Reb's hung up around everywhere. This old man passed by me with a jumpsuit covered with a giant Confederate flag pattern and said "Hotty Toddy." I know that he meant this as a greeting to a fellow comrade, but it did not feel that way to me. I did not feel like we were comrades, I mean what a slap in the face. A FULL CONFEDERATE FLAG JUMPSUIT AND YOU GREET ME AS IF WE ARE ON THE SAME TEAM?! We are not. Because the people, who waved the flag you are celebrating, fought to uphold an institution that dehumanized and oppressed my people. I was told that The Grove was supposed to be where I'd be able to bond with my fellow students and have a blast in the name of the football season. I hated it. And I will never go back.[23]

Confederate rhetoric continues to damage southern universities and colleges, to counteract and offset many other efforts to welcome and support students from underrepresented groups. It divides white people from Black people, fortifying the separation of the races, even after stronger mechanisms of racism have faded away. The American legal system has successfully opened doors for African Americans. Many oppressive laws and policies have been eliminated or improved. But language and symbols are more difficult to overturn.

By the 1970s, Eubanks and other Black students were attending UM without facing violence of the kind encountered by James Meredith. By the early 2000s, Black families were attending football games and cheering on the "Rebels." By the 2010s, a Black sophomore who obviously loved his school was bold enough to let down his guard and party in the Grove. Yet all of these people were forced to confront "symbols like the Confederate flag, symbols that most blacks found offensive and that contributed to a hostile, racially polarizing environment."[24] Confederate rhetoric is divisive and punitive, and that reality is obvious to those in the minority. When recognized and acted on by those in the majority, the situation improves, if only incrementally. When ignored or denied, the situation stagnates or worsens.

At this point, it is worthwhile to return to a fundamental precept of this study: history, in the broad sense, does not create words and symbols; history, in the broad sense, is created by words and symbols. They are the mechanisms for moving people to action and thereby for changing the directions of institutions, towns, cities, states, regions, and nations. In this view of history, small institutions like universities become significant anchors by which individuals are connected to the bedrock of their communal identities. Regional or national identity is not far behind and is intertwined with, dependent on, the identities formed within these smaller institutions. Thus, a communal attachment to the bust of Stephen D. Lee at Mississippi State University can reveal much about statewide and regional dynamics. Lee and his nineteenth- and early twentieth-century admirers and compatriots were witnessing on behalf of the South for a particular purpose. They were creating evidence for an argument, worrying about audiences of both the present and the future. As Bradford Vivian has shown, such witnessing can be a major force in "creating or sustaining the impression, if not the reality, of a particular social, political, and moral community."[25] This has been true in the US South, where those in power across the decades have simply accepted, without much scrutiny or questioning, the accounts of witnesses like Lee and other Confederate rhetors.

If white southerners have fallen into a pattern of passive remembering, then Black southerners have not enjoyed the privilege of that option. For them, confederate rhetoric has always been punitive and damaging. Eubanks could not ignore the Confederate flag hung in his dorm room. The Black family McNeal observed at the UM football game could not ignore the words "The South Will Rise Again!" And I suspect that despite the façade of tranquility and the minimizing dismissals of President Keenum, some Black students at Mississippi State have not been able to ignore the looming and central presence of Stephen D. Lee on their campus. The new South has increasing numbers of new witnesses: African Americans with long memories but with only recent access to the witness stands of public life. Their testimonies are changing the case, correcting the incomplete, false, and often hateful record.

Their testimonies are forming the future public memories of the region. In Mississippi, writers like Kiese Laymon, Angie Thomas, Natasha Trethewey, Jesmyn Ward, Ralph Eubanks, and many other people of color (from all walks of life) are now witnessing about the full reality of their home state and region.

Such witnessing is extraordinarily powerful and can, over time, change the South's established system of racism. But such witnessing must be supported and joined and celebrated (and thus sustained or memorialized) by those in formal positions of power, by those presiding over the court, to extend Vivian's metaphor. White southerners must be willing to correct the record, to question the validity and motives of witnesses from the past, people like Jubal Early and Stephen D. Lee, who regarded themselves as victims and who spent decades constructing a one-sided argument for Old South glory and for the sanctity of whiteness. Their evidence—confederate rhetoric—remains all around us, living on and influencing our individual and communal identities.

All contemporary southerners can play a role in recognizing these injustices and in correcting the record. In the next chapter, I offer examples of ongoing rhetorical reformation and ideas for prosecuting further progress. If previous generations could use rhetoric to create and sustain a racist system, then current southerners could certainly use rhetoric to create and sustain a system of equality and justice. We are all witnesses, and future generations will be listening to our testimonies and living for a long time with our evidence.

CHAPTER 7

Reasons for Hope?

Scholars of Language and a New South Rhetoric

SCHOLARS OF LANGUAGE AND COMMUNICATION have much to offer in the ongoing and complicated work of understanding how racism has been enacted and enforced in the United States. Indeed, this has already been a fruitful part of this vast field, one that has produced illuminating scholarship on issues of race.[1] But scholars of language and communication are not always in agreement over the urgency of this mission or the methodologies best suited to undertake it. Debates within key professional organizations have highlighted this professional discord. Writing in the *Journal of Communication* in 2018, scholars Paula Chakravartty, Rachel Kuo, Victoria Grubbs, and Charlton McIlwain documented the disturbing underrepresentation of first authors of color, editors of color, and race-related keywords in leading communication journals. Their article "#CommunicationSoWhite" asked communication scholars "to pay more attention to the persistent marginalization of racial and ethnic minorities in today's complex media systems" and to collectively address the "absence of non-White scholars from the canon of communication across all subfields."[2] The article launched a critical conversation about race that has continued within the field.

In 2019, a related real-world controversy erupted between the Executive Committee of the National Communication Association and some of NCA's most senior members, namely, a group of veteran professors who had earned honorary status as Distinguished Scholars. Although the debate began over issues of representation—there was only one scholar of color among the group of some seventy Distinguished Scholars—it grew to include arguments over other NCA structures and processes, which some members had come to regard as exclusionary and racist. In an influential blog post, scholar Ragan Fox invoked "#CommunicationSoWhite" and suggested that NCA was little more than "a system of meritocracy that is set up to continue rewarding straight white dudes." Professor Stephen Llano called for NCA to reboot itself, and he criticized the organization in its current form as "saddled with a bunch of nonsense that only gets in the way of the importance of getting teachers, professionals, and scholars together to identify shared issues and interesting ideas. NCA," wrote Llano, "seems to be a place that is designed to give prestige and power to people who already have it." Llano argued that the group should begin to empower "new people with new ideas" and should refocus its attention on "blind spots . . . to invest, quite directly, in new ways to see and do communication." Within a few days of the initial eruption, Bernadette Marie Calafell, communication scholar and chair of Critical Race and Ethnic Studies at Gonzaga, coauthored an open letter—soon signed by hundreds of scholars—that reiterated previous findings that "our discipline has a race problem." Calafell and her colleagues offered many ideas for addressing the problems in the organization, including that "NCA should pursue the creation of endowed research awards for critical scholarship in race, gender, and other marginalized identities and topics. Honoring such work in an intentional and conspicuous way will further codify the organization's commitment to diversity."[3]

This controversy within NCA became heated and often personal. Scholars were called out by name. Letters and statements were volleyed from all sides throughout the month of June.[4] There were direct appeals for editorial positions and professional honors to be revoked. There was a suggestion that certain scholarly journals should be boycotted. At times, while reading the arguments as they unfolded in tweets, letters, and blog posts, I felt like a voyeur watching the most passionate of fights within a family's supposedly private home. But this vigorous debate was far more consequential than a family squabble. The future of one of the field's largest and most interdisciplinary organizations was in question. Would issues of race and racism become central to the mission of communication and its related disciplines—or would these topics remain secondary subjects of inquiry?

Months before this controversy in NCA, there was similar seismic activity in another major professional organization. In his 2019 Chair's Address at the Conference on College Composition and Communication Annual Convention, Asao Inoue purposefully and provocatively divided his audience by race, speaking first to people of color and then to "the White folks in the room." In so doing, he surfaced the inequities of power that persist, even among a group of language scholars and faculty. Part of Inoue's point was that white people continue to have more linguistic and semiotic power and privilege and that they should reflect on this reality. Another part of his point was that white scholars often fail to use that power in productive ways, choosing instead to remain comfortable in their positions of "language supremacy." When he pointedly addressed his white colleagues in the large hall in Pittsburgh, Inoue was challenging and provocative:

> How does it feel to be the problem? How does it make you feel to be the one in the way of progress, no matter what you have said or what your agendas are, how hard you worked, or how sincere you are? It's unfair, isn't it? You are good people. And yet you are the problem, but you don't want to be. Think about that for a minute. You can be a problem even when you try not to be. Sit and lament in your discomfort and its sources. Search. If our goal is a more socially just world, we don't need more good people. We need good changes, good structures, good work that makes good changes, structures, and people.[5]

For me, these challenges to academic orthodoxies—these calls to open up scholarly traditions and to confront racial inequities on all fronts—are timely and invigorating. Rather than representing instability and turmoil, these healthy challenges to the status quo represent, from my perspective, an evolutionary moment in the many fields occupied by language scholars. My own hope is that all of us will work together from our various inherited positions to trace, expose, understand, and document the ways in which words and symbols have contributed to America's exclusionary history, all with an activist's eye toward healing that history within our various regions and communities.

It is within this context that I hope this book can make a small contribution. Writing from my own position as a white male, cishet, tenure-track scholar who has held multiple administrative positions at a research university, I recognize that I have enjoyed layered levels of privilege and power within my life and profession. I ask myself then, what will I do with that privilege and power? What I have attempted to do in this book is to leverage my insider's view to better understand whiteness, language, and power in my own region of the country. While I am still learning my craft as a scholar, I have pulled zealously—but hopefully responsibly—from critical discourse analysis, communication studies, rhetoric, and memory studies to look from my own position at the problem of racism in the US South. One certain conclusion is that scholars of language have much to contribute to the active field of southern studies, which is proudly interdisciplinary and inviting. In a region where language and power swirl together in continually complicated ways, there are many opportunities for rhetorical research and study.

Scholars of rhetoric and communication know the significance of everyday words and symbols and have many useful tools for examining just how those words and symbols create local meaning and reify local identities. As

I hope I have demonstrated in this book, commonplace lexical choices and popular symbolic orthodoxies are worth our attention. If we are interested in understanding human behaviors and human societies, then we must better understand real-world human investments in words and symbols. Most personal portfolios of such investments are heavily weighted toward the local. Individuals are likely to interact daily with the words and symbols associated with their alma maters, favorite sports teams, or employers. As Norman Fairclough has pointed out, "Most discourse has a more local character, being located in or on the edges of particular institutions—the family, schools, neighborhoods, workplaces, courts of law, etc. We [as scholars of language] have to honour the specificity of such institutional domains."[6] These local domains are the places where identities emerge through language, where communal concepts are formalized, and where public memories are shaped, preserved, and enacted. Language scholars are well positioned to study these quotidian and local processes.

Furthermore, as we consider language and its relationship to power in our society, we should persist in focusing on local domains. Again, the potential for effective action lies nearby, within our own communities. Societies do not move unless individuals are moved, and language and symbols are the energy of those movements. When power inequities create problems for societies—racism in the US South, for example—then some antidotes to those inequities must inevitably reside in language and symbols. As this book has shown, confederate rhetoric has been a stubborn, pernicious, and stabilizing force in the history of the US South. It has been a key mechanism in the preservation and prosecution of racism through its power to simplify race as a binary, to punish southerners in the Black minority, to reward white people, and to protect and house Old South sentiments. Those operations are occurring to this very day within southern institutional settings. So, if we are interested in overturning destructive orthodoxies, we must expose their full and problematic power through sustained and careful analysis.

Doing so will open a number of curative possibilities within our communities. In the US South, for example, there are many white people who are not yet equipped to confront inherited language or symbols that run counter to their hopes and dreams for the region. They continue to accept the commonsensical notion that visible examples of confederate rhetoric—like statues, flags, mascots, building names, and the like—are nothing more than inert relics of some distant past. Such passive acceptance among the white majority has been common throughout previous decades in the US South, and it has been a terribly regressive force. Consider, for example, the many white people who did not think twice about blackface photos in yearbooks in past decades.

Or consider the many white people who to this very day are able to stroll by Confederate statues without feeling disturbed or bothered, without noticing the complexity and power of those rhetorical beacons.

Writers have accounted for such white insensitivity in various ways. Sociologist Robin DiAngelo sees obliviousness as one symptom of "white fragility," a complex in which many white people retreat toward color blindness in order to avoid discomfort and to sidestep racial responsibility. Like Asao Inoue, DiAngelo urges white people to consider their own racial positionality, not as exceptional or "woke" individuals but as parts of a problematic collective. Until more white people in society can reflect honestly on their own complicity within racist institutions, those institutions cannot be fully repaired. "The racial status quo is comfortable for white people," writes DiAngelo, "and we will not move forward in race relations if we remain comfortable."[7]

Mitch Landrieu, who served as mayor of New Orleans from 2010 to 2018, comes to a similar conclusion in his memoir, recalling that he drove by the Jefferson Davis monument in New Orleans for many years without ever really registering it. As a white person, Landrieu had the privilege of (dis) regarding such monuments as inert historical relics. Landrieu was forty years old before he had a moment of "transformative awareness," a moment catalyzed by conversations with Terence Blanchard and Wynton Marsalis, African American men from New Orleans who spoke direct truth to Landrieu about the monuments and their impact on people of color. Like DiAngelo, Landrieu used his book to challenge other white people to actively consider notions beyond those that are comfortable and immediately commonsensical. Both writers offer prescriptions for antiracism that are not about white guilt or "gotcha" politics; instead, they are about improving the world for the present and for the future. According to DiAngelo, more white people must "break with white silence and solidarity, to stop privileging the comfort of white people over the pain of racism for people of color, to move past guilt and into action."[8] In the realm of linguistic practices, such action would mean raising objections to words and symbols that are comfortable for white people but painful for people of color. In the US South specifically, this action would mean exposing and revising confederate rhetoric. Otherwise, confederate rhetoric will continue to perform injurious cultural work in the maintenance of white supremacy.

By thinking in unorthodox ways about traditional, commonplace linguistic and symbolic practices, scholars of language can perhaps provoke localized white majorities to pay closer attention, to look beyond their commonsensical and comfortable perspectives. Such work is ongoing, of course, across fields as diverse as rhetoric, communication, literary studies, history, and sociology.

The hope is that over time scholars can encourage disturbances and catalyze actual reforms. In the US South, such work must be widespread and sustained, if there is any hope for overcoming more than a century of sociolinguistic inertia. As Asao Inoue said in his address, it is too easy for white majorities to ignore the "conditions of White language supremacy," to consider objections only on their surface and then to "turn and go in their White world, a world that rewards their silence and hesitation."[9] In the US South, this incentivized acceptance and passivity has hindered white majorities within local institutions from fully listening to Black minorities. It is this ease of ignorance that has led to the kind of minimization and dismissal of confederate rhetoric documented throughout this book. More often than not, white southerners have not been willing to listen to unpalatable truths. More typical responses have ranged from defensive to retreating, from proclamations of "Heritage, Not Hate" to genteel silence. Operating from positions of linguistic and symbolic power, white people can simply ignore—or work around—the need for linguistic and symbolic change.

White people in the US South do, in fact, maintain great power and control over the semiotic practices of the region. If they begin to think differently about their investments in harmful words and symbols, then those investments might be reconsidered. Fairclough is right that educators and educational institutions should strive "toward educating people about the sociolinguistic order they live in . . . to equip them with what has . . . become, because of the enhanced social and cultural role of language and because of the technologisation of discourse, an essential prerequisite for effective democratic citizenship, the capacity for critique of language."[10] Unfortunately, in the US South, many universities are not only neglecting the teaching of that prerequisite, but they are continuing through outdated co-curricular practices the teaching of its opposite: the passive acceptance of language. They are encouraging students and other stakeholders to be linguistic bystanders, rather than linguistic activists. When the president of Mississippi State defended Stephen D. Lee in 2017—as historical person, as statue, as building, as student award, as symbol—and then called Lee a leader of reconciliation, he was forwarding an incomplete and misleading viewpoint. He was ignoring key parts of Lee's problematic biography, and he was encouraging the acceptance and continuation of a harmful status quo.[11]

In this book, I have called attention to many such examples when leaders, students, alumni, and other stakeholders at southern universities have allowed or enabled confederate rhetoric to flourish on their campuses. As I have argued, this is a common and long-standing problem across the region, a problem with deep historical roots and dynamic present-day consequences.

One consequence has been the perpetuation of a false and limiting racial binary that is strategically straightforward and overly simplified: white or Black, Black or white. The truth, of course, is that race is complex, varied, and sometimes variable. Thinking scientifically, for example, race is not binaristic at all. Indeed, it is so complicated as to be virtually meaningless as a category. But this is not a book about science. It is, instead, a book about perceptions, language, symbols, and their generative power within the particular context of the US South, where race has almost always been oversimplified. Indeed, the binary of white and Black has been constructed and strengthened by white southerners using many tools, including Old South words and symbols, that simplifying but powerful collective that I call confederate rhetoric. Confederate rhetoric has been a principal mechanism for reifying the binary of race and for elevating white supremacist ideology. Like all binaries, the white/Black binary that is dominant in the US South eliminates the middle ground. It forces individuals into one category or another.

If any reader objects to this oversimplification of race as it is discussed in relation to confederate rhetoric, I can only concede that your objection is both valid and correct. Pretending that race is a binary is harmful and limiting. It can often be a method for imprisoning identities and punishing minorities. And this oversimplification has, of course, made life extraordinarily complicated and costly for non-Black and non-white southerners who fall outside the racial binary. So yes, the racial binary enforced in the US South is false and damaging. For so long, however, it has been operative and consequential.

A stark example of the cost of a reinforced racial binary can be seen in the experience of Medgar Evers. When Evers was a young boy in Mississippi, he had a "good" friend, a neighbor who was his age.

> I grew up with a white playmate, a kid next door who practically lived at my house. In the long, hot summers we would do all the things that kids do—play hide and seek, talk about our big plans for growing up, swap the little personal treasures that boys grow friendly over, and argue over his double-barreled stopper gun. Then, one day, my friend stopped coming by. In a little while, he began to get nasty. Finally, out in the street with a group of his friends, he called me "nigger." The split had come. The lines were drawn, black on one side and white on the other.

These kinds of cruel punishments have always been a part of life for Black people in Mississippi and the South. Through confederate rhetoric, they remain a part of life in many situations to this very day. Even on college campuses, African American students are still subjected to the periodic deployment of the n-word. Sociologists at the University of Mississippi, Kirk Johnson, Willa Johnson, James Thomas, and John Green, documented fifty-one "references to students being called nigger" in the 2014/15 academic year alone.[12] Other examples from earlier in this book prove that the n-word—perhaps the most hurtful and overt single word in the confederate rhetoric vocabulary—remains active on many other college campuses too.

While the deployment of the n-word is still common, much more frequent these days are other, less overt reminders of the Old South. At UM, for example, the white/Black binary is invoked and reinforced through the presence of rhetoric like the Confederate statue,[13] the unofficial but frequent appearance of the Confederate flag (and its spin-offs), the unexamined and uncontextualized name "Ole Miss," the nostalgic Frank Everett quote affixed to the wall of the student union, and other prevalent symbols of campus "community." Racial lines remain drawn by words and symbols. The false binary continues to be enforced.

After the boyhood experience described above, Medgar Evers fought against Mississippi's racial "split" for the rest of his life. When he wanted to attend the University of Mississippi for law school, he was denied on the basis of his race.[14] Thanks to the courage and persistence of civil rights heroes like Evers, laws and policies have since been changed, and African American students are now able to attend UM. Progress has been made. When Black students arrive on campus these days, however, they still face some of the same rhetorical discouragements faced by Evers and his generation. Many Black students continue to feel a "split," to use Evers's words, with "black on one side and white on the other." The ongoing existence of this racial divide at the university has been proven by the sociologists Kirk Johnson, Willa Johnson, James Thomas, and John Green. Their 2018 report was based on surveys of 621 UM students, and it documented 1,381 troubling incidents, many of which involved confederate rhetoric. As those scholars concluded, "These incidents occurred throughout the campus in classrooms, in Greek houses and dormitories, and in public spaces such as the Grove and the Student Union."[15] When it comes to words and symbols, the evidence for presence and harm is being clearly voiced by students and scholars alike.

Yet many white people often fail to listen to ugly truths, even when those truths are found through methodological research conducted by academic specialists at their own institutions. At UM, when the aforementioned team of sociologists released *Microaggressions at the University of Mississippi*, then chancellor Jeffrey Vitter questioned the validity of the report by attacking sociological methods. He made these critiques publicly through an op-ed published in the campus newspaper.[16] Therein, Vitter shifted blame and suspicion onto the authors of the study—his own faculty experts—suggesting that they should have de-anonymized their data and shared it with "local authorities" or with university staff. Vitter undercut and questioned an empirical report, when he could have embraced and used its many insights to improve his campus climate. In so doing, the chancellor was echoing the sentiments of some alumni and students in the white majority at UM who preferred to emphasize racial progress and harmony while downplaying any remnants of racism and discord. These majority voices engaged in the spin of public relations rather than in the accountability and reconciliation of public history.

It is my hope that scholars of language will listen to leaders like Marie Calafell, Asao Inoue, and others who have critiqued the field of communication and its orthodoxies. I hope that the community of communication scholars will turn together to race as one of its principal subjects and will take intentional steps to address inequities within its professional organizations. I believe it is important that this community unite to provide scholarly support to sociologists, historians, literary scholars, and others who are and have been more vigorously pursuing antiracist scholarship and activism. These subjects merit and require many insights and organized reinforcement. For inspiration, one can look to ongoing work by organizations like the Coalition for Community Writing based in Boulder, where Veronica House and colleagues have created an international group of writing teachers interested in using language to promote dialogue and change within local communities. This growing organization has been active for years now and sponsors conferences, teaching materials, workshops, and a research journal. One can also look to newer organizations and journals. In the US South, for example, Donald Unger (now at the University of Mississippi) and Liz Lane at the University of Memphis are founding editors of *Spark: A 4C4Equality Journal*, which highlights activism within rhetoric, writing, and literacy studies. Journals like *Spark* are gathering places for language scholars interested in engaged research that can impact and improve local communities. Race and power are often at the forefront of such scholarship.

For most people within the modern US South, there is an understandable fatigue around issues of race. It can be a depressing topic for everyone involved. This is certainly true at the University of Mississippi, where many white stakeholders feel unfairly singled out when it comes to racial conflicts and controversies. As I mentioned earlier in this book, one common target for blame is the national media. Racism is everywhere, goes this argument, so why does UM receive so much negative attention? It is a complaint trotted out after every publicized episode of racial conflict, after every eruption of confederate rhetoric. In 2009, for example, when a white student used the n-word on camera, the video went viral and the story made national news. Commenting on the coverage of this incident in *Deadspin*, a self-identified alum under the username Kjerome posted a typical complaint:

> As a graduate of Ole Miss, I would be willing to travel to other universities in the sec and see how many young idiots I could find that would throw down on a few N-bombs for you tube. By the way this young man isn't from Mississippi. Maybe the racism that so many accuse the University of Mississippi of, exist on all your campuses. You think? We just continue to be everyone's favorite target. I travel quite a bit and I see the confederate flag from Naples, Florida all the way to West Virginia. So I'm sure there are plenty of shallow ignorant people like this young man all over the United States.[17]

Kjerome expressed a multilayered sensitivity that was clearly defensive and dismissive. He placed blame on the media, on other southern universities, on students at UM who were not from Mississippi, and on disembodied and delocalized shallowness and ignorance. Within the white community at UM, this kind of argument has proven quite powerful over the years, and scholars of rhetoric and language are in the best position to expose, trace, understand, and defuse such fallacies. While such arguments are common, they are also little more than excuse making. They are not credible ways of denying the reality, scale, and longevity of racism within an institution like UM. When those in the white majority use such rhetorical strategies to dismiss eruptions of racism, to minimize the importance and consequentiality of Old South words and symbols, they are often successful in slowing or stalling reforms. Such diversionary arguments need to be countered and corrected.

What I am suggesting is a movement to highlight confederate rhetoric within local institutions and to make white denials, obfuscations, and minimizations much more difficult. This can and should be done in a positive spirit, one that de-emphasizes individual blame or guilt but rewards individual listening, engagement, and change. Traditionalists should be given room for conversion and redemption. Otherwise, the lifespan of confederate rhetoric—and of racism—will be much, much longer. Projects to highlight and change confederate rhetoric will need to be local and nuanced, as confederate rhetoric is often different from place to place and is often hidden or deeply embedded within the life of an institution. In raising awareness of confederate rhetoric, scholars will need to be evenhanded and objective, creating space for improvements while also acknowledging and supporting extant movements led by progressive students, faculty, staff, and community members across the region who are already protesting Confederate statues and other forms of confederate rhetoric. Such work is difficult and is meeting resistance, in part because, as this book has shown, confederate rhetoric is deeply ingrained and protected.

When harmful words and symbols related to the Old South become entrenched as commonsensical and traditional, they concomitantly become resistant to reevaluation. Thus, the defenders of confederate rhetoric have certain advantages. The white majority in any southern community is likely to have considerable appetite for denial and delay but little appetite for reappraisal and change. This is simply another way of saying that the white majority is often far too comfortable. When individuals or leaders from the white majority overcome this inertia and step forward to criticize confederate rhetoric, those voices should be amplified and acknowledged.

Kate Kellum, a professor and administrator at the University of Mississippi, offers an encouraging example, a model for how white people of some privilege and power can become active participants in reconciling or retiring Old South words and symbols. Kellum's great-great-great-grandfather was Senator James Z. George of Mississippi. Known as a primary architect of Jim Crow, Senator George did more than perhaps anyone else to disenfranchise Black people and to preserve government-sponsored racism in the nineteenth century and beyond. His legal and political innovations—and their terrible consequences—were highly effective in Mississippi and were quickly adopted by other southern states. As his descendant, Kellum in 2017 encouraged the University of Mississippi to contextualize a campus building named in George's honor. Rather than blindly defending her family name or remaining comfortably silent, Kellum took a public stand: "We, as a society, have to continue to evolve and behave in ways consistent with our current environment. . . . I'm not saying forget history, but history has a place, and it may not be on the names of our buildings."[18] Kellum was willing to endure some discomfort and to look unflinchingly at her own family history. She stepped out and advocated for symbolic progress over symbolic preservation.

Scholars have a role to play in encouraging and celebrating this kind of advancement. At times, they may even be able to catalyze profound reconsiderations, but that type of scholarly engagement will require methodical patience and careful analysis, in addition to some level of local knowledge. Scholars of language should thus turn purposefully to their local communities, to the everyday, to the personal. Methods and models already exist for this kind of excavation and analysis, of course, and I have drawn on some of them in the chapters of this book.

Scholars Rasha Diab, Beth Godbee, and Thomas Ferrell have offered another interdisciplinary method that could be useful to scholars of language in their research efforts and that could be fruitfully extended into classrooms, campuses, and broader public communities. Diab, Godbee, and Ferrell have articulated a framework for enacting antiracism through a particular kind of dialogue, one scaffolded and repeatable. Their model recognizes the affordances of personal, confessional storytelling, but also moves well beyond such disclosures of positionality, which on their own can limit and stall rhetors and listeners. One goal of the model is to enact dialogue about race while limiting the possibilities for angry denials or unmindful dismissals on the part of those in the sociolinguistic majority. Instead, this framework seeks to foster transformative dialogue through "three interdependent rhetorical moves that have the potential to re-design, transform, and move us closer toward racial justice." Most notably, this framework for antiracism requires members of any community to embrace "a willingness to be disturbed."[19]

It seems to me that such a willingness to be disturbed has been a common absence, a missing component, in many of the most disheartening stories noted in this book, stories in which Old South words and symbols have erupted, done harm, and then have been inadequately understood or engaged by those in positions of power. If members of the white majority are not purposeful in their willingness to be disturbed, then minimization, dismissals, and denials will remain the easiest of defaults. If members of the white majority often refuse to listen to minority voices within their communities—like those of Payton Head at Mizzou or many of the 621 students at the University of Mississippi who contributed to the microaggressions report—then they will fail to understand the depth and breadth of the race problem extant within their communities. White majorities within southern universities should stop treating eruptions of confederate rhetoric as anachronistic or isolated incidents. Instead, they should listen to the realities often communicated by Black students and others, realities that run counter to their most traditional and idealized conceptions of themselves. When minority members of communities speak up, when they attempt to disabuse those in privileged positions, members of the majority should be ready to listen. They should be ready to be disturbed.

The reality of southern universities is that hateful words and symbols are not contrary to but consistent with historical campus values or traditions. Diab, Godbee, and Ferrell's framework emphasizes that rhetors and listeners must be prepared for this kind of racial truth and turbulence. Members of the white majority, for example, must be prepared to imagine sociolinguistic realities beyond those they have inherited. Ultimately, in the name of improving communities, regions, and the world, members of the white majority must make new commitments to racial justice. Once those commitments are made, they must be clearly articulated—not left vague or unstated—and communities must move purposefully together from open dialogue and articulation to concrete action and improvement.

Through frameworks like this one, southern communities might be able to break recursive cycles in which confederate rhetoric creates problems, becomes isolated, buried, or minimized, and then simply emerges again to create more problems. The goal is "an everyday educational process toward racial justice [that] works against the macro-logics of oppression."[20] Through their teaching and research, scholars of language can contribute to the cultivation of a willingness to be disturbed within many members of the white majority in regions like the US South, where those majorities continue to matriculate in regional universities before graduating to influential careers and positions of leadership. In other words, southern educators can and should look for ways to inspire critical thought about language, to influence their own schools and communities to move, whenever possible, away from confederate rhetorical practices.

And, of course, many educators have already begun to undertake this challenge, and their work provides great reasons for hope. Even in the US South—and even at UM—linguistic and semiotic progress can be made and harmful traditions can be disrupted and changed. Susan Glisson and her team at the Winter Institute for Racial Reconciliation spent years working from the University of Mississippi. They stimulated educational programs, community dialogues, outreach projects, and scholarly research, all to create "a world where people honestly engage in their history in order to live more truthfully in the present . . . where people of all identities are treated equally . . . where healing and reconciliation are commonplace and social justice is upheld and honored." Created in 1999 and later named for former Mississippi governor William Winter, a politician and public servant who "helped implement sweeping changes in educational reform as well as race relations in his beloved state of Mississippi," the institute was housed for more than fifteen years at UM. Under Glisson's leadership, much of the Winter Institute's work was rhetorical in nature and groundbreaking within the region. For example, the institute encouraged and advised leaders at the University of Mississippi, the University of Georgia, and the University of Alabama to issue public apologies for their histories of excluding African Americans.[21]

Such projects of linguistic and symbolic redress are possible even from UM, where the confederate rhetorical backdrop is pervasive. Of course, most of these projects to date have been led by white progressives like Glisson and Winter, people with enough agency and protection to function "within a paternalistic framework (dominated by a ruling white hierarchal structure)." Indeed, a weak but perceptible tradition of such internal resistance can be traced within most southern institutions. At UM, even during the 1960s, there was "a small cadre of liberal faculty members who served as gadflies in a school, community, and state that were highly conservative by a huge majority." In his book about UM professor Evans Harrington, Robert Hamblin lists nine or ten professors who challenged racial orthodoxies during the 1960s.[22] While their victories were few, the efforts of such progressives should be celebrated as cornerstones of future activism. They perhaps softened the defenses for modern dissenters like the embattled sociologists mentioned earlier in this chapter. On the UM campus today, the Critical Race Studies Group[23] and Slavery Research Group[24] are active and productive, all fighting in their own ways—and from their own disciplines—against the orthodox language practices of an institution that is resistant and slow to change.

Indeed, reconciliation work remains controversial and contested. If confederate rhetoric has proven obdurate at UM, reconciliation projects have proven malleable and impermanent. The Winter Institute, after all of its international acclaim and local progress, became a lightning rod. Some university stakeholders were proud of its work; some were critical. Under Chancellor Vitter, the Winter Institute was dissociated from the university and moved quietly off campus to Jackson, Mississippi, in 2018. Glisson and many other staffers were replaced, and the institute now operates as an independent organization. Although beyond the scope of this book, the Winter Institute's split from UM seems to be a complicated story deserving of further scholarly attention.[25]

For me, Asao Inoue is someone I have long regarded as a thought leader in composition and rhetoric. His charge to the audience at the annual meeting of the Conference on College Composition and Communication in 2019 disturbed and excited me because it revealed a new clearing to work from my own position of white privilege and power to contribute to the meaningful project of antiracism. There are landmines in this kind of thinking, which does risk the perpetuation of the false and harmful white/Black binary and which could tempt white people like me toward the dangers of white saviorism.[26] But overall, there are also tremendous opportunities in this kind of thinking. In arguing for a renewal of white responsibility, Inoue and others are simply acknowledging that white people in America still maintain disproportionate economic, social, linguistic, and semiotic control, as well as other benefits of a privileged racial identity. If traditional limiters like confederate rhetoric are to be purged, once and for all, white people will have to be active participants. As Inoue suggests, it is time for white Americans to use their positions of power and privilege to further ameliorate our country's racism—to extend the legal and social victories of the civil rights movement into the sociolinguistic realm. White people have the power to retire Old South words and symbols, for example, and scholars of language should advocate for those retirement plans.

Although such projects may have seemed unrealistic in the past, there are good reasons to believe that many white southerners in the younger generations stand ready to yield the confederate rhetoric that is part of their inheritance. In 2019 at the University of Mississippi, for example, the Associated Student Body Senate approved a resolution to relocate the Confederate statue that stands near the main entrance of the campus. Their vote was unanimous: 47–0.[27] Although now a somewhat diverse body, the ASB Senate remains predominantly white, with many representatives coming from fraternities and sororities, traditional bastions of whiteness and conservativism. This vote from this body is a marker of real progress.

Also ongoing are acts of linguistic and semiotic protest and resistance on the part of Black southerners. This tradition deserves continued attention from scholars in a number of fields, as Black resistance has been responsible for substantial progress and change. These are heroic and inspiring stories, many of which have already been told by historians and social scientists. Language scholars can mine these existing stories to chart the linguistic and semiotic depths of African American resistance. Whereas African Americans in the South are usually forced to quietly absorb confederate rhetoric—to simply endure symbolic and linguistic punishments doled out by white people and their institutions—many African Americans from different eras have mounted subtle and savvy defenses against confederate rhetoric. One well-documented example from UM came in 1982, when student John Hawkins, the university's first African American cheerleader, decided not to carry the ubiquitous Confederate battle flag onto the football field. At the time, carrying and waving the flag were essential duties of UM cheerleaders, and so Hawkins's brave refusal drew attention and stirred controversy. The Ku Klux Klan came to Oxford for a public rally, and the national media covered the short-lived but heated debate. Hawkins had opened a pathway for symbolic progress, but he paid something for his resistance. After enduring the draining episode, he decided to end his career as a UM cheerleader. He later called that period in his life "a lonely moment."[28] Such stories of bravery are rich opportunities for further study, and there are surely many more examples waiting to be found by scholars interested in linguistic and symbolic activism and resistance.

In our current era, more and more African Americans are unwilling to stand for linguistic slights and aggressions, and social media often amplifies (to some extent) their minority voices. When Alexia Washington, a UM student, went with some of her fellow African American friends to a new drive-through daiquiri bar near campus in 2019, an unnamed employee typed the following description of their car into the computerized cash register: "Black bitches in silver car." That demeaning phrase was printed on the receipt, which Washington later noticed. She posted the offensive receipt on Facebook, writing, "I seek justice for this hate crime, and I will no longer remain silent. I've lived in Oxford for 5 years, and I'm still having to deal with this type of ignorance. I'm not a rude or hateful person. I was not rude when I was at this establishment and was greeted with this kind of service. I will not stand for it." Her post gained significant attention within the community and region. Wylie Coleman, the owner of the drive-through daiquiri bar, offered a well-received apology and fired the employee who committed the offense.[29] This is one recent example of a long tradition of Black rhetorical resistance in the South, where many brave African Americans have refused to accept the words or symbols of white supremacy. Often invisible and surely much richer than has thus far been documented, this tradition of resistance, with some power to erode confederate rhetoric, deserves more attention from scholars of language.

Derrick Harriell, an accomplished scholar and poet, is currently an associate professor at the University of Mississippi. As an African American man, Harriell lives daily with the extant racism of the US South. Through his powerful and insightful poetry, he sometimes illuminates that racism and its effects on characters of color. In his poem "Links Rd to HWY 6 to Jackson Ave," which is set on three connected roads in Oxford that lead to the UM campus, the speaker of the poem is jolted by a passing vehicle: "front confederate tag tells all I need to know / about the soul of this South / get it young country / bumpkin / make grandpa proud / push that pedal / like propaganda / like a hate you can't understand."[30] Distilled within these few lines of poetry are truths that have taken me thousands of lines of prose to explore. It's one reason that I chose the poem as an epigraph for this book. Harriell's speaker feels the pain and exclusion communicated by the Confederate flag on the front bumper of the passing car or truck. The speaker hears emphasized hatred when the driver accelerates aggressively ("get it . . . push that pedal"). Harriell is narrating a familiar scene in the US South, and he is telling us something important about white aggression. Young white men who display antagonistic symbols on their cars or trucks may be unremarkable to most white people, but they are jarring and discouraging reminders of racism to more attuned passersby.

If the many white students at southern universities who continue to display the Confederate flag—on cars, shirts, coolers, hats, stickers, and so on—would read Harriell's poem and truly consider it, would some of them abandon the old symbol? I think so. Might such direct interventions within southern university curricula lessen the displays of confederate rhetoric on and around these campuses? I think so.

Perhaps such optimism seems unrealistic or naïve, but Eli Saslow offers evidence for hope in his book *Rising Out of Hatred*, which documents the awakening of Derek Black, a one-time wunderkind of American white nationalism. The godson of David Duke, Black was born into a tradition of racism and hatred. As a young man, he embraced and embodied that tradition, helping the white nationalist movement spread its ugly messages across the burgeoning internet. Black not only displayed confederate rhetoric, he created and disseminated it. By his teenage years, he had become an innovative and effective propagandist, a national leader highly regarded by the KKK and other hate groups. But, as Saslow documents, Black underwent a transformation, turning quite improbably into a proponent for racial inclusion and multicultural understanding. His evolution was radical in its sweep, and it began during his freshman year of college. In his public disavowal letter of 2013, Black explained his conversion: "It has become clear to me that white nationalism is not a movement of positive identity or of asserting cultural values, but of constant antagonism. . . . Advocating for white nationalism means that we are opposed to minority attempts to elevate themselves to a position equal to our own. It is an advocacy that I cannot support, having grown past my bubble, talked to the people I affected, read more widely, and realized the impact my actions had on people I never wanted to harm. I am sorry."[31] This conversion proves that progress is possible, even in extreme cases.

My larger point is that examples of Black resistance to confederate rhetoric and examples of white voluntary relinquishment of confederate rhetoric should be celebrated and multiplied. Furthermore, southerners should begin looking for new words and symbols that can unite everyone—and that are free of ideational or ideological baggage. One shining example comes from Mississippi, where a movement is underway to replace with a more inclusive design the state flag, which in 2019 still contained an inset of the Confederate flag. Although at the time of this writing the movement has not yet achieved its ultimate goal, it has enjoyed real progress. Starting in 2019, Mississippians could purchase "Stennis Flag" license plates for their cars and trucks. The Stennis design is free of the Confederate emblem and was created by artist Laurin Stennis, the granddaughter of segregationist Senator John Stennis.[32] The Stennis Flag represents both familial and communal strides, and its appearance as an option for a Mississippi state license plate gives forward-looking

Mississippians some limited but public power to declare support for a unifying symbol. The Stennis Flag plates are reconciliatory rhetoric with some potential to help emerge a Mississippi identity shared equally by white and Black people, an identity free of anger and provocation. Just imagine the speaker from Harriell's poem encountering the Stennis Flag plate on a passing car rather than the Confederate flag plate. Driving into the UM campus, the speaker would register hope and hospitality rather than dread and hatefulness.

Language and symbols can divide white and Black people. They can deepen discord and refresh racism. But language and symbols can also perform more salubrious work. In the US South, promoting substitutions for outworn confederate rhetoric is one straightforward way to pursue the remaining promises of the civil rights movement. At institutions like the University of Mississippi of today, are those in power catalyzing such reforms or delaying or neglecting them? I think again of Jackie Certion, my colleague who has done so much to help students at our university. As detailed in chapter 1, Jackie read a WPA interview of her great-great-grandmother, a woman born into slavery who spoke about serving her "Ole Miss," the wife of the man who enslaved her. Inspired by her ancestor's words, Certion quietly abandoned using the term "Ole Miss," even while continuing to serve the institution as an influential advisor, mentor, and educator. Like John Hawkins in 1982, does Jackie Certion feel lonely in her principled position? I don't know for sure, but I do know that she is working every day within an institution whose very name antagonizes and discomforts her. Why is this necessary? Why are Jackie Certion's white colleagues and friends within what is sometimes called the "Ole Miss family" allowing such a thing? Is it tradition? Heritage? Obliviousness?

Alienation and community are not reconcilable concepts. Within southern universities, more white people need to recognize truths spoken by peers like Jackie Certion, Derrick Harriell, and Asao Inoue. More white people need to listen fully to uncomfortable messages, look beyond their inherited positions of contentment, and be willing to be disturbed for a good cause. Building truly inclusive communities is within reach, perhaps for the first time in southern history. Many of the remaining barriers are constructed of words and symbols.

As a region, the US South has much to be proud about and to build on: tremendous reserves of hospitality, diversity, ecology, agriculture, food, literature, art, and more. Institutions like the University of Mississippi have made real and substantial progress on many fronts, and they are now home to diverse student and faculty populations that often enjoy meaningful and inclusive educational and co-curricular experiences together, experiences that are sometimes free of racial overtones or undertones. Yet, as this book has shown, predominant words and symbols at UM do not yet match the most promising moments of the institution's present or future. In words and symbols, it is time for places like "Ole Miss" to become places like "New Miss." It is time for confederate rhetoric to be recognized, retired, and permanently replaced.

Epilogue

Russian Confederate Rhetoric

The Russian scholar Mikhail Bakhtin built significant parts of the intellectual foundation for understanding words and their power. He demonstrated, for example, that language—even in its smallest parts—is always responsive to, or anticipatory of, other language. Bakhtin viewed "language as responsive to the social world . . . shaped and influenced by the discourse of others."[1] It was Bakhtin's insights that inspired intertextuality and that gave rise to critical discourse analysis and other interpretative approaches that consider language as social, dynamic, and always able to exert power on human beings. In other words, it would not be hyperbole to suggest that a Russian made possible much of the analysis undertaken in this book.

While the majority of my analysis of confederate rhetoric has centered on symbols and phrases tied to university campuses within the US South, my research on the subject has recently pointed to a significant and interesting link between confederate rhetoric and Bakhtin's home country of Russia. There, Russians have been using insights about language for darker, geopolitical purposes, essentially weaponizing the divisive potential of confederate rhetoric. As a contemporary adversary of the United States, Russia under the Putin regime has repeatedly deployed divisive words and symbols to stoke American institutional and regional identity conflicts. As mentioned in the preface to this book, US agencies, entrepreneurial journalists, and others have gathered strong evidence proving that Russia launched a strategic and orchestrated influence campaign prior to the 2016 American presidential election. This campaign is ongoing, and Russia's weapons have been words and symbols deployed mostly through social media. The operation has been based in St. Petersburg, Putin's hometown, and the Russian operatives have used digital fronts and false flags to make it appear as if Americans are arguing online with other Americans—and to catalyze actual arguments and discord among real Americans.[2]

These multimodal attacks have succeeded in their breadth and depth, fooling tens of millions of Americans across all major social media platforms. Far more research needs to be completed before we understand, even partially, the specific consequences of Russia's covert rhetorical campaign. But it is clear that during this same period our country has become sharply divided. Extremists in America have been mobilized and reinvigorated. From 2012 to 2018, right-wing terrorist attacks increased measurably.[3] Again, scholars have not established causality between the Russian operations and these alarming American realities—or other more specific outcomes, such as Donald Trump's election—but some impact seems certain. Decades of research in rhetoric, communication, and other fields have revealed that words and symbols shape human behavior and influence communal identities. The Russians have lately been using linguistic and semiotic forces for manipulative purposes.

Some southerners dismiss confederate rhetoric as an outdated concern, choosing to minimize or ignore its continuing power within American society. They argue, for example, that Confederate monuments and flags should be left alone. Those symbols, they say, are simply inactive relics of history that can do no harm in modern America. Russian agents charged with sowing discord in the United States obviously disagree. Russian social media content creators crafted and deployed confederate rhetoric during the 2010s. Their use of Confederate phrases, symbols, and imagery should serve as a stark corrective to any and all Americans who claim to be oblivious to the power of confederate rhetoric. As detailed in a report from the Office of the Director of National Intelligence released January 6, 2017, "Moscow's influence campaign followed a Russian messaging strategy that blends covert intelligence operations—such as cyber activity—with overt efforts by Russian Government agencies, state-funded media, third-party intermediaries, and paid social media users or 'trolls.'" The declassified version of this assessment provides tantalizing details of Russia's efforts "to undermine public faith in the US democratic process." The report, which was prepared with information gathered by the Central Intelligence Agency, the Federal Bureau of Investigation, and the National Security Agency, locates the recent Russian operation along a continuum of "longstanding" efforts to "undermine the US-led democratic order," but the report also concludes that the recent operation was "a significant escalation in directness, level of activity, and scope of effort."[4]

Further insights about Russia's influence campaign were presented on February 16, 2018, when Special Counsel Robert Mueller filed an indictment against the Internet Research Agency, Concord Management, Yevgeniy Prigozhin, and other Russian fronts and agents. Mueller charged that Russian agents, "posing as U.S. persons and creating false U.S. personas, operated social media pages and groups designed to attract U.S. audiences. These groups and pages, which addressed divisive U.S. political and social issues, falsely claimed to be controlled by U.S. activists when, in fact, they were controlled by [Russian] Defendants."[5] Mueller's indictment quotes from the Russian agents themselves, demonstrating that their stated goals included sowing discord in the US and spreading "distrust toward the candidates and the political system in general." Again, the Russian technique for pursuing these outcomes was to deploy provocative words and symbols across social media, and operatives took full advantage of confederate rhetoric, tapping purposefully into an existing tradition with a proven record of motivating white people and punishing Black people. Their memes, which attracted millions of engagements on Twitter, Instagram, and Facebook, featured slogans like "The South Will Rise Again," "Heritage, Not Hate," and "Kiss My Rebel Ass," words paired almost always with images of the Confederate battle flag, guns, trucks, Confederate soldiers, and so on.

While some details are not yet known about Russia's covert social media campaign, we do know that it was expansive and entrepreneurial. Working from a complex of Internet Research Agency (IRA) offices in St. Petersburg, Russian operatives managed to infiltrate and influence social networks across the United States. Russian memes and messages reached and fooled tens of millions of Americans. These Russian agents were not content to simply create online disharmony and discord, however. According to the Mueller Report, IRA operatives "organized and promoted political rallies inside the United States while posing as U.S. grassroots activists." The first known rally was a "confederate rally" in Houston in November 2015. Posting on Instagram under the "Stand for Freedom" alias, a Russian operative initiated the idea for this rally with a post on November 3: "Good evening buds! Well I am planning to organize a confederate rally . . . in Houston on the 14 of November and I want more people to attend."[6] As in dozens of other documented cases, the Russian operatives thus attempted to prod real Americans into the streets of real American cities.

In each case, after announcing the date of a rally, the IRA would then send "a large number of direct messages to followers of its social media account asking them to attend the event. From those who responded . . . the IRA then sought a U.S. person to serve as the event's coordinator." As Mueller's analysis of dozens of these operations found, "the IRA account operator would tell the U.S. person that they personally could not attend the event due to some preexisting conflict or because they were somewhere else in the United States. The IRA then further promoted the event by contacting U.S. media about the event and directing them to speak with the [duped American] coordinator."[7]

Sometimes this template for moving agitated Americans from the online world into the real world proved effective.

In May 2016, Russian operatives, posing as the "Heart of Texas" Facebook group, organized another rally in Houston. The event creator claimed that the rally aimed to protest "Islamization." When Mike Glenn, a reporter at the *Houston Chronicle*, arrived at the Islamic Da'wah Center in downtown Houston to cover the rally, he found about ten protesters on one side of the street yelling at about fifty counterprotesters on the other side of the street. Reflecting a few years later, Glenn remembered, "I couldn't find the rally organizers. No 'Heart of Texas.' I thought that was odd, and mentioned it in the article: What kind of group is a no-show at its own event? Now I know why. Apparently, the rally's organizers were in Saint Petersburg, Russia." Pictures taken that day show what Glenn did find: protesters with "White Power" T-shirts, Confederate flags, and a "White Lives Matter" banner. When he asked those protesters how they learned about the rally, they showed him the "Heart of Texas" Facebook page. One of the posts there encouraged Texans to bring their firearms to the event. On the street that day, Glenn did indeed see one protester "with an AR-15 rifle hanging from his shoulder strap."[8] There was no outbreak of violence, but the rally received significant press attention in the region. Confederate rhetoric was once again performing its cultural work.

This is an alarming story. To me, one that is much more worrying than whether Donald Trump, an individual, albeit a powerful one, colluded with Russia or committed some other kind of crime. Yes, as candidate and president, Trump has often used covert and overt confederate rhetoric and other rhetoric of exclusion and hatred. And yes, Trump's tactics and vocabulary have often mirrored those used by the Russian agents in St. Petersburg. But there is seemingly no evidence that Trump coordinated knowingly with the expansive Russian misinformation campaign. What is clear is that both the Russian operatives and Trump mined the same tradition of confederate rhetoric to rally a certain segment of the US electorate, to sow discord and dissent, and to invigorate latent anger, especially among white Americans. That professional agitators and social media operatives working across the world in Russia were able to move Americans into the streets—sometimes with guns in hand—with only the incentives of words and symbols should give all Americans pause.

The Russian operation, which has been waged digitally and which has thus left behind millions of breadcrumbs, also provides language scholars with a rich trove of data that needs to be untangled and better understood. These Russian content creators did not run this kind of operation only once or twice. As the *New York Times* reported in 2018, "The Russian attempt at long-distance choreography was playing out in many cities across the United

States. Facebook has disclosed that about 130 rallies were promoted by 13 of the Russian pages, which reached 126 million Americans with provocative content on race, guns, immigration and other volatile issues."[9] The question of how that content impacted behavior, attitudes, and emotions provides an important opportunity for future research. To this end, perhaps companies like Facebook will share relevant digital data with American scholars. Given that social media companies rely on the localization—even the individualization—of data transmitted on their networks, they likely have extraordinarily rich data sets related to the Russian attacks. Some data has already been released, giving scholars potential projects for decades to come.

As far as I know, no one has yet established a connection between the Russian campaign and the now infamous "Unite the Right" rally in Charlottesville. Although, by 2017, Russian operatives had certainly taken strides to invigorate white supremacists and other extremists throughout the United States. We do not yet know if—or to what extent—Russian operatives supported the planning for Charlottesville. When I think about that terrible event, however, I think first about something fundamental and quite obvious: it was confederate rhetoric that did the work of *uniting* the right. When white supremacists Richard Spencer and Jason Kessler, both UVA graduates, teamed up to organize the rally, they repeatedly emphasized their goal of defending Charlottesville's Robert E. Lee monument, which city leaders had recently debated removing. This focus on the Lee monument was a wise decision, as this particular example of confederate rhetoric did, in fact, unite many different groups within the sphere of white supremacy. A huge turnout in Charlottesville was the result. Both Spencer and Kessler have routinely espoused some horrifying and violent ideologies. In 2013, for example, Richard Spencer publicly advocated for remaking America into an all-white "entho-state so that our people can come home again, can live amongst family and feel safe and secure." His followers often engage in "Hail Hitler" salutes, which in recent years have been joined by "Hail Trump" salutes, sometimes led by Spencer himself. But he also routinely softens his rhetoric when speaking to mainstream audiences. He has publicly acknowledged the usefulness of "plausible deniability." In other words, Spencer thinks rhetorically and strategically. When prosecuting racist arguments, he and other extremist leaders often adapt their messages to appeal to various internal and external audiences. In planning the Charlottesville rally, they seized on the statue of Lee, hoping to gain more attention and to amplify their message within mainstream circles. Given that the president of the United States used his bully pulpit in the days following the Charlottesville rally to legitimize and tacitly support the "very fine people on both sides" and to publicly extol Robert E. Lee, Spencer and the other white supremacists who united around confederate rhetoric were (not surprisingly) very pleased with the results of the event.[10]

Scholars Ivo Strecker and Stephen Tyler have stated succinctly that "while rhetoric is the instrument with which we describe, it is also the means by which we *create* culture." This idea has been around since antiquity, but it feels like an essential starting point from which to begin understanding the America of the Trump era. Writing in 2009, Peter Oesterreich predicted the continuing importance of a rhetorical lens: "After the twentieth century media-led globalization, the task of promoting a process of transcultural understanding is an outstanding issue for the twenty-first century. This is even more important since the presence of diverse cultures, whose opposing worldviews are rooted in different traditions, may be a source of future social unrest." In such a situation of potential conflict, rhetoric will be active and formative, either serving to palliate or aggravate cultural divisions and discord. To return to a metaphor introduced earlier in this book, Lillian Smith warned that southerners "cannot get along without symbols. . . . They are full of strange power and can destroy us when used improperly. . . . They need to be handled as carefully as nuclear energy."[11] Donald Trump, the Russian operatives of the IRA, and the organizers of the white supremacist rally in Charlottesville all understood the tremendous nuclear power of confederate rhetoric. They have been mobilizing that power to explode harmony within America and to slow progress toward the creation of a stronger, more unified culture.

Concluding Call for Linguistic and Symbolic Activism

Confederate rhetoric has played—and continues to play—a negative role in the South's cultural stasis or regression. In overt and covert ways, confederate rhetoric continues to create and re-create a culture in which whiteness is celebrated and rewarded while Blackness is marginalized and punished. Again, this process is happening on the local level, and college towns are often flashpoints: places like Charlottesville, Athens, Columbia, Tuscaloosa, and Oxford.

The Russian social media campaign to sow American discord is one very worrying reason to turn scholarly attention to the ways discourse plays out within communities like that of the University of Mississippi. Through a fuller understanding of a particular southern university community, we might be able to better understand the US South and, indeed, the country. Discourse is local, and discourse is powerful. America's enemies seem to believe that words and symbols can be used strategically to stoke dissent and to catalyze division, and they have thus far been affirmed in their belief. It would seem wise, then, for scholars to better understand if and how those enemies have been successful. Are the correlations above—between a deluge of Russian memes and a flood of American hatred—rooted in any traceable causalities? It is a pressing question.

We should also care about analyses of discourse in the US South because previous failures almost always contain lessons for future successes. If language and symbols divide, then language and symbols can surely unite. As I suggested in chapter 7, leaders in the South have opportunities to break old linguistic and semiotic patterns, to confront words and symbols that are beloved by some but abominated by others. This work is difficult, and it will surely displace some white stakeholders who cannot or will not adjust their vocabularies, who cannot or will not transfer some of their ideational and emotional investments away from confederate rhetoric. Ultimately, however, this work will liberate everyone in the community by removing symbolic and linguistic barriers that have sown division and enforced oppression for many decades. This book has highlighted how Old South words and symbols have slowed progress and propagated racism within southern university communities. The far better story lies ahead: how new South words and symbols might accelerate progress and propagate unity and true equality within those same communities.

But we should not be naïve or prematurely optimistic. This book has charted just how entrenched and stubborn traditions of harmful Old South words and symbols have become at predominantly white southern universities. The good news is that rhetorical traditions are controlled by rhetors, and new generations of white southern rhetors today have the sociolinguistic power to change direction. Just as previous generations of white southerners made purposeful and sustained investments in Old South words and symbols, current generations can liquidate those investments and use their linguistic power and privilege to construct (ideally in full partnership with southerners of all races) more mindful and inclusive portfolios. As Asao Inoue and others have suggested, this work will require white people to move voluntarily and quickly from positions of relative comfort and silence to positions of frequent discomfort and advocacy. Just as the construction of confederate rhetoric has been a project accomplished by the white majority over many decades, the dismantling of confederate rhetoric must also be—in large part—a project undertaken by the white majority in the coming years. For the region to strengthen and improve beyond the real but incomplete victories of the civil rights era, white southerners must make new contributions to progress.

In the realm of words and symbols, white people in the US South will have daily opportunities to eschew confederate rhetoric and to deploy, instead, rhetorical hospitality: to use words and symbols to reject racism and to overtly signal acceptance and inclusion. In the region—especially in its most powerful institutions, including its predominantly white universities—white people still maintain the power to welcome people of color into "their" white spaces, which have forever been controlled and dominated by whiteness (fig. 22). This kind of rhetorical action is the opposite of measures taken recently by the Russian government and by white supremacists like Richard Spencer. Just as

FIGURE 22. Table of food in the Grove at the University of Mississippi before the football game versus the University of Alabama on October 4, 2014. Colonel Rebel's name and image evoke the Civil War and a glorified view of antebellum plantation life. The mascot was officially retired in 2010 but remains popular and highly visible within the community. In this image, confederate rhetoric complicates the southern tradition of hospitality. Would everyone, black and white, feel welcome at this table? (Photograph taken by William DeShazer for the *New York Times*, October 31, 2014, https://www.nytimes.com.)

confederate rhetoric has done so much harm, a new southern rhetoric holds tremendous potential to transform and improve the region. If rhetoric can traumatize and damage, then rhetoric can also soothe and heal.

Sometime around 2014, a white fraternity at the University of Mississippi was planning a party when the following discussion took place within the all-white space of a campus fraternity house. It was later reported by a white person who was present: "The idea of t-shirts for an event came up. A boy said 'we are going to invite all the black fraternities and sororities and then send them to a cotton field and make them pick cotton for our shirts, the only downside is that we'll have to whip them.' The entire room went silent and a few other boys laughed but most people just didn't know what to say about this offensive topic. He then continued to say how they would have to be kicked out before the actual party started."[12] As this book has made clear, such imaginative re-creations of racist tableaus and tropes are not isolated incidents at UM (or at other southern universities). They are, instead, predictable encores within a persistent rhetorical performance. In the above moment, the white student who later reported the exchange—and likely other white people in the room—found the fraternity member's comments offensive, but they remained silent. (The only audible reaction was supportive laughter from a few others.) We know from many examples from other eras that racist rhetoric only grows stronger when left unchallenged. Traditions of confederate rhetoric cannot be changed with silence, and thus much responsibility for disrupting scenes like the one above will fall on present-day white people within all-white, private spaces. Bravery and defiance will be required to speak up, to advocate, to ally oneself with minorities who are invisible, underrepresented, or consistently marginalized. But rhetorical disruptions are clearly necessary for a region still weighed down by racism. White discomfort must be followed by white disruption.

In many cases, only white people in the US South have the power and opportunity to change linguistic and symbolic practices like confederate rhetoric. When attacked by Black southerners or outsiders, confederate rhetoric has persistently adapted and survived. As examples throughout this book have demonstrated, confederate rhetoric has often become commonsensical or mainstream. It has often been successfully defended as harmless, or even charming, and minimized as natural and beyond reproach. It has often survived and thrived, protected even by well-intentioned white people who simply fail to recognize its actual impacts on audiences other than themselves.

So, I end this book with a call for activism from a group that has been far too passive for far too long: white southerners of all ages within institutions like the University of Mississippi. It is time to refresh and reinvent our rhetoric. It is time to improve the region through internally aggressive confrontations with outmoded words and symbols. Those words and symbols are standing in the way of full southern hospitality and progress. They are hurting our African American neighbors and holding back our individual communities. Confederate rhetoric has become a tradition, and it is time to upgrade and improve that tradition. Just as previous generations used words and symbols to shape their future South, current generations can use words and symbols to shape their own future South. The "nuclear" power of language is available and limitless. We can and should innovate linguistically and symbolically. We can and should reconstruct better and more inclusive communities. Improving our words and symbols will improve our region.

Postscript

Chanelle Benz closes her great Mississippi novel *The Gone Dead* with a meditation on the power of language: "Words have blood in them; they can make fate take shape when they pass from a mouth into a heart." *Heritage and Hate* is nothing if not a long argument for this very truth. The story of the US South is in part a story of blood-infused words and symbols built by previous generations of white southerners to shape fate, to preserve racism, to offer some hearts the salve of nostalgia, and to punish other hearts with the poison of hatred.

I began writing this book in 2016, and I finished in 2019. When Minneapolis policemen killed George Floyd in 2020, I watched the resulting firestorm spread southward and burn away some of the worst words and symbols that were my subjects. The fire is now ongoing, and it is exhilarating to watch. Like most everyone else, I cannot turn away from the coverage as more and more Confederate statues fall, as more old buildings are stripped of their racist namesakes, as even the Mississippi flag is designed anew. That so many prominent examples of confederate rhetoric are now being reconsidered says something very good about our society. That so much Black blood needed to be spilled in order to spark this widespread reconsideration says something reprehensible about our same society. A good bit of our nastiest rhetorical underbrush is now going up in smoke, but why did it take so long?

At least in the present moment, it seems that George Floyd's murder might become a culminating American tragedy. As I write this postscript in the summer of 2020, the country continues to heave in anger and disgust. Protesters are gathering nightly in big cities like Atlanta and Portland, and even in small towns like Oxford, Mississippi. The Black Lives Matter movement has gained in strength and popularity and acceptance. It is no longer a marginalized concern. Many hopeful commentators on television speak of a turning point. As one common protest sign reads, "Enough!" Black Americans and their allies rally to commemorate George Floyd and all the other Black people killed in that long and senseless procession: Trayvon Martin, Tamir Rice, Michael Brown, Eric Garner, Breonna Taylor, and on and on. Today's protesters are making a stand, and they seem to be achieving a real and heartening acceleration of racial progress from sea to shining sea.

In the US South, it did not take long for the protesters to turn toward confederate rhetoric. Suddenly in this environment it is much harder for old racist symbols to hide in plain sight. Yes, protesters are pulling down prominent markers like monuments and statues, but they are also scrutinizing and helping retire less overt reminders of the Old South. The Dixie Chicks have dropped their outdated adjective: no more Dixie. Disney is removing the Old South nostalgia from its Splash Mountain ride in Orlando. School boards around the region, including the Franklin County School Board in Tennessee, are reconsidering their "rebel" mascots. This is a moment filled with many positive developments. There is a groundswell of sorts in which Old South words and symbols are being reconsidered and revised at a record pace.

In my most optimistic moments, I think that perhaps all of the old destructive rhetoric—like the confederate rhetoric that I wrote about in this book—will be washed away at once. Perhaps it will all be gone by 2021. Maybe the old defenders of Dixie will surrender their symbols once and for all. Maybe we are now living through a rhetorical Appomattox. Maybe no white southerner will ever again argue that Confederate symbols—like the rebel flag—are about heritage, not hate.

But then, in my clearer and more realistic moments, I remember what I have learned while researching and writing this book. Confederate rhetoric is deeply embedded in southern institutions, including the region's predominantly white universities. In some ways, white people built those very institutions using these terrible symbols. They created sturdy foundations and guaranteed that generations of white students would form their individual and communal identities by relying on these words and symbols. Confederate rhetoric is ubiquitous and consequential, and it has performed its cultural work for more than a century. And so it will not be easy to alter southern orthodoxies, to shift deep-rooted discourses that remain commonsensical and controlling. I hope that I am wrong, but I do not believe that all remaining confederate rhetoric will be retired within this single summer or year or decade.

Yes, we are living in a time of accelerated progress, but history tells us that such progress is always recursive. Appomattox was hardly the end of the conflicts and hatreds it was meant to put to rest. Already white resistance is reemerging, and there has been backpedaling. President Trump is a case in point. He is helping the old cause, utilizing confederate rhetoric and summoning some of the old orthodoxies for his own political purposes. Recently, when pressed by a reporter, Trump refused to acknowledge, much less condemn, the hateful consequences of the Confederate battle flag. "It depends on who you're talking about, when you're talking about," said Trump. "When people proudly had their Confederate flags they're not talking about racism. They love their flag, it represents the South. They like the South. . . . I say it's freedom of many things, but it's freedom of speech." A few weeks before, Trump had mocked NASCAR for its decision to prohibit the Confederate flag from races.[1]

We must listen to Trump, for he is amplifying some significant percentage of southerners—and Americans—who have been more or less silent during this summer of protest and progress. These white people are often savvy enough to keep their "politically incorrect" opinions to themselves. There have been viral and violent exceptions, but much of the resistance is reserved at this point. During this turbulent summer, millions of white southerners remain reticent. They hold their tongues and wait in silence while feeling more or less satisfied with the status quo. Fairly or not, these white people continue to control the legal, social, and political systems of the region. They still have the power to ignore the tumult, the headlines, the protests. They can politely look away. They can go to the beach, even during the pandemic. They can avoid incendiary racial topics and tough conversations. They can remain noncommittal when someone says, "Black lives matter," or when someone else says, "All lives matter."

We should all be concerned about these silent white southerners, for they are enacting the inertia that has repeatedly limited racial progress and slowed lasting change. How do we engage the silent South in conversation and education? How do we convince and enlist more white southerners to care more actively about racial equality and justice? Black Lives Matter has perhaps made some progress this summer, recruiting new white people of conscience into the streets. But we will need a menu of approaches to convert white southerners en masse.

Within liberal circles, there is an ongoing debate about the most effective tactics for achieving racial progress. Some advocates for change believe first and foremost in radicalization. Marching. Chanting. Never compromising. Some, on the other hand, believe first and foremost in racial reconciliation. Sitting. Talking. Patiently engaging. One approach is loud and confrontational. The other is quiet and conciliatory. Which is best? The truth is that we probably need both. Radical voices provide pressure toward change. Reconciliation programs provide safe avenues for moving toward that change.

I wrote earlier in this book about the William Winter Institute for Racial Reconciliation in Mississippi. Staff there facilitate Welcome Table programs for local organizations and communities. People of all races gather together to share stories, talk openly and safely about race, and build relationships with each other. The programs break down barriers and promote new kinds of unity and togetherness. In addition to the Winter Institute, other wonderful organizations promote and produce racial reconciliation. Dave Tell and his colleagues at the Emmett Till Memory Project engage white and Black people through historical tours, social media campaigns, multimodal publications, and traditional panels and programs.

Such advocacy projects raise awareness, amplify new and diverse voices, and provide inspiration to people of all colors who want our country and region to be better. Inspiration will be important in the coming years, especially if I am right in my pessimistic prediction that the battle over Old South words and symbols will not be completely won anytime soon.

This summer, I've found great inspiration close to home, in Mississippi, where neighbors, colleagues, students, and friends have pulled together to protest the state's long-standing tradition of racism. White, Black, rich, poor, old, young: they've been fighting for years, but since George Floyd's murder in faraway Minneapolis, these Mississippians are gaining in number and winning more battles.

It's not the Mississippi that you see in the movies. Thank God. It's far more complicated and beautiful. There is more hope. I live, of course, in Oxford, home to the University of Mississippi, where I teach and where I'm now writing this postscript. I know people like Curtis Hill. Curtis came to Oxford to study English and writing. He is a young Black man from a small Delta town. He was not born into wealth or privilege. He's the first in his family to go to college. In the Mississippi of the movies, Curtis might be shy and unassuming—he might "know his place."

In the real Mississippi, though, Curtis Hill is bold and ambitious. He is studying, reading, and networking. He is making his place, and he moves through the world with his head held high and his eyes toward the future. He is speaking and writing his truth.[2]

Last year, before the mass protests of this summer, I worried that Curtis might get arrested or expelled. I saw him on social media in a video that went viral. It depicted a protest of his own. In the video, it was dusk on our beautiful campus, and Curtis and his classmate Tyler Yarbrough were dressed up. They were carrying a big bullet-riddled metal sign through the famous Grove. At first, I had lots of questions about what I was watching, but I knew immediately which sign that was. It had been big news over the past month or two.

It was the Emmett Till historical marker that normally stood on the banks of the Tallahatchie River, some seventy miles from campus. It had been placed there to mark the site where the white men who murdered Till dumped his brutalized body. There is perhaps no more terrible or infamous moment from the civil rights era.

Emmett Till was fourteen years old in 1955 and was visiting family in Mississippi. Probably on a dare, he said something flirtatious to Carolyn Bryant, a white woman. She told her husband, embellishing the details. Her husband and his brother then went looking for young Till a few nights later. They beat him, murdered him, used barbed wire to tie a heavy cotton gin blade around his neck, and sunk his body in the river.

I recognized the historical marker right away because not long ago, in the spring of 2019 and a few months before Curtis and Tyler carried it across campus, three other University of Mississippi students—white fraternity men—had used this same historical marker in another way. Back then, it was still standing beside the river. The white fraternity brothers drove out there in the dark with their guns. Perhaps they shot the marker up themselves. Perhaps it was already shot up. Either way, they had their picture taken before the bullet-riddled sign, posing with smiles on their faces and guns in hand like hunters displaying their kill. That hateful photo of the vandalized Till marker appeared on social media, it was "liked" a few hundred times, and eventually university administrators discovered it. Reportedly, the white students were punished by a mere suspension from their fraternity.

Months later, when Curtis and Tyler were filmed carrying that same marker across campus, they had just been part of a panel discussion about the earlier episode. They had gathered with other students and community members to talk about the actions and consequences of their three white classmates. The panel was sponsored by the Emmett Till Memory Project, and the participants wanted to know more about the photograph of the white students with their guns. Why had they been standing so happily and proudly beside the bullet-riddled marker? Why had the university been slow to respond? Why was there not more outrage, more condemnation? Someone from the Memory Project had brought the marker to Oxford for the panel discussion. It served as a chilling prop during the session. After the panel was over, on the spur of the moment, Curtis and Tyler lifted the marker and began to walk with their friends toward the Confederate monument, which was then still standing at the center of campus.

It was not a short walk, and it was hot. Curtis cut his hand on the ragged edge of one of the bullet holes. He and Tyler were sweating. Strangers began to notice. There were dozens of bystanders on campus, football fans getting ready for tomorrow's football game and for the world-famous tailgate. Some faces were friendly; some were not. People were watching and filming. Curtis and Tyler marched on.

When they arrived at the Confederate statue, they stood silently with the disfigured Till marker. (The photographer Suzi Altman, on campus for the panel discussion, captured compelling photos of this moment, which can now be found online.) Curtis and Tyler stood with stoic faces as they brought two symbols together. They had created a complex and instructive juxtaposition. One symbol was the Confederate statue that has stood on campus since 1906, that honors the ideals of the Confederacy, and that idealizes systemic racism. The other symbol was the marker commemorating Emmett Till, the young person whose horrific lynching was fuel for countless activists and allies in the civil rights movement. Curtis and Tyler created this tableau of contradictions, and they stood there for a few moments in silence and dignity. In my opinion, it was a masterful composition, a clarion call for change.

As I write these words now, not quite a year since that moment, the Confederate statue at the University of Mississippi has finally been moved to another spot on campus. It no longer stands prominently in the place where Curtis and Tyler created their silent protest. The move was not a perfect solution, and local arguments continue, but that is a story for another time. Today, the statue no longer stands at the entrance to the university. It no longer greets every visitor. It no longer defines the university in the same way that it did for so long. Perhaps most importantly, students—new generations—no longer have to walk past it on their way to class. It is mostly out of sight, and it is no longer the symbolic centerpiece of confederate rhetoric on campus. This is a tremendously important milestone for our modest institution, a moment of real and undeniable racial progress.

There was so much activism and effort that led to the movement of this single Confederate statue.[3] Over many years, inspiring figures in our Mississippi community have argued, protested, prayed, organized, petitioned, and beseeched for the removal of that Confederate monument. The tactics were many, and the process was long. George Floyd's murder certainly accelerated the victory. But like many recent victories, this has been a prolonged story of progress through local and sustained effort. So many good people from town and gown fought to bring down the Confederate monument at "Ole Miss." They often fought silent, stubborn, and strong enemies. This summer, they finally won.

Of course, my favorite moment in this meandering tale, the one that for me will always mark the true end of the statue's reign, was created by Curtis and Tyler. Through their bravery and wisdom, they summarized a seemingly interminable argument over an influential artifact of confederate rhetoric. They moved the ole toward the new, and they used rhetoric to push our community toward a much better fate.

Notes

Preface

1. Laurie Gries, *Still Life with Rhetoric: A New Materialist Approach for Visual Rhetorics* (Logan: Utah State University Press, 2015), 287.

2. Philip N. Howard, Bharath Ganesh, Dimitra Liotsiou, John Kelly, and Camile François, *The IRA, Social Media and Political Polarization in the United States, 2012–2018* (Oxford: Computational Propaganda Project, University of Oxford, 2018), 6 (statistics), 8, 39 (quotation), https://comprop.oii.ox.ac.uk; Nicholas Fandos, Cecilia Kang, and Mike Isaac, "House Intelligence Committee Releases Incendiary Russian Social Media Ads," *New York Times*, November 1, 2017, https://www.nytimes.com.

3. Renee DiResta, Kris Shaffer, Becky Ruppel, David Sullivan, Robert Matney, Ryan Fox, Jonathan Albright, and Ben Johnson, *The Tactics and Tropes of the Internet Research Agency* (New Knowledge, 2019), 50 (quotation), https://disinformationreport.blob.core.windows.net/disinformation-report/NewKnowledge-Disinformation-Report-Whitepaper.pdf; Scott Shane, "These Are the Ads Russia Bought on Facebook in 2016," *New York Times*, November 1, 2017, https://www.nytimes.com.

4. Shane, "Ads Russia Bought"; Patrick Warren quoted in Oliver Roeder, "Why We're Sharing 3 Million Russian Troll Tweets," *FiveThirtyEight*, July 31, 2018, https://fivethirtyeight.com; US House of Representatives Permanent Select Committee on Intelligence, "Exposing Russia's Effort to Sow Discord Online: The Internet Research Agency and Advertisements," 2018, https://intelligence.house.gov/social-media-content/.

5. Chas Danner, "More than Half of Russian Facebook Ads Focused on Race," *New York Magazine*, May 12, 2018, http://nymag.com.

6. Walker Percy quoted in James C. Cobb, *Away Down South: A History of Southern Identity* (Oxford: Oxford University Press, 2005), 208.

7. Angie Thomas (@angiecthomas), "Aaaand this is why I'm moving," Twitter, January 19, 2019, 9:52 a.m., https://twitter.com/angiecthomas/status/1086652519303008257; Giacomo Bologna, "Mississippi Department of Revenue Deletes Robert E. Lee Tweet after Backlash," *Clarion-Ledger*, January 17, 2019, https://www.clarionledger.com.

8. V. S. Naipaul quoted in Anthony Walton, *Mississippi: An American Journey* (New York: Knopf, 1996), 187; Richard Grant, *Dispatches from Pluto: Lost and Found in the Mississippi Delta* (New York: Simon and Schuster, 2015), 2.

9. Kwame Anthony Appiah, *Cosmopolitanism: Ethics in a World of Strangers* (New York: Norton, 2007), xiv.

10. Isabel Wilkerson, *The Warmth of Other Suns: The Epic Story of America's Great Migration* (New York: Vintage Books, 2011), 31.

11. Walton, *Mississippi*, 158.

12. Clarence L. Mohr, introduction to *Education*, ed. Mohr, vol. 17, *The New Encyclopedia of Southern Culture* (Chapel Hill: University of North Carolina Press, 2001), 7.

Introduction

1. Jan Blommaert, *Discourse: A Critical Introduction* (Cambridge: Cambridge University Press, 2005), 3.

2. I acknowledge the productive turn within southern studies to the Global South, and I believe that some of the interpretative strategies developed in this book might contribute to such broader notions of the South, but I also remain preoccupied and focused on the traditionally bounded region known as the US South or the American South.

3. Michael Montgomery and Ellen Johnson, "Language in the South," in *Language*, ed. Montgomery and Johnson, vol. 5, *The New Encyclopedia of Southern Culture* (Chapel Hill: University of North Carolina Press, 2006), 1.

4. C. Van Woodward, *The Burden of Southern History*, 3rd ed. (Baton Rouge: Louisiana State University Press, 1993), 25.

5. Lillian Smith, *Killers of the Dream* (New York: W. W. Norton, 1994), 244.

6. Charles Reagan Wilson, "Whose South?," *Southern Cultures* 22, no. 4 (Winter 2016).

7. Jane H. Hill, *The Everyday Language of White Racism* (Chichester, UK: Wiley and Sons, 2008), 41.

8. Grace Elizabeth Hale, *Making Whiteness: The Culture of Segregation in the South, 1890–1940* (New York: Random House, 1998), 8–9. Hale broadens this conclusion to America as a whole. See also Hale, "Bounding Consumption," chap. 4 in *Making Whiteness*.

9. Norman Fairclough, *Language and Power*, 3rd ed. (New York: Routledge, 2015), 49.

10. Bryan Stevenson, *Just Mercy* (New York: Spiegel and Grau, 2015), 299.

11. The adjective "affectionate" is ubiquitous in explanations of the term "Ole Miss." See, for example, the "About UM" page on the university's website, which still featured the adjective in its explanation at the time of this writing.

12. Editorial, "Experience Informs Our Consciousness," *Daily Mississippian*, February 19, 2014, http://thedmonline.com.

13. A. C. Thompson and Karim Hajj, "A New Generation of White Supremacists Emerges in Charlottesville," *ProPublica*, August 13, 2017, https://www.propublica.org.

14. Delece Smith-Barrow, "Ole Miss Grapples with Its Links to Slavery and Racism," *Clarion-Ledger*, March 7, 2018, https://www.clarionledger.com.

15. Greg Dickinson, Carole Blair, and Brian L. Ott, *Places of Public Memory: The Rhetoric of Museums and Memorials* (Tuscaloosa: University of Alabama Press, 2010), 6.

16. Tammie M. Kennedy, Joyce Irene Middleton, and Krista Ratcliffe, *Rhetorics of Whiteness* (Carbondale: Southern Illinois University Press, 2016), 5.

17. Bradford Vivian, *Commonplace Witnessing: Rhetorical Invention, Historical Remembrance, and Public Culture* (Oxford: Oxford University Press, 2017), 203.

18. Thomas Walter Reed, *History of the University of Georgia* (Athens: University of Georgia, 1949), 24–25.

19. Charles W. Eagles, *The Price of Defiance: James Meredith and the Integration of Ole Miss* (Chapel Hill: University of North Carolina Press, 2009), 13, 14 (Curtis Wilkie quotation), 16.

20. University of Alabama, *Corolla, 1961*, http://purl.lib.ua.edu/35222.

Chapter 1

1. Stuart Stevens, "Between Ole Miss and Me," *Daily Beast*, October 30, 2015, updated April 13, 2017, https://www.thedailybeast.com ("most Southern"); John Talty, "Mississippi Rising: How Ole Miss, Mississippi State Are Capitalizing on a Historic Football Season," *Al.com*, October 31, 2014, updated March 5, 2019, https://www.al.com ("good, Southern, friendly feel"); Ole Miss Sports Productions, "We Are Ole Miss: A Conversation between Athletics Director, Ross Bjork, and Chancellor, Dan Jones," online video, Vimeo, 2014, retrieved and transcribed December 15, 2016; *Daily Mississippian*, November 2, 1929 ("so beautiful and appropriate").

2. Charles Eagles quoted in Alan Blinder, "Racist Episodes Continue to Stir Ole Miss Campus," *New York Times*, February 20, 2014, https://www.nytimes.com.

3. Jackie Certion, email message to author, January 2017. Quoted with permission.

4. Norman Fairclough, *Critical Discourse Analysis: The Critical Study of Language*, 2nd ed. (London: Routledge, 2010), 57 ("ideology invests language"), 67 ("naturalized, automatized"); Norman Fairclough, *Language and Power*, 3rd ed. (London: Routledge, 2015), 108 ("least visible").

5. Jan Blommaert, *Discourse: A Critical Introduction* (Cambridge: Cambridge University Press, 2005), 33 (quotation), 34.

6. Allen Cabaniss, *The University of Mississippi: Its First Hundred Years* (Hattiesburg: The University and College Press of Mississippi, 1971), 117; David G. Sansing, *The University of Mississippi: A Sesquicentennial History* (Jackson: University Press of Mississippi, 1999), 168; Charles W. Eagles, *The Price of Defiance: James Meredith and the Integration of Ole Miss* (Chapel Hill: University of North Carolina Press, 2009), 17.

7. Laurie Gries, *Still Life with Rhetoric: A New Materialist Approach for Visual Rhetorics* (Logan: Utah State University Press, 2015), 290.

8. Catherine Jones, "Reconstruction and Redemption," in *Social Class*, ed. Larry J. Griffin and Peggy G. Harris, vol. 20, *The New Encyclopedia of Southern Culture* (Chapel Hill: University of North Carolina Press, 2012), 230.

9. Edward L. Ayers, *The Promise of the New South: Life after Reconstruction* (Oxford: Oxford University Press, 2007), viii.

10. Grace Elizabeth Hale, *Making Whiteness: The Culture of Segregation in the South, 1890–1940* (New York: Random House, 1998), 65.

11. "Elma Meek Gave University Its Name, 'Ole Miss,' Long Probe of Students Reveals," *Commercial Appeal*, October 11, 1936.

12. University of Mississippi, *Ole Miss, 1897*, dedication page.

13. Rory McVeigh, "Structural Incentives for Conservative Mobilization: Power Devaluation and the Rise of the Ku Klux Klan, 1915–1925," *Social Forces* 77, no. 4 (1999): 1464.

14. John Sharp Williams, "Issues of the War Discussed," November 1904, excerpted in *The Confederate and Neo-Confederate Reader: The "Great Truth" about the "Lost Cause,"* ed. James Loewen and Edward Sebesta (Jackson: University Press of Mississippi, 2010), 301.

15. Hale, *Making Whiteness*, 153.

16. Franklin E. Moak, *A History of the Alumni Association of the University of Mississippi 1852–1986* (Oxford: Alumni Association of the University of Mississippi, 1986), 53.

17. Office of Institutional Research, Effectiveness, and Planning, University of Mississippi, "Enrollment at the University of Mississippi since 1848," retrieved December 15, 2016, http://irep.olemiss.edu/institutional-research/enrollment-data/.

18. Gries, *Still Life with Rhetoric*, 287.

19. Anthony J. Stanonis, introduction to *Dixie Emporium: Tourism, Foodways, and Consumer Culture in the American South*, ed. Stanonis (Athens: University of Georgia Press, 2008), 5.

20. J. B. Webb's poem printed in University of Mississippi, *Ole Miss, 1905*, 7; Williams, "Issues of the War Discussed," 302.

21. Karen Cox, "Branding Dixie: The Selling of the American South, 1890–1930," in Stanonis, *Dixie Emporium*, 51; UM catalog quoted in Nadine Cohodas, *The Band Played Dixie: Race and the Liberal Conscience at Ole Miss* (New York: Free Press, 1997), 12; Curtis Wilkie, *Dixie: A Personal Odyssey through Events That Shaped the Modern South* (New York: Scribner, 2002), 82.

22. Fairclough, *Critical Discourse Analysis*, 67.

23. Gries, *Still Life with Rhetoric*, 287.

24. University of Mississippi, *Ole Miss, 1911*, 1.

25. Editorial, "Gem Which Pleased All—Ole Miss," *Mississippian*, January 11, 1913, 4; University of Mississippi, *Ole Miss, 1925*, 11, 13.

26. James C. Cobb, *Away Down South: A History of Southern Identity* (Oxford: Oxford University Press, 2005), 12.

27. W. Fitzhugh Brundage, *The Southern Past* (Cambridge, MA: Harvard University Press, 2005), 4.

28. L. A. Smith, "Origin of 'Ole Miss,'" *Ole Miss Alumni News*, 1932, 12.

29. Equal Justice Initiative, *Lynching in America: Confronting the Legacy of Racial Terror, Report Summary*, 2nd ed. (Montgomery, AL: EJI, 2015), 4, 12.

30. University of Mississippi, *Ole Miss, 1945*, 41.

31. Ole Miss Department of Public Relations, "Ole Miss Origin," October 29, 1947, print memo, University of Mississippi Department of Archives and Special Collections.

32. Eagles, *Price of Defiance*, 58.

33. William Winter, afterword to *Riot: Witness to Anger and Change*, by Edwin E. Meek (Oxford: Yoknapatawpha Press, 2015), 135.

34. Fairclough, *Critical Discourse Analysis*, 67.

35. Cohodas, *The Band Played Dixie*, 37, 38 (quotation).

36. Gries, *Still Life with Rhetoric*, 39–42.

37. John Cossar quoted in Al Poval, *A Time Remembered: Ole Miss, 1945–1970, an Oral History* (Oxford: Nautilus, 2016), 202–3.

38. Allen Cabaniss, "Memo to the Committee on the 125th Anniversary Observance: An Open Letter Containing a Humble Petition," n.d., Gerald Walton Collection, Special Collections, University of Mississippi Libraries.

39. Joan Bailey, "An Ode to Ole Miss," *Ole Miss Alumni Review* 55, no. 3 (Summer 2006), 30.

40. Bailey, "Ode to Ole Miss," 30; Staff Reports, "The University of Mississippi or Ole Miss," *Vicksburg Post*, November 11, 2006, https://www.vicksburgpost.com.

41. Frank E. Everett Jr. quoted in Bailey, "Ode to Ole Miss," 30.

42. Sansing, *University of Mississippi*, 322–23; W. Ralph Eubanks, "The Unhealed Wounds of a Mass Arrest of Black Students at Ole Miss, Fifty Years Later," *New Yorker*, February 23, 2020, https://www.newyorker.com.

43. Staff Reports, "University of Mississippi or Ole Miss."

44. Everett quoted in Bailey, "Ode to Ole Miss," 30.

45. James Meredith, *Three Years in Mississippi* (Bloomington: Indiana University Press, 1966), 3, 260–62.

46. Bailey, "Ode to Ole Miss," 30.

47. Bailey, "Ode to Ole Miss," 30.

Chapter 2

1. Julian Shakespeare Carr, "Unveiling of Confederate Monument at University," June 2, 1913, Julian Shakespeare Carr Papers (#00141), Southern Historical Collection, Wilson Library, University of North Carolina at Chapel Hill, https://exhibits.lib.unc.edu/items/show/5519; postcard depicting the unveiling of the Confederate Monument, June 2, 1913, in Orange County, North Carolina Postcard Collection (P052), North Carolina Collection Photographic Archives, Wilson Library, University of North Carolina at Chapel Hill, https://exhibits.lib.unc.edu/exhibits/show/silent-sam/item/3670; UNC University Archives, Guide to Resources about UNC's Confederate Monument, "Timeline," https://exhibits.lib.unc.edu/exhibits/show/silent-sam/timeline.

2. UNC University Archives, Guide to Resources about UNC's Confederate Monument, "Timeline."

3. Andy Thomason, "Protesters Tear Down Chapel Hill's Divisive Confederate Monument," *Chronicle of Higher Education*, August 20, 2018, https://www.chronicle.com; Jesse James Deconto and Alan Blinder, "Silent Sam Confederate Statue Is Toppled at University of North Carolina," *New York Times*, August 21, 2018. https://www.nytimes.com.

4. Susan Svrluga, "Silent Sam Will Stay Off the University of North Carolina Campus as the School Turns the Statue Over to a Confederate Group," *Washington Post*, November 27, 2019, https://www.washingtonpost.com.

5. Lily Jackson, "Is Auburn's Response to Ivey Blackface Incident Enough?" *Al.com*, August 30, 2019, https://www.al.com; Susan Svrluga, "Mizzou Chancellor Responds after Student-Body President Is Called the N-word," *Washington Post*, September 17, 2015, https://www.washingtonpost.com; Savannah Sicurella, "UGA Fraternity Suspended after Racist Video Goes Viral," *Red & Black*, March 23, 2019, https://www.redandblack.com; Kristi L. Nelson, "UT: One Student from 'Blackface' Snapchat Image No Longer Enrolled; Brother Speaks Out," *Knoxville News Sentinel*, March 6, 2019, https://www.knoxnews.com; John Murawski, "Racial Slur Scrawled on Center for Black Culture at Duke University," *News & Observer*, August 25, 2018, https://www.newsobserver.com.

6. Richard Bauman, "Language, Identity, Performance," *Pragmatics* 10 (2000): 1–5.

7. Jerry Mitchell, "Ole Miss Students Face Possible Civil Rights Investigation after

Posing with Guns in front of Emmett Till Memorial," Mississippi Center for Investigative Reporting, July 25, 2019, https://www.mississippicir.org.

8. David G. Sansing, *The University of Mississippi: A Sesquicentennial History* (Jackson: University Press of Mississippi, 1999), 270.

9. Saxon Nelson, "Ole Miss Class of 2017 Aims to Establish Hotty Toddy Plaque," *Hotty Toddy*, August 26, 2016, http://hottytoddy.com.

10. For an example of the Hotty Toddy as part of a wedding celebration, see "Hotty Toddy - Wedding Reception," posted by Matt Williams, July 20, 2014, YouTube, https://youtu.be/moaWm6--lIw.

11. Ruth Serven, "A 'Radical Form of Resistance': MU Activists on Looking Back and Moving Forward," *Missourian*, November 7, 2016, https://www.columbiamissourian.com; Anthony James, Amanda Bennett, and Patrick Maddox, "How Does It Feel to Be a Problem," dir. Patrick Maddox, 2015, Vimeo, https://vimeo.com/145380616; Kurt Edward Kemper, *College Football and American Culture in the Cold War Era* (Champaign: University of Illinois Press, 2009), 119.

12. Mary Bucholtz and Kira Hall, "Identity and Interaction: A Sociocultural Linguistic Approach," *Discourse Studies* 7, no. 4–5 (2005): 588.

13. John Oddo "Discourse-Based Methods across Texts and Semiotic Modes: Three Tools for Micro-Rhetorical Analysis," *Written Communication* 30, no. 3 (2013): 236–75; J. R. Martin and P. R. R. White, *The Language of Evaluation: Appraisal in English* (Basingstoke: Palgrave Macmillan, 2005).

14. Adam Hodges, "'Yes, We Can': The Social Life of a Political Slogan," in *Contemporary Critical Discourse Studies*, ed. Christopher Hart and Piotr Cap (London: Bloomsbury, 2014). See also Mikhail Mihaïlovich Bakhtin, "The Problem of Speech Genres," in *Speech Genres and Other Late Essays*, ed. Michael Holquist and Caryl Emerson (Austin: University of Texas Press, 1986); Michael Silverstein, "Indexical Order and the Dialectics of Sociolinguistic Life," *Language & Communication* 23 (2003): 193–229; and Bauman, "Language, Identity, Performance."

15. James K. Gentry, "Tailgating Goes Above and Beyond at the University of Mississippi," *New York Times*, October 31, 2014, https://www.nytimes.com.

16. Bucholtz and Hall, "Identity and Interaction," 587, 607.

17. Bucholtz and Hall, "Identity and Interaction," 607, 589.

18. Bucholtz and Hall, "Identity and Interaction," 589.

19. Edwin Smith, "Understanding the History and Significance of 'Hotty Toddy,'" *University of Mississippi News*, April 9, 2014, https://news.olemiss.edu; "What Does Hotty Toddy Mean?," posted by Ole Miss News, November 10, 2010, YouTube, https://www.youtube.com/watch?v=JfpirH7BEwE&feature=emb_logo.

20. Thomas Reardon, "Hotty Toddy & Other Traditions," in *The Ole Miss Experience*, ed. Leslie Banahan (Oxford: Nautilus, 2012), 151–59.

21. Doug Ward, "Ole Miss Tailgating," *espn.com*, October 27, 2010, http://www.espn.com.

22. Stuart Stevens, *The Last Season: A Father, a Son, and a Lifetime of College Football* (New York: Knopf, 2015), 6.

23. Blaire Jackson and Jenna Artz quoted in Emmie Harmon, "Hotty Toddy History," *Daily Mississippian*, October 3, 2014, http://thedmonline.com; Bucholtz and Hall, "Identity and Interaction," 588.

24. Bucholtz and Hall, "Identity and Interaction," 585–86.

25. James C. Cobb, *Away Down South: A History of Southern Identity* (Oxford: Oxford University Press, 2005), 197.

26. Franklin Moak, *A History of the Alumni Association of the University of Mississippi* (Oxford: Alumni Association of the University of Mississippi, 1986), 106; Sansing, *University of Mississippi*, 270; Charles W. Eagles, *The Price of Defiance: James Meredith and the Integration of Ole Miss* (Chapel Hill: University of North Carolina Press, 2009), 58.

27. Joshua I. Newman, "Army of Whiteness? Colonel Reb and the Sporting South's Cultural and Corporate Symbolic," *Journal of Sport & Social Issues* 31 (2007): 315–39; Sarah Fowler and Daniel Paulling, "Ole Miss Marching Band Drops 'Dixie' from Game Day," *Clarion-Ledger*, August 19, 2006, http://www.clarionledger.com; Susan Svrluga, "Ole Miss Takes Down Its State Flag with Confederate Emblem," *Washington Post*, October 26, 2015, https://www.washingtonpost.com.

28. Leslie Larson, "Ole Miss Students Yell Out Racial Slurs in Campus Riot Protesting Obama's Reelection," *Daily Mail*, November 7, 2016, http://www.dailymail.co.uk; Leslie Banahan and K. B. Melear, *Incident Review Committee Public Report* (University of Mississippi, January 25, 2013), 8–11, https://news.olemiss.edu; R. L. Nave, "Ole Miss Student Describes Campus Disturbance," *Jackson Free Press*, November 9, 2012, http://www.jacksonfreepress.com.

29. Banahan and Melear, *Incident Review Committee Public Report*, 10.

30. Banahan and Melear, *Incident Review Committee Public Report*, 14.

31. Nadine Cohodas, *The Band Played Dixie: Race and the Liberal Conscience at Ole Miss* (New York: Free Press, 1997), 210.

32. James Meredith delivered his 1982 speech in Fulton Chapel, the same campus building where blackface performances had been staged in previous decades. See, for example, figure 10 in chapter 1.

33. Eagles, *Price of Defiance*, 302 (quotation), 304; Russell Barrett, *Integration at Ole Miss* (Chicago: Quadrangle Books, 1965), 107 (quotation). For a comprehensive history of the integration of the University of Mississippi, see Eagles, *Price of Defiance*.

34. William Doyle, *American Insurrection: James Meredith and the Battle of Oxford, Mississippi, 1962* (New York: Anchor, 2003), 66 (quotation), 277; Edwin Meek in "Ed Meek and Curtis Wilkie," episode of *Conversations*, aired July 3, 2016, on Mississippi Public Broadcasting; Curtis Wilkie quoted in Edwin E. Meek, *Riot: Eyewitness to Anger and Change* (Oxford: Yoknapatawpha Press, 2015), 127.

35. Doyle, *American Insurrection*, 135; Eagles, *Price of Defiance*, 353.

36. Doyle, *American Insurrection*, 137.

37. Alex A. Alston and James L. Dickerson, *Devil's Sanctuary: An Eyewitness History of Mississippi Hate Crimes* (Chicago: Lawrence Hill Books, 2009), 90–91.

38. Alexis C. Madrigal, "Outside the White House, a Celebration of Osama Bin Laden's Death," *Atlantic*, May 2, 2011, https://www.theatlantic.com.

39. Oddo, "Discourse-Based Methods," 237.

40. Oddo, "Discourse-Based Methods," 251–52.

41. Keith Yellin, *Battle Exhortation: The Rhetoric of Combat Leadership* (Columbia: University of South Carolina Press, 2008), 43.

42. Chuck Rounsaville, "Stan Sandroni: Rebel Radio Icon Had His Own Brand," *Rebel Nation Magazine*, August 12, 2015, https://rebelnationmagazine.com; Emily

Howerton Pratt, February 20, 2013, public Facebook post, www.facebook.com/adodsons/posts/; "Drink of the Week: Hot Toddy," *Bows & Beaus: A Southern Lifestyle Magazine*, November 1, 2017, https://bowsandbeausliving.com.

43. Associated Press, "Ole Miss Tweaks Fight Song," *espn.com*, October 23, 2009, http://www.espn.com.

44. For a fascinating primer on gendered Grove etiquette from an insider's perspective, see "Women of the Grove," posted by Ashley Barnett, October 16, 2013, YouTube, https://www.youtube.com/watch?v=zoaXcqnUZb8. It has been viewed more than fifty-five thousand times.

45. Al Poval, *A Time Remembered: Ole Miss, 1945–1970, an Oral History* (Oxford: Nautilus, 2016), 125.

46. Jonathan Hunt, "From Cacemphaton to Cher: Foul Language and Evidence in the Rhetorical Tradition," *Relevant Rhetoric* 3 (2012), http://relevantrhetoric.com.

47. Nelson, "Ole Miss Class of 2017."

48. Norman Fairclough, *Critical Discourse Analysis: The Critical Study of Language*, 2nd ed. (London: Routledge, 2010), 533.

Chapter 3

1. Ruth Serven, "A 'Radical Form of Resistance': MU Activists on Looking Back and Moving Forward," *Columbia Missourian*, November 7, 2016, https://www.columbiamissourian.com; University of Missouri, "What Is Mizzou?," accessed February 2017, https://missouri.edu/about/what-is-mizzou.php.

2. Monica Kast, "University of Tennessee Condemns Blackface Photo with Racist Text Believed to Be Students," *Knoxville News Sentinel*, February 28, 2019, https://www.knoxnews.com; Wayne T. Davis, "Denouncing Hate and Racism," statement from the Office of the Chancellor, University of Tennessee at Knoxville, March 1, 2019, accessed May 7, 2019, https://chancellor.utk.edu/2019/03/01/denouncing-hate-and-racism/.

3. Anemona Hartocollis, "Long After Protests, Students Shun the University of Missouri," *New York Times*, July 9, 2017, https://www.nytimes.com/.

4. For a stark example from the University of Mississippi, see the official Vimeo page of the university, where highly polished and professionally produced films, made at some considerable cost by university employees, often have fewer than eight hundred views. Compare this to amateur efforts on YouTube and other platforms. The "Drunk Girl in the Grove" video, for example, has garnered more than one million views in its various versions.

5. Payton Head's post from September 12, 2015, reprinted at People Power Assemblies, November 11, 2015, Facebook post, https://www.facebook.com/PeoplesPowerAssemblies/posts/932921543409524.

6. Emily Gallion, Lucille Sherman, and Allyson Sherwin, "MSA President Payton Head Combats Campus Discrimination," *Maneater*, September 16, 2015, https://www.themaneater.com.

7. Nana Naskidashvili, "Students March through MU Student Union in Protest of Racial Injustice," *Columbia Missourian*, October 1, 2015, https://www.columbiamissourian.com; Cathy Scroggs quoted in Lisa Gutierrez, "MU Student Body Leader Payton Head Writes Emotional Response to Being Called the N-word," *Kansas City Star*, September 17, 2015, https://www.kansascity.com; Susan Svrluga, "What the Student-Body President

Did After He Was Called the N-word—Again," *Washington Post*, September 16, 2015, https://www.washingtonpost.com.

8. Eduardo Bonilla-Silva, *Racism without Racists* (Lanham, MD: Rowman and Littlefield, 2006), 77.

9. Black alumni statement quoted in Jamelle Bouie, "The Mizzou Football Team May Be Just the Beginning," *Slate*, November 9, 2015, http://www.slate.com.

10. Clay Travis, "Is the Entire Mizzou Protest Based on Lies?" *Outkick the Coverage*, November 11, 2015, https://www.outkickthecoverage.com; Grizzly999, comment on tigerboard.com, November 7, 2015, accessed January 2018 (no longer publicly accessible).

11. Bonilla-Silva, *Racism without Racists*, 93, 105.

12. Susan Svrluga, "Mizzou Chancellor Responds after Student-Body President Is Called the N-word," *Washington Post*, September 17, 2015, https://www.washingtonpost.com. The chancellor's statement is reprinted in full in this article.

13. Chancellor Loftin's statement reprinted in Svrluga, "Mizzou Chancellor Responds."

14. Naskidashvili, "Students March."

15. R. Bowen Loftin, "Racism at Mizzou," Office of the Chancellor, University of Missouri, October 5, 2015, accessed February 26, 2017, https://chancellor.missouri.edu/news/racism-at-mizzou/.

16. Mikhail Mihaĭlovich Bakhtin, "Problem of Speech Genres," in *Speech Genres and Other Late Essays*, ed. Michael Holquist and Caryl Emerson (Austin: University of Texas Press, 1986), 94, 93.

17. Jan Blommaert, *Discourse: A Critical Introduction* (Cambridge: Cambridge University Press, 2005), 131.

18. Kasia Kovacs, "Common Questions about Jonathan Butler's Hunger Strike," *Columbia Missourian*, November 8, 2015, https://www.columbiamissourian.com; Matt Pearce, "University of Missouri President, Chancellor Resign over Racial Turmoil," *Baltimore Sun*, November 9, 2015, https://www.baltimoresun.com; Krishnadev Calamur, "What's Happening at the University of Missouri?," *Atlantic*, November 9, 2015, https://www.theatlantic.com.

19. Staff, "Update: Protesters Meet UM System President outside Kansas City Fundraiser," *Columbia Missourian*, November 6, 2015, https://www.columbiamissourian.com.

20. Beatriz Costa-Lima and Hannah Sturtecky, "More Than This Moment: Jonathan Butler Talks about the Movement," *Columbia Missourian*, November 16, 2015, https://www.columbiamissourian.com. Butler was quoted in the *Columbia Missourian* in the days after the homecoming protest: "We disrupted the parade specifically in front of Tim Wolfe because we need him to get our message. We've sent emails, we've sent tweets, we've messaged, but we've gotten no response back from the upper officials at Mizzou." Ruth Serven and Ashley Reese, "In Homecoming Parade, Racial Justice Advocates Take Different Paths," *Columbia Missourian*, October 10, 2015, https://www.columbiamissourian.com.

21. Tim Wolfe, "Presidential Resignation Speech," November 9, 2015, American Rhetoric Online Speech Bank, http://www.americanrhetoric.com/speeches/timwolferesignation.htm.

22. Cynthia Frisby, "Too Many Times to Count: My Experiences of Racism at the University of Missouri," *Huffington Post*, November 9, 2015, https://www.huffingtonpost.com; Staff, "MU Black Alumni, Others Support Protesters, Decry Continued Racism," *Columbia Missourian*, November 9, 2015, https://www.columbiamissourian.com.

23. University of Missouri, *2020 Vision for Excellence: The Strategic Plan of the University of Missouri* (University of Missouri, 2011), 6, 7, https://mospace.umsystem.edu/xmlui/.

24. University of Missouri, *2020 Vision for Excellence*, 2.

25. Carolyn R. Miller, Amy J. Devitt, and Victoria J. Gallagher, "Genre: Permanence and Change," *Rhetoric Society Quarterly* 48, no. 3 (2018): 269–77.

26. Janese Heavin, "Two Arrested in Cotton Ball Incident," *Columbia Daily Tribune*, March 3, 2010, http://www.columbiatribune.com.

27. Luke Udstuen, "Townhall Meeting Responds to BCC Tampering," *Maneater*, March 2, 2010, https://www.themaneater.com.

28. Alan Scher Zagier, "Missouri Students Apologize for Cotton Ball Prank," *Diverse Issues in Higher Education*, March 8, 2010, http://diverseeducation.com.

29. Lysaundra Campbell quoted in Zagier, "Missouri Students Apologize"; University of Missouri News Bureau, "Statement from University of Missouri Chancellor Brady Deaton," February 26, 2010, https://munews.missouri.edu.

30. Chad Garrison, "The Mystery of Lloyd Gaines," *Riverfront Times*, April 4, 2007, https://www.riverfronttimes.com.

31. Hartocollis, "Long After Protests."

CHAPTER 4

1. Jane H. Hill, *The Everyday Language of White Racism* (Chichester, UK: Wiley and Sons, 2008), 41.

2. Norman Fairclough, *Critical Discourse Analysis: The Critical Study of Language*, 2nd ed. (London: Routledge, 2010), 44.

3. There are countless high schools that continue to call themselves "Rebels" and countless companies that feature "Old South" or "Dixie" in their name. Rarely do such names draw attention.

4. Fairclough, *Critical Discourse Analysis*, 44.

5. The adjective "affectionate" or the adverb "affectionately" are used repeatedly in UM publications. See, for example, the "History and Tradition" section in the guide to commencement at http://commencement.olemiss.edu/history-and-tradition/.

6. Anonymous lawyer and University of Mississippi alumnus, conversation with author, December 2016, Oxford, MS.

7. Leslie Larson, "Ole Miss Students Yell Out Racial Slurs in Campus Riot Protesting Obama's Reelection," *Daily Mail*, November 7, 2012, http://www.dailymail.co.uk; Leslie Banahan and K. B. Melear, *Incident Review Committee Public Report* (University of Mississippi, January 25, 2013), https://news.olemiss.edu; R. L. Nave, "Ole Miss Student Describes Campus Disturbance," *Jackson Free Press*, November 9, 2012, http://www.jacksonfreepress.com; Robbie Brown, "Anti-Obama Protest at Ole Miss Turns Unruly," *New York Times*, November 7, 2012, https://www.nytimes.com.

8. Sean Higgins, Allen Hamilton, Kimbrely Dandridge, Brian Barnes, Kendrick Hunt, Kate Kellum, Lauren Wright, and Josh Moore, "An Open Letter to Students, Faculty and Alumni of the University of Mississippi," excerpted in Michael Harrelson, "Ole Miss 'Not a Safe Haven for Hate,' Student Leaders Say," *Hotty Toddy*, November 12, 2012, https://hottytoddy.com; Chancellor Dan Jones's email to the campus community, quoted in Jenna Johnson, "Obama's Re-election Sparks Racially Charged Protest at Ole Miss," *Washington Post*, November 7, 2012, https://www.washingtonpost.com.

9. Larson, "Ole Miss Students."

10. Edwin Smith, "UM Commemorates 50 Years of Integration," *University of Mississippi News*, September 25, 2012, https://news.olemiss.edu.

11. Emily Le Coz, "Racial Slurs after Election Night Prompt Vigil at Mississippi College," *Reuters*, November 8, 2012, https://www.reuters.com/.

12. Coach Hugh Freeze quoted in Steven Godfrey, "Riot Rhythm: Ole Miss and Its Football Recruits Believe There's Nothing to See Here," *SB Nation*, November 15, 2012, https://www.sbnation.com.

13. Diana Hacker and Nancy Sommers, *A Writer's Reference*, 8th ed. (Boston: Bedford/St. Martin's, 2015), 89 (quotation); Walter S. Minot, "A Rhetorical View of Fallacies: Ad Hominem and Ad Populum," *Rhetoric Society Quarterly* 11, no. 4 (Autumn 1981), 222–35.

14. Lacey Russell, "Faculty Express Concern," *Daily Mississippian*, November 15, 2012, http://thedmonline.com.

15. Banahan and Melear, *Incident Review Committee Public Report*, 5 ("erroneously suggested"), 5–6n5 ("student media," Kym Clark), 12 ("Local media"), 10n13 ("NOT a 'riot'").

16. Kerry Brian Melear and Leslie Banahan, "The Election Night Incident," in *Responding to Campus Protests: A Practitioner's Resource*, Legal Links: Connecting Student Affairs and Law, vol. 1, no. 2 (Education Law Association and the NASPA, 2014).

17. Staff editorial, "Experience Informs Our Consciousness," *Daily Mississippian*, February 19, 2014, http://thedmonline.com.

18. Extended Sensitivity and Respect Committee, *Report, Findings, and Recommendations of the Extended Sensitivity and Respect Committee* (University of Mississippi, 2016), 2, https://olemiss.edu. This version of the report also includes Chancellor Jones's response.

19. ESRC, *Report*, 10.

20. ESRC, *Report*, 16.

21. ESRC, *Report*, 14, 16.

22. Barbara Harris Combs, Kirsten Dellinger, Jeffrey T. Jackson, Kirk A. Johnson, Willa M. Johnson, Jodi Skipper, John Sonnett, James M. Thomas, Critical Race Studies Group, University of Mississippi, "The Symbolic Lynching of James Meredith: A Visual Analysis and Collective Counter Narrative to Racial Domination," *Sociology of Race and Ethnicity* 2, no. 3 (2016): 338; Alan Blinder, "Racist Episodes Continue to Stir Ole Miss Campus," *New York Times*, February 20, 2014, https://www.nytimes.com. For the best and most provocative analysis of this episode, see Combs et al., "The Symbolic Lynching of James Meredith."

23. Amelia Camurati, "Former Ole Miss Student to Plead Guilty over Noose on James Meredith Statue," *Hotty Toddy*, March 24, 2016, https://hottytoddy.com; United States of America v. Graeme Phillip Harris 3:15CR022 18 U.S.C. 245(b)(2).

24. Adam Ganucheau, "Chancellor Awaits Reports, Discusses Campus Diversity," *Daily Mississippian*, April 28, 2014, http://thedmonline.com.

25. Dan Jones, "Action Plan on Consultant Reports and Update on the Work of the Sensitivity and Respect Committee," August 1, 2014, http://diversity.olemiss.edu.

26. Jones, "Action Plan."

27. Fairclough, *Critical Discourse Analysis*, 67.

28. Bart Wilbanks, "Calling for Resignation of Dan Jones," GoPetition, August 8, 2014, https://www.gopetition.com/petitions/calling-for-resignation-of-dan-jones.html;

Clara Turnage, "Has the IHL Board Repaired Its Relationship with the University of Mississippi?," *Daily Mississippian*, April 3, 206, http://thedmonline.com.

29. Ole Miss Sports Productions, "We Are Ole Miss: A Conversation between Athletics Director, Ross Bjork, and Chancellor, Dan Jones," online video, Vimeo, 2014, retrieved and transcribed December 15, 2016.

30. Commenters 19 and 33, both of whom signed and posted on August 9, 2014, in Wilbanks, "Calling for Resignation of Dan Jones."

31. "The Ghost of Jay Cutler," August 16, 2014, 4:21 p.m., comment on Red Cup Rebellion, "How Much Does Dan Jones Love the Term 'Ole Miss'?," posted by smeargle, August 16, 2014, https://www.redcuprebellion.com.

32. University of Mississippi, "Vision, Mission and Core Values," https://olemiss.edu/aboutum/mission.html.

33. Fairclough, *Critical Discourse Analysis*, 532.

34. Hill, *Everyday Language of White Racism*, 41; Fairclough, *Critical Discourse Analysis*, 44.

35. Democracy in Color, *The Trump Administration's Record of Racism: The First 200+ Documented Examples* (Democracy in Color, 2018), http://democracyincolor.com/recordofracism; Center on Extremism, *New Hate and Old: The Changing Face of American White Supremacy* (Anti-Defamation League, 2018), https://www.adl.org; Eugene Robinson, "Trump's Rhetoric Stokes Hate. He Never Thinks of the Consequences," *Washington Post*, April 19, 2019, https://www.washingtonpost.com.

36. Democracy in Color, "Summer 2017," in *The Trump Administration's Record of Racism.*

37. "Time Is Getting Close to Miss Stands Event," February 20, 2019, video Facebook post, accessed and transcribed February 27, 2019, Facebook.com/confederate901.

38. James Paul Gee and Michael Handford, introduction to *The Routledge Handbook of Discourse Analysis*, ed. Gee and Handford (Abingdon, UK: Routledge, 2015).

Chapter 5

1. Edwin Smith, "Meet James 'Blind Jim' Ivy," University of Mississippi News, March 4, 2014, https://news.olemiss.edu; Charles W. Eagles, *The Price of Defiance: James Meredith and the Integration of Ole Miss* (Chapel Hill: University of North Carolina Press, 2009), 43; David G. Sansing, *The University of Mississippi: A Sesquicentennial History* (Jackson: University Press of Mississippi, 1999), 275 (quotation). For more information about Ivy's life, see Eagles, *Price of Defiance*, 43–46.

2. Curtis Wilkie, *Dixie: A Personal Odyssey through Events That Shaped the Modern South* (New York: Scribner, 2002), 96.

3. Sansing, *University of Mississippi*, 276; Joshua I. Newman, "Army of Whiteness? Colonel Reb and the Sporting South's Cultural and Corporate Symbolic," *Journal of Sport & Social Issues* 31, no. 4 (November 2007): 322; Eagles, *Price of Defiance*, 45–46; Michael Oriard, *King Football: Sport and Spectacle in the Golden Age of Radio and Newsreels, Movies and Magazines* (Chapel Hill: University of North Carolina Press, 2001), 259.

4. Anthony James, "Paternalism's Demise: Blind Jim Ivy and Ole Miss, 1896–1955," *Mississippi Folklife* 28, no. 1 (Winter/Spring 1995), 19.

5. Kurt Edward Kemper, *College Football and American Culture in the Cold War Era*

(Champaign: University of Illinois Press, 2009), 121 (quotations, University of Georgia and University of Alabama examples); Oriard, *King Football*, 258 (Auburn University example).

6. J. R. Cofield, "Ex-Marine and Blind Jim," 1944, Cofield Collection of the University of Mississippi Libraries, https://egrove.olemiss.edu/cofield/221/. For another image of this sort, see James, "Paternalism's Demise," 22.

7. James, "Paternalism's Demise," 19–21.

8. Jan Blommaert, *Discourse: A Critical Introduction* (Cambridge: Cambridge University Press, 2005), 135.

9. Bill Dabney, "Major Gift Will Assist Freshmen Entering UM," University of Mississippi News, December 29, 2017, https://news.olemiss.edu.

10. Eagles, *Price of Defiance*, 46.

11. Sansing, *University of Mississippi*, 276; Newman, "Army of Whiteness?," 323.

12. James, "Paternalism's Demise," 19.

13. Laurie Gries, *Still Life with Rhetoric: A New Materialist Approach for Visual Rhetorics* (Logan: Utah State University Press, 2015), 90.

14. Brian Ferguson, "About Us," Colonel Rebel Foundation, https://www.colonelreb.org/.

15. Clay Travis (@ClayTravis), Twitter, August 11, 2018. This engagement far outdoes the official @OleMissSports tweet of that same day, which introduced Tony the Landshark and which has garnered only 151 retweets and 475 likes.

16. Nadine Cohodas, *The Band Played Dixie: Race and the Liberal Conscience at Ole Miss* (New York: Free Press, 1997), 162; William Doyle, *An American Insurrection: James Meredith and the Battle of Oxford, Mississippi, 1962* (New York: Anchor, 2003), 112.

17. Robert Khayat, *The Education of a Lifetime* (Oxford, MS: Nautilus, 2013), 157, 160.

18. Khayat, *Education of a Lifetime*, 161, 162, 163.

19. Tommy Tuberville quoted in Khayat, *Education of a Lifetime*, 153; Gina Holland, "Tuberville: Lose the Rebel Flag," *Daily Journal* (Tupelo, MS), September 26, 1997, www.djournal.com; Tuberville quoted in Donald P. Baker, "Point of Contention on Ole Miss Campus," *Washington Post*, October 5, 1997, https://www.washingtonpost.com; John M. Coski, *The Confederate Battle Flag: America's Most Embattled Emblem* (Cambridge, MA: Belknap Press of Harvard University Press, 2005), 228–29.

20. Coski, *Confederate Battle Flag*, 219.

21. Coski, *Confederate Battle Flag*, 228.

22. Gries, *Still Life with Rhetoric*, 57, 61.

23. Neil R. McMillen, "Citizens' Council," in *History*, ed. Charles Reagan Wilson, vol. 3 of *The New Encyclopedia of Southern Culture* (Chapel Hill: University of North Carolina Press, 2006), 273; Fred T. Jennings, ed., *Citizens Informer* 3, no. 7 (July 1975): 5. For more on the Council of Conservative Citizens and its support of segregation academies, see Heidi Beirich, "White Supremacist Group Backs Private Academies in Mississippi," Southern Poverty Law Center, October 28, 2010, https://www.splcenter.org.

24. Melton v. Young, Civil Action 6018, United States District Court for the Eastern District of Tennessee, Southern Division, January 13, 1977, 1 ("to protest"), 3, 8 ("cavalcade of cars"), 11 ("impromptu pep rally"); Coski, *Confederate Battle Flag*, 208.

25. Coski, *Confederate Battle Flag*, 20.

26. Lee High School (website), https://leehs.fcps.edu/; Robert E. Lee High School, Baytown, Texas, *The Lee Traveler, 1973*, 188–89, digitized by Sterling Library, https://www.flickr.com/photos/98317021@N02/albums/72157634667310139/page1; Central High School (website), http://www.centralr3.org/rebel1/index.php/student/schools/high-school; Effingham County High School (website), https://www.effinghamschools.com/page/1806; photo by gagirl_88, September 26, 2008, Digital Photography Challenge Contest Site, https://www.dpchallenge.com/image.php?IMAGE_ID=725888; Vestavia Hills Brand (website), https://vhbrand.com/.

27. Coski, *Confederate Battle Flag*, 211.

28. Frances Robles, Jason Horowitz, and Shaila Dewan, "Dylan Roof, Suspect in Charleston Shooting, Flew the Flags of White Power," *New York Times*, June 18, 2015, https://www.nytimes.com; Kyle Whitmire, "John Oliver Ridicules Vestavia Hills for Rebel Mascot," *Al.com*, July 13, 2015, https://www.al.com; Knight Eady Creative Agency, *Vestavia Hills High School: Brand and Identity Guide* (Birmingham, AL: Knight Eady, 2016), https://static.vhbrand.com/pdf/VHHS-BrandBook.pdf.

29. John Naughton, "Five Iowa Schools Use Rebels Nickname," *Des Moines Register*, July 22, 2015, https://www.desmoinesregister.com; Benjamin Fearnow, "High School Alumni Debate Confederacy, Racism as Students Vote to Keep 'Rebel' Mascot," *Newsweek*, June 12, 2018, https://www.newsweek.com; Gabriel San Roman, "How the Confederate Flag and Johnny Rebel Fell at Anaheim's Savanna High School," *Orange County Weekly*, June 25, 2015, www.ocweekly.com; Ali Chiasson, "Go Rebels? No Rebels? Georgetown High School Considers Changing Controversial Team Name," *CBC News*, February 22, 2017, https://www.cbc.ca.

30. James C. Cobb, *Away Down South: A History of Southern Identity* (Oxford: Oxford University Press, 2005), 219.

31. Comments from users cdh72469 and SCBAMA on "SEC Coaches, Players Share Strong Opinion on Race Relations in College Football," by Brad Crawford, 2015, Saturday Down South, https://www.saturdaydownsouth.com.

32. Blommaert, *Discourse*, 152.

33. Chancellor's Advisory Committee on History and Context, University of Mississippi, https://context.olemiss.edu/.

Chapter 6

1. Alan Blinder and Jonathan Martin, "Governor Admits He Was in Racist Yearbook Photo," *New York Times*, February 1, 2019, https://www.nytimes.com.

2. Scott Jaschik, "Yearbook Review Finds Dean with Confederate Flag," *Inside Higher Ed*, February 25, 2019, https://www.insidehighered.com.

3. Perhaps Northam and Allman should be punished, although both present complicated cases. Allman has worked for decades from her positions of influence to make Wake Forest more diverse and to increase the number of African American students and graduates at her alma mater. Even Northam, as a professional politician, has been mildly progressive on some matters related to race, taking a hard line, for example, on the need to relocate Confederate monuments to museums. Societies are constantly updating rules of propriety and enforcing those rules. Should Northam and Allman lose their positions of power? That question will be decided by the voters in Northam's case and by the Wake Forest administration in Allman's.

4. Bradford Vivian, *Commonplace Witnessing: Rhetorical Invention, Historical Remembrance, and Public Culture* (Oxford: Oxford University Press, 2017), 6–7.

5. Jubal A. Early, "Speech to the Southern Historical Society," August 14, 1873, in *The Confederate and Neo-Confederate Reader: The "Great Truth" about the "Lost Cause,"* ed. James W. Loewen and Edward H. Sebesta (Jackson: University Press of Mississippi, 2010), 270.

6. Sharon A. Sharp, "Southern Historical Society," in *History*, ed. Charles Reagan Wilson, vol. 3 of *The New Encyclopedia of Southern Culture* (Chapel Hill: University of North Carolina Press, 2006), 335; Richard D. Starnes, "Forever Faithful: The Southern Historical Society and Confederate Historical Memory," *Southern Cultures* 2, no. 2 (Winter 1996): 178.

7. Gary W. Gallagher, "Jubal A. Early, the Lost Cause, and Civil War History: A Persistent Legacy," in *The Myth of the Lost Cause and Civil War History*, ed. Gary W. Gallagher and Alan T. Nolan (Bloomington: Indiana University Press, 2010), 36 (quotation), 51–52.

8. Stephen D. Lee, "The Negro Problem," in Loewen and Sebesta, *Confederate and Neo-Confederate Reader*, 293.

9. *Mississippi Encyclopedia Online*, s.v. "Stephen D. Lee," https://mississippiencyclopedia.org.

10. Lee, "The Negro Problem," 286, 289, 290, 291.

11. Office of the Chancellor, University of Arkansas, "Daniel H. Hill," https://chancellor.uark.edu; Starnes, "Forever Faithful," 178, 179.

12. Much of the discussion in this chapter centers on the white men who were organizing southern witnessing in the postbellum years. For more information on the women who were engaged in this work, see Karen L. Cox, *Dixie's Daughters: The United Daughters of the Confederacy and the Preservation of Confederate Culture* (Gainesville: University Press of Florida, 2003).

13. Charles W. Eagles, *The Price of Defiance: James Meredith and the Integration of Ole Miss* (Chapel Hill: University of North Carolina Press, 2009), 55.

14. Caption to "Perfect Finish," photo of Stephen D. Lee Scholars at Mississippi State commencement, May 9, 2016, https://www.msstate.edu/state-spotlight/2016/05/perfect-finish/.

15. Mark Keenum quoted in Hannah East, "Confederate Statues on College Campuses Stir Up Controversy," *Reflector*, September 25, 2017, http://www.reflector-online.com.

16. W. Ralph Eubanks, *Ever Is a Long Time: A Journey into Mississippi's Dark Past* (New York: Basic Books, 2003), 135, 144.

17. SCBAMA comment on "SEC Coaches, Players Share Strong Opinion on Race Relations in College Football," by Brad Crawford, 2015, Saturday Down South, https://www.saturdaydownsouth.com; Paul Bond, "'Dukes of Hazzard' Star Rips TV Land for Dropping Show," *Hollywood Reporter*, July 1, 2015, https://www.hollywoodreporter.com; Eubanks, *Ever Is a Long Time*, 144, 145.

18. Eubanks, *Ever Is a Long Time*, 146–47.

19. James Paul Gee, *How to Do Discourse Analysis* (London: Routledge, 2011), 176.

20. Indeed, following the multimillion dollar expansion of the Ole Miss Student Union in 2019, Everett's quote was scheduled to be reinstalled on the building's central staircase. Excerpts were painted in large letters along the walls of the renovated bookstore in the building.

21. Elam Miller, welcome address, University of Mississippi orientation sessions, summer 2018, witnessed by the author.

22. Roun McNeal quoted in Shelia Byrd, "Ole Miss Seeks to Silence 'Rising South' Chant," Fox News, October 22, 2009, https://www.foxnews.com.

23. Kirk A. Johnson, Willa M. Johnson, James M. Thomas, and John J. Green, *Microaggressions at the University of Mississippi* (UM Race Diary Project, October 2018), 19.

24. Johnson et al., *Microaggressions*, 145.

25. Vivian, *Commonplace Witnessing*, 203.

Chapter 7

1. For example, see Alexandra Hidalgo and Donnie Jackson Sackey, eds., special issue, *Present Tense: A Journal of Rhetoric and Society* 5, no. 2 (2015). See also John T. Gagnon, "How Cultural Rhetorics Can Change the Conversation: Towards New Communication Spaces to Address Human Trafficking," *Poroi* 12, no. 2 (2016), https://doi.org/10.13008/2151-2957.1245.

2. Paula Chakravartty, Rachel Kuo, Victoria Grubbs, and Charlton McIlwain, "#CommunicationSoWhite," *Journal of Communication* 68, no. 2 (April 2018): 254–66, https://doi.org/10.1093/joc/jqy003.

3. Ragan Fox, "In Response to Martin J. Medhurst's Embarrassing Editorial in Rhetoric and Public Affairs," *Ragan Fox* (blog), June 11, 2019, https://raganfox.blog; Stephen M. Llano, "NCA Reboot," *New York City Sophist* (blog), June 16, 2019, https://sophist.nyc; Bernadette Marie Calafell et al., "Letter to Leadership in the Field of Communication," accessed October 8, 2020, https://docs.google.com/forms/d/e/1FAIpQLSfMyosNWkZvTu7TK5JsZxx4bpYO_vJp_3f2ERozw5QWnaJN8w/viewform?fbclid=IwAR0uuI6cOxyH_2Xp5I0sYrMZQYMCyWF-Qn4jqbbaAY8V3pAasnfmbL8zaog.

4. Although some of these statements were posted only on social media and have since been lost or deleted, many have been archived by an anonymous scholar at a website titled "2019 #Communicationsowhite Controversy" (accessed October 8, 2020, http://2019commsowhitecontroversy.simplesite.com/442746685).

5. Asao Inoue, "How Do We Language So People Stop Killing Each Other, or What Do We Do about White Language Supremacy?," Chair's Address at the Annual Convention of the Conference on College Composition and Communication, Pittsburgh, PA, March 14, 2019, 7.

6. Norman Fairclough, *Critical Discourse Analysis: The Critical Study of Language*, 2nd ed. (London: Routledge, 2010), 63.

7. Robin DiAngelo. *White Fragility: Why It's So Hard for White People to Talk about Racism* (Boston: Beacon Press, 2018), 14.

8. Mitch Landrieu, *In the Shadow of Statues: A White Southerner Confronts History* (New York: Penguin, 2018), 40; DiAngelo, *White Fragility*, 150.

9. Inoue, "What Do We Do about White Language Supremacy?," 9, 6.

10. Fairclough, *Critical Discourse Analysis*, 532.

11. Hannah East, "Confederate Statues on College Campuses Stir Up Controversy," *Reflector*, September 25, 2017, http://www.reflector-online.com. Thus far, the synchronization strategy has been successful at Mississippi State, but I suspect that it is only a matter of time before Stephen D. Lee as confederate rhetoric erupts at the school, causing some open turmoil and division.

12. Medgar Evers, "Why I Live in Mississippi," in *Nonfiction*, ed. Dorothy Abbot, vol. 2 of *Mississippi Writers: Reflections of Childhood and Youth* (Jackson: University Press of Mississippi, 1986), 209; Kirk A. Johnson, Willa M. Johnson, James M. Thomas, and John J. Green, *Microaggressions at the University of Mississippi* (UM Race Diary Project, October 2018), 7.

13. As of this writing, the Confederate statue remains at the center of the UM campus. Perhaps it will be removed by the time of publication. The story of its protesters and defenders deserves an entire book of its own.

14. Charles W. Eagles, *The Price of Defiance: James Meredith and the Integration of Ole Miss* (Chapel Hill: University of North Carolina Press, 2009), 72–79. In telling the story of how Medgar Evers was prevented admission into the University of Mississippi Law School, Eagles illuminates many of the tactics used by southern institutions to formalize and implement racism. There is no better introduction to institutionalized racism than this story, with its various twists and turns.

15. Johnson et al., *Microaggressions*, iii.

16. Jeffrey S. Vitter, "Guest Column: Ole Miss Chancellor Jeffrey Vitter," *Daily Mississippian*, October 11, 2018, https://thedmonline.com.

17. Kjerome, November 13, 2009, 8:39 p.m., comment on "The Louts Will Rise Again," by Tommy Craggs, Deadspin, https://deadspin.com.

18. Stephanie Saul, "Ole Miss Edges Out of Its Confederate Shadow, Gingerly," *New York Times*, August 9, 2017, https://www.nytimes.com; Kate Kellum quoted in Lasherica Thornton, Sara Doan, and Pierce Morrison, "University Professor, Relative of Former US Senator Leads Charge to Contextualize George Hall," *Daily Mississippian*, January 30, 2018, https://thedmonline.com.

19. Rasha Diab, Beth Godbee, and Thomas Ferrell, "Making Commitments to Racial Justice Actionable," in *Performing Antiracist Pedagogy in Rhetoric, Writing, and Communication*, ed. Frankie Condon and Vershawn Ahsanti Young (Fort Collins: University Press of Colorado, 2016), 25, https://wac.colostate.edu/books/atd/antiracist/.

20. Diab, Godbee, and Ferrell, "Making Commitments," 37.

21. Winter Institute, "Mission, Vision, and Values," https://winterinstitute.org/about/mission-vision-values; Otis W. Pickett, "We Were All Prisoners of the System: William Winter, Susan Glisson, and the Founding of the William Winter Institute for Racial Reconciliation," *Southern Quarterly* 54, no. 1 (Fall 2016): 151, 165.

22. Pickett, "We Were All Prisoners," 152; Robert W. Hamblin, *Living in Mississippi: The Life and Times of Evans Harrington* (Jackson: University Press of Mississippi, 2017), 31.

23. The Critical Race Studies Group at the University of Mississippi "aims to serve as a source of expert opinion and professional support for administrators, students, scholars, community leaders, and journalists regarding racial and race-related concerns." This interdisciplinary working group was founded and first housed within UM's Department of Sociology and Anthropology. Critical Race Studies Group, "About," University of Mississippi, https://socanth.olemiss.edu/critical-race-studies-group.

24. Professors Shennette Garrett-Scott, Jeff Jackson, Charles Ross, Jodi Skipper, and Anne Twitty lead the University of Mississippi Slavery Research Group (https://slaveryresearchgroup.olemiss.edu/). It was founded in 2013 by Ross and Jackson, along with Professors Kirsten Dellinger and Joe Ward.

25. Staff, "UM's Relationship with the Winter Institute Was Not Black and White," *Daily Mississippian*, October 11, 2018, https://thedmonline.com.

26. Teju Cole warns of a "White Savior Industrial Complex" that blinds white people with good hearts to "the patterns of power behind the isolated 'disasters.'" Cole urges readers away from sentimental thinking that overemphasizes the potential positive impacts of white philanthropy, when isolated and satisfying (for white people). Cole's context is Africa, but his warnings are relevant to racial reconciliation efforts in the United States. Teju Cole, "The White-Savior Industrial Complex," *Atlantic*, March 21, 2012, https://www.theatlantic.com.

27. Daniel Payne, "Resolution to Relocate Ole Miss's Confederate Monument Passes ASB Senate," *Daily Mississippian*, March 5, 2019, https://thedmonline.com.

28. John Hawkins, "One Student Led Rejection of Confederate Flag at Ole Miss," interview by Rachel Maddow, *Rachel Maddow Show*, MSNBC, June 24, 2015, https://www.msnbc.com. The Department of African American Studies at the University of Mississippi, with support from the University Libraries Archives and Special Collections, has assembled the "Timeline of African American Experience at UM." This multimedia website includes an entry about John Hawkins and his heroic refusal to carry the Confederate flag.

29. Kenneth Niemeyer, "Community Reacts to Racist Receipt," *Daily Mississippian*, June 13, 2019, https://thedmonline.com. As an educator and parent, I must mention my opinion that a drive-through daiquiri bar seems like a bad idea for a number of obvious reasons.

30. Derrick Harriell, "Links Rd to HWY 6 to Jackson Ave," in *Stripper in Wonderland* (Baton Rouge: LSU Press, 2017), 34.

31. Eli Saslow, *Rising Out of Hatred: The Awakening of a Former White Nationalist* (New York: Doubleday, 2018), 219.

32. John Bowden, "Mississippi Governor Signs Bill Permitting License Plates with Alternative Flag without Confederate Symbol," *Hill*, April 17, 2019, https://thehill.com.

Epilogue

1. Adrian Blackledge, "Discourse and Power," in *The Routledge Handbook of Discourse Analysis*, ed. James Paul Gee and Michael Handford (London: Routledge, 2015), 617.

2. Nicholas Fandos, Cecilia Kang, and Mike Isaac, "House Intelligence Committee Releases Incendiary Russian Social Media Ads," *New York Times*, November 1, 2017, https://www.nytimes.com.

3. Renee DiResta, Kris Shaffer, Becky Ruppel, David Sullivan, Robert Matney, Ryan Fox, Jonathan Albright, and Ben Johnson, *The Tactics and Tropes of the Internet Research Agency* (New Knowledge, 2019), https://disinformationreport.blob.core.windows.net/disinformation-report/NewKnowledge-Disinformation-Report-Whitepaper.pdf; Glenn Geher, "The Polarization of America," *Psychology Today*, August 14, 2018, https://www.psychologytoday.com; Cynthia Miller-Idriss, "The Global Rise of Right-Wing Extremism," American University College of Arts and Sciences News, April 3, 2019, https://www.american.edu/cas/news; Seth G. Jones, *The Rise of Far-Right Extremism in the United States* (Center for Strategic and International Studies, November 7, 2018), https://www.csis.org.

4. Office of the Director of National Intelligence, *Background to "Assessing Russian Activities and Intentions in Recent US Elections": The Analytic Process and Cyber Incident Attribution* (Office of the Director of National Intelligence, January 6, 2017).

5. United States of America v. Internet Research Agency LLC et al., February 16, 2018.

6. Peter Finn, ed., *The Mueller Report*, presented with related materials by *The Washington Post* (New York: Scribner, 2019), 87.

7. Finn, *Mueller Report*, 87.

8. Mike Glenn, "A Houston Protest, Organized by Russian Trolls," *Houston Chronicle*, February 20, 2018, https://www.houstonchronicle.com.

9. Scott Shane, "How Unwitting Americans Encountered Russian Operatives Online," *New York Times*, February 18, 2018, https://www.nytimes.com.

10. Ian Shapira, "Inside Jason Kessler's Hate-Fueled Rise," *Washington Post*, August 11, 2018, https://www.washingtonpost.com ("ethno-state"); Daniel Lombroso and Yoni Appelbaum, "Hail Trump: White Nationalists Salute the President-Elect," *Atlantic*, November 21, 2016. https://www.theatlantic.com; Josh Harkinson, "Meet the White Nationalist Trying to Ride the Trump Train to Lasting Power," *Mother Jones*, October 27, 2016, https://www.motherjones.com/ ("plausible deniability"); Glenn Thrush and Maggie Haberman, "Trump Gives White Supremacists an Unequivocal Boost," *New York Times*, August 15, 2017, https://www.nytimes.com.

11. Ivo Strecker and Stephen Tyler, introduction to *Culture and Rhetoric*, ed. Strecker and Tyler (New York: Berghahn Books, 2009), 2; Peter L. Oesterreich, "Homo Rhetoricus," in Strecker and Tyler, *Culture and Rhetoric*, 57; Lillian Smith, *Killers of the Dream* (New York: W. W. Norton, 1994), 244.

12. Kirk A. Johnson, Willa M. Johnson, James M. Thomas, and John J. Green, *Microaggressions at the University of Mississippi* (UM Race Diary Project, October 2018), 12.

Postscript

1. Doina Chiacu, "Trump Says Confederate Flag Proud Symbol of U.S. South," Reuters, July 19, 2020, https://ca.reuters.com.

2. Curtis Hill, "Equity, Justice and Inclusion: Why We Carried Emmett Till's Memorial," *Clarion-Ledger*, January 19, 2020, https://www.clarionledger.com.

3. Ellie Campbell, "A Week in the Life of Ole Miss: February 2019 and the Fight to Take Down the Confederate Statue," *Activist History Review*, December 16, 2019, https://activisthistory.com.

Bibliography

Alston, Alex A., and James L. Dickerson. *Devil's Sanctuary: An Eyewitness History of Mississippi Hate Crimes*. Chicago: Lawrence Hill Books, 2009.

Appiah, Kwame Anthony. *Cosmopolitanism: Ethics in a World of Strangers*. New York: Norton, 2007.

Ayers, Edward L. *The Promise of the New South: Life after Reconstruction*. Oxford: Oxford University Press, 2007.

Bakhtin, Mikhail Mihaïlovich. "The Problem of Speech Genres." In *Speech Genres and Other Late Essays*, edited by Michael Holquist and Caryl Emerson, 60–102. Austin: University of Texas Press, 1986.

Banahan, Leslie, and K. B. Melear. *Incident Review Committee Public Report*. University of Mississippi, January 25, 2013. https://news.olemiss.edu.

Barrett, Russell H. *Integration at Ole Miss*. Chicago: Quadrangle Books, 1965.

Bauman, Richard. "Language, Identity, Performance." *Pragmatics* 10 (2000): 1–5.

Blackledge, Adrian. "Discourse and Power." In *The Routledge Handbook of Discourse Analysis*, edited by James Paul Gee and Michael Handford, 616–27. London: Routledge, 2015.

Blommaert, Jan. *Discourse: A Critical Introduction*. Cambridge: Cambridge University Press, 2005.

Bonilla-Silva, Eduardo. *Racism without Racists*. Lanham, MD: Rowman and Littlefield, 2006.

Brundage, W. Fitzhugh. *The Southern Past*. Cambridge, MA: Harvard University Press, 2005.

Bucholtz, Mary, and Kira Hall. "Identity and Interaction: A Sociocultural Linguistic Approach." *Discourse Studies* 7, no. 4–5 (2005): 585–614.

Cabaniss, Allen. *The University of Mississippi: Its First Hundred Years*. Hattiesburg: The University and College Press of Mississippi, 1971.

Center on Extremism. *New Hate and Old: The Changing Face of American White Supremacy*. Anti-Defamation League, 2018. https://www.adl.org.

Chakravartty, Paula, Rachel Kuo, Victoria Grubbs, and Charlton McIlwain. "#CommunicationSoWhite." *Journal of Communication* 68, no. 2 (April 2018): 254–66. https://doi.org/10.1093/joc/jqy003.

Cobb, James C. *Away Down South: A History of Southern Identity*. Oxford: Oxford University Press, 2005.

Cohodas, Nadine. *The Band Played Dixie: Race and the Liberal Conscience at Ole Miss*. New York: Free Press, 1997.

Combs, Barbara Harris, Kirsten Dellinger, Jeffrey T. Jackson, Kirk A. Johnson, Willa M. Johnson, Jodi Skipper, John Sonnett, James M. Thomas, Critical Race Studies Group, University of Mississippi. "The Symbolic Lynching of James Meredith: A Visual Analysis and Collective Counter Narrative to Racial Domination." *Sociology of Race and Ethnicity* 2 no. 3 (2016): 338–53.

Coski, John M. *The Confederate Battle Flag: America's Most Embattled Emblem*. Cambridge, MA: Belknap Press of Harvard University Press, 2005.

Cox, Karen L. "Branding Dixie: The Selling of the American South, 1890–1930." In *Dixie Emporium: Tourism, Foodways, and Consumer Culture in the American South*, edited by Anthony J. Stanonis, 50–68. Athens: University of Georgia Press, 2008.

———. *Dixie's Daughters: The United Daughters of the Confederacy and the Preservation of Confederate Culture*. Gainesville: University Press of Florida, 2003.

Democracy in Color. *The Trump Administration's Record of Racism: The First 200+ Documented Examples*. Democracy in Color, 2018. http://democracyincolor.com/recordofracism.

Diab, Rasha, Beth Godbee, and Thomas Ferrell. "Making Commitments to Racial Justice Actionable." In *Performing Antiracist Pedagogy in Rhetoric, Writing, and Communication*, edited by Frankie Condon and Vershawn Ahsanti Young, 19–39. Fort Collins: University Press of Colorado, 2016. https://wac.colostate.edu/books/atd/antiracist/.

DiAngelo, Robin. *White Fragility: Why It's So Hard for White People to Talk about Racism*. Boston: Beacon Press, 2018.

Dickinson, Greg, Carole Blair, and Brian L. Ott. *Places of Public Memory: The Rhetoric of Museums and Memorials*. Tuscaloosa: University of Alabama Press, 2010.

DiResta, Renee, Kris Shaffer, Becky Ruppel, David Sullivan, Robert Matney, Ryan Fox, Jonathan Albright, and Ben Johnson. *The Tactics and Tropes of the Internet Research Agency*. New Knowledge, 2019. https://disinformationreport.blob.core.windows.net/disinformation-report/NewKnowledge-Disinformation-Report-Whitepaper.pdf.

Doyle, William. *An American Insurrection: James Meredith and the Battle of Oxford, Mississippi, 1962*. New York: Anchor, 2003.

Eagles, Charles W. *The Price of Defiance: James Meredith and the Integration of Ole Miss*. Chapel Hill: University of North Carolina Press, 2009.

Equal Justice Initiative. *Lynching in America: Confronting the Legacy of Racial Terror, Report Summary*. 2nd ed. Montgomery, AL: EJI, 2015.

Eubanks, W. Ralph. *Ever Is a Long Time: A Journey into Mississippi's Dark Past*. New York: Basic Books, 2003.

Evers, Medgar. "Why I Live in Mississippi." In *Nonfiction*, edited by Dorothy Abbot, 209–34. Vol. 2 of *Mississippi Writers: Reflections of Childhood and Youth*. Jackson: University Press of Mississippi, 1986.

Extended Sensitivity and Respect Committee. *Report, Findings, and Recommendations of the Extended Sensitivity and Respect Committee*. University of Mississippi, 2016. https://olemiss.edu.

Fairclough, Norman. *Critical Discourse Analysis: The Critical Study of Language*. 2nd ed. London: Routledge, 2010.

———. *Language and Power*. 3rd ed. New York: Routledge, 2015.

Finn, Peter, ed. *The Mueller Report*. Presented with related materials by *The Washington Post*. New York: Scribner, 2019.

Gagnon, John T. "How Cultural Rhetorics Can Change the Conversation: Towards New Communication Spaces to Address Human Trafficking." *Poroi* 12, no. 2 (2016). https://doi.org/10.13008/2151-2957.1245.

Gallagher, Gary W. "Jubal A. Early, the Lost Cause, and Civil War History: A Persistent Legacy." In *The Myth of the Lost Cause and Civil War History*, edited by Gary W. Gallagher and Alan T. Nolan, 35–59. Bloomington: Indiana University Press, 2010.

Gee, James Paul. *How to Do Discourse Analysis*. London: Routledge, 2011.

Gee, James Paul, and Michael Handford. Introduction to *The Routledge Handbook of Discourse Analysis*, edited by Gee and Handford, 1–6. Abingdon, UK: Routledge, 2015.

Grant, Richard. *Dispatches from Pluto: Lost and Found in the Mississippi Delta*. New York: Simon and Schuster, 2015.

Gries, Laurie. *Still Life with Rhetoric: A New Materialist Approach for Visual Rhetorics*. Logan: Utah State University Press, 2015.

Hacker, Diana, and Nancy Sommers. *A Writer's Reference*. 8th ed. Boston: Bedford/St. Martin's, 2015.

Hale, Grace Elizabeth. *Making Whiteness: The Culture of Segregation in the South, 1890–1940*. New York: Random House, 1998.

Hamblin, Robert W. *Living in Mississippi: The Life and Times of Evans Harrington*. Jackson: University Press of Mississippi, 2017.

Harriell, Derrick. "Links Rd to HWY 6 to Jackson Ave." In *Stripper in Wonderland*, 34. Baton Rouge: LSU Press, 2017.

Hidalgo, Alexandra, and Donnie Jackson Sackey, eds. *Present Tense: A Journal of Rhetoric and Society* 5, no. 2 (2015).

Hill, Jane H. *The Everyday Language of White Racism*. Chichester, UK: Wiley and Sons, 2008.

Hodges, Adam. "'Yes, We Can': The Social Life of a Political Slogan." In *Contemporary Critical Discourse Studies*, edited by Christopher Hart and Piotr Cap, 346–64. London: Bloomsbury, 2014.

Howard, Philip N., Bharath Ganesh, Dimitra Liotsiou, John Kelly, and Camile François. *The IRA, Social Media and Political Polarization in the United States, 2012–2018*. Oxford: Computational Propaganda Project, University of Oxford, 2018. https://comprop.oii.ox.ac.uk.

Hunt, Jonathan. "From Cacemphaton to Cher: Foul Language and Evidence in the Rhetorical Tradition." *Relevant Rhetoric* 3 (2012). http://relevantrhetoric.com.

Inoue, Asao. "How Do We Language so People Stop Killing Each Other, or What Do We Do about White Language Supremacy?" Paper presented at the Annual Meeting of the Conference on College Composition and Communication, Pittsburgh, PA, March 14, 2019.

James, Anthony. "Paternalism's Demise: Blind Jim Ivy and Ole Miss, 1896–1955." *Mississippi Folklife* 28, no. 1 (Winter/Spring 1995): 17–24.

Jennings, Fred T., ed. *Citizens Informer* 3, no. 7 (July 1975).

Johnson, Kirk A., Willa M. Johnson, James M. Thomas, and John J. Green. *Microaggressions at the University of Mississippi*. UM Race Diary Project, October 2018.

Jones, Catherine. "Reconstruction and Redemption." In *Social Class*, edited by Larry J. Griffin and Peggy G. Harris, 230–35. Vol. 20 of *The New Encyclopedia of Southern Culture*. Chapel Hill: University of North Carolina Press, 2012.

Jones, Seth G. *The Rise of Far-Right Extremism in the United States*. Center for Strategic and International Studies, November 7, 2018. https://www.csis.org.

Kemper, Kurt Edward. *College Football and American Culture in the Cold War Era*. Champaign: University of Illinois Press, 2009.

Kennedy, Tammie M., Joyce Irene Middleton, and Krista Ratcliffe. *Rhetorics of Whiteness*. Carbondale: Southern Illinois University Press, 2016.

Kerschbaum, Stephanie L. *Toward a New Rhetoric of Difference*. Urbana, IL: Conference on College Composition and Communication/National Council of Teachers of English, 2014.

Khayat, Robert. *The Education of a Lifetime*. Oxford, MS: Nautilus, 2013.

Landrieu, Mitch. *In the Shadow of Statues: A White Southerner Confronts History*. New York: Penguin, 2018.

Lee, Stephen D. "The Negro Problem." In Loewen and Sebesta, *The Confederate and Neo-Confederate Reader: The "Great Truth" about the "Lost Cause,"* 286–93.

Loewen, James, and Edward Sebesta, eds. *The Confederate and Neo-Confederate Reader: The "Great Truth" about the "Lost Cause."* Jackson: University Press of Mississippi, 2010.

Martin, J. R., and P. R. R. White. *The Language of Evaluation: Appraisal in English*. Basingstoke, UK: Palgrave Macmillan, 2005.

McMillen, Neil R. "Citizens' Council." In *History*, edited by Charles Reagan Wilson, 273–74. Vol. 3 of *The New Encyclopedia of Southern Culture*. Chapel Hill: University of North Carolina Press, 2006.

McVeigh, Rory. "Structural Incentives for Conservative Mobilization: Power Devaluation and the Rise of the Ku Klux Klan, 1915–1925." *Social Forces* 77, no. 4 (1999): 1461–96.

Meek, Edwin E. *Riot: Witness to Anger and Change*. Oxford: Yoknapatawpha Press, 2015.

Melear, Kerry Brian, and Leslie Banahan. "The Election Night Incident." In *Responding to Campus Protests: A Practitioner's Resource*, Legal Links: Connecting Student Affairs and Law, vol. 1, no. 2, pp. 9–12. Education Law Association and NASPA, 2014.

Meredith, James. *Three Years in Mississippi*. Bloomington: Indiana University Press, 1966.

Miller, Carolyn R., Amy J. Devitt, and Victoria J. Gallagher, "Genre: Permanence and Change." *Rhetoric Society Quarterly* 48, no. 3 (2018): 269–77.

Minot, Walter S. "A Rhetorical View of Fallacies: Ad Hominem and Ad Populum." *Rhetoric Society Quarterly* 11, no. 4 (Autumn 1981): 222–35.

Moak, Franklin E. *A History of the Alumni Association of the University of Mississippi 1852–1986*. Oxford: Alumni Association of the University of Mississippi, 1986.

Mohr, Clarence L. Introduction to *Education*, edited by Mohr, 1–30. Vol. 17 of *The New Encyclopedia of Southern Culture*. Chapel Hill: University of North Carolina Press, 2001.

Montgomery, Michael, and Ellen Johnson. "Language in the South." In *Language*, edited by Montgomery and Johnson, 1–27. Vol. 5 of *The New Encyclopedia of Southern Culture*. Chapel Hill: University of North Carolina Press, 2006.

Newman, Joshua I. "Army of Whiteness? Colonel Reb and the Sporting South's Cultural and Corporate Symbolic." *Journal of Sport & Social Issues* 31, no. 4 (November 2007): 315–39. https://doi.org/10.1177/0193723507307814.

Oddo, John. "Discourse-Based Methods across Texts and Semiotic Modes: Three Tools for Micro-Rhetorical Analysis." *Written Communication* 30, no. 3 (2013): 236–75.

Oesterreich, Peter L. "Homo Rhetoricus." In *Culture and Rhetoric*, edited by Ivo Strecker and Stephen Tyler, 49–58. New York: Berghahn Books, 2009.

Office of the Director of National Intelligence. *Background to "Assessing Russian Activities and Intentions in Recent US Elections": The Analytic Process and Cyber Incident Attribution*. Office of the Director of National Intelligence, January 6, 2017.

Oriard, Michael. *King Football: Sport and Spectacle in the Golden Age of Radio and Newsreels, Movies and Magazines*. Chapel Hill: University of North Carolina Press, 2001.

Ownby, Ted. *Hurtin' Words: Debating Family Problems in the Twentieth-Century South*. Chapel Hill: University of North Carolina Press, 2018.

Pickett, Otis W. "We Were All Prisoners of the System: William Winter, Susan Glisson, and the Founding of the William Winter Institute for Racial Reconciliation." *Southern Quarterly* 54, no. 1 (Fall 2016): 150–69.

Poval, Al. *A Time Remembered: Ole Miss, 1945–1970, an Oral History*. Oxford: Nautilus, 2016.

Reardon, Thomas. "Hotty Toddy & Other Traditions." In *The Ole Miss Experience*, edited by Leslie Banahan, 145–57. Oxford: Nautilus, 2012.

Reed, Thomas Walter. *History of the University of Georgia*. Athens: University of Georgia, 1949.

Sansing, David G. *The University of Mississippi: A Sesquicentennial History*. Jackson: University Press of Mississippi, 1999.

Saslow, Eli. *Rising Out of Hatred: The Awakening of a Former White Nationalist*. New York: Doubleday, 2018.

Sharp, Sharon A. "Southern Historical Society." In *History*, edited by Charles Reagan Wilson, 334–35. Vol. 3 of *The New Encyclopedia of Southern Culture*. Chapel Hill: University of North Carolina Press, 2006.

Silverstein, Michael. "Indexical Order and the Dialectics of Sociolinguistic Life." *Language & Communication* 23 (2003): 193–229.

Smith, Lillian. *Killers of the Dream*. New York: W. W. Norton, 1994.

Stanonis, Anthony J. Introduction to *Dixie Emporium: Tourism, Foodways, and Consumer Culture in the American South*, edited by Stanonis, 1–16. Athens: University of Georgia Press, 2008.

Starnes, Richard D. "Forever Faithful: The Southern Historical Society and Confederate Historical Memory." *Southern Cultures* 2, no. 2 (Winter 1996): 177–94.

Stevens, Stuart. *The Last Season: A Father, a Son, and a Lifetime of College Football*. New York: Knopf, 2015.

Stevenson, Bryan. *Just Mercy*. New York: Spiegel and Grau, 2015.

Strecker, Ivo, and Stephen Tyler. Introduction to *Culture and Rhetoric*, edited by Strecker and Tyler, 1–20. New York: Berghahn Books, 2009.

University of Missouri. *One Mizzou, 2020 Vision for Excellence: The Strategic Plan of the University of Missouri*. University of Missouri, 2011. https://mospace.umsystem.edu/xmlui/.

Vivian, Bradford. *Commonplace Witnessing: Rhetorical Invention, Historical Remembrance, and Public Culture*. Oxford: Oxford University Press, 2017.

Walton, Anthony. *Mississippi: An American Journey*. New York: Knopf, 1996.

Wilkerson, Isabel. *The Warmth of Other Suns: The Epic Story of America's Great Migration*. New York: Vintage Books, 2011.

Wilkie, Curtis. *Dixie: A Personal Odyssey through Events That Shaped the Modern South*. New York: Scribner, 2002.

Williams, John Sharp. "Issues of the War Discussed." November 1904. Excerpted in Loewen and Sebesta, *The Confederate and Neo-Confederate Reader: The "Great Truth" about the "Lost Cause,"* 301–3.

Wilson, Charles Reagan. "Whose South?" *Southern Cultures* 22, no. 4 (Winter 2016). https://www.southerncultures.org.

Winter, William. Afterword to *Riot: Witness to Anger and Change*, by Edwin E. Meek, 135–38. Oxford: Yoknapatawpha Press, 2015.

Woodward, C. Van. *The Burden of Southern History*. 3rd ed. Baton Rouge: Louisiana State University Press, 1993.

Yellin, Keith. *Battle Exhortation: The Rhetoric of Combat Leadership*. Columbia: University of South Carolina Press, 2008.

Index

Page numbers in italics refer to figures.